Prison Violence

Prison Violence

Edited by

Albert K. Cohen
George F. Cole
Robert G. Bailey

University of Connecticut

Lexington Books
D.C. Heath and Company
Lexington, Massachusetts
Toronto   London

Library of Congress Cataloging in Publication Data
Main entry under title:

Prison violence.

 Papers presented at a conference co-sponsored by the Corrections
Program of the University of Connecticut and the Connecticut Dept.
of Correction, held May 30 to June 1, 1975, at the New England Center,
Durham, N. H.
 Includes indexes.
 1. Prison violence—Addresses, essays, lectures. I. Cohen, Albert
Kircidel. II. Cole, George F., 1935-   III. Bailey, Robert G. IV. Con-
necticut. University. Corrections Program. V. Connecticut. Dept. of
Correction.
HV9025.P74   365'.641   75-24561
ISBN 0-669-00185-6

Published simultaneously in Canada

Printed in the United States of America

International Standard Book Number: 0-669-00185-6

Library of Congress Catalog Card Number: 75-24561

Contents

List of Figures and Tables

Figure

Table

Preface

Although prisons have always been violent places, the revolt at Attica, the death of George Jackson in Soledad, the homosexual rapes in the sheriff's vans of Philadelphia, and the countless suicides of inmates in American correctional institutions have again focused public attention on this vital problem. From May 30 to June 1, 1975 the Corrections Program of The University of Connecticut and the Connecticut Department of Correction co-sponsored a conference on prison violence at The New England Center, Durham, New Hampshire. Invited were academics, correctional officials, and ex-offenders from throughout the nation. The conference was concerned with both collective and individual violence but primarily the latter—between inmates and between inmates and staff—because it has not received as much attention as the former.

The book contains many of the papers given at the conference as well as edited and paraphrased versions of the dicussions. As the reader will note from the serious tone of the presentations, the participants adhered to the conference guideline that "the idea is not to talk about the terrible things about prison as though violence naturally followed, but to deal with these things—and those not so terrible—from the standpoint of the ways in which they contribute . . . to the production of violence." Emphasis was placed upon achieving a better understanding of the problem of suggesting policies that might be implemented to reduce violence.

Leonard Oshinsky, then director of the Corrections Program, provided the necessary leadership to bring the idea of the conference to fruition. In preparing this book we have been aided by a grant from The University of Connecticut Research Foundation and the expert assistance of Helen Hauschild and Lisa Ferriere. To these people we are most thankful.

Conference Participants

Robert G. Bailey, Corrections Program, The University of Connecticut

Lawrence A. Bennett, Chief of Research, California Department of Corrections

Robert Brooks, Chief, Program Development, Connecticut Department of Correction

Peter Buffum, Staff Sociologist, Pennsylvania Prison Society

Albert K. Cohen, University Professor, Department of Sociology, The University of Connecticut

George F. Cole, Professor, Department of Political Science, The University of Connecticut

John P. Conrad, Senior Fellow, The Academy of Contemporary Problems

Desmond Ellis, Professor, Department of Sociology, York University

Edith E. Flynn, Professor of Criminology, College of Criminal Justice, Northeastern University

Colin Frank, Administrator, Mental Health Services, U. S. Bureau of Prisons

John Irwin, Professor, Department of Sociology, San Francisco State University

James B. Jacobs, Professor, Cornell University

Edwin I. Megargee, Professor, Department of Psychology, Florida State University

Kenneth E. Moyer, Professor, Department of Psychology, Carnegie-Mellon University

William G. Nagel, Executive-Vice President, Institute of Corrections, The American Foundation, Inc.

Lloyd Ohlin, Professor, Harvard Law School

Sheldon Olson, Professor, Department of Sociology, University of Texas

James W. L. Park, Chief, Research and Planning Services, California Department of Corrections

Richard Steinert, Superintendent, Connecticut Correctional Institution—Enfield

George W. Sumner, Deputy Superintendent, Correctional Training Facility—North, Soledad, California

Hans Toch, Professor of Psychology, School of Criminal Justice, State University of New York at Albany

Stanton Wheeler, Professor, Yale Law School

Richard W. Wilsnack, Professor, Department of Sociology, Indiana University

Wendy Wolfson, Professor, Department of Sociology, Bates College

Part I

Perspectives on Prison Violence

1

Prison Violence: A Sociological Perspective

Albert K. Cohen

The Uses and Meaning of Violence

One obstacle to a better understanding of violence is the common assumption that it is abnormal, perverse, and pathological. Most people believe that *violence* is the use of force (the attacker clobbering someone with a shovel) or an attempt to accomplish something by threat of force (the robber brandishing a gun). But they tend to restrict their actual use of the word to *illicit* violence, and this helps to prevent their appreciation of the commonalities and continuity between licit and illicit violence, and indeed between violent and nonviolent behavior. Most violence is in fact ordinary, commonplace, and socially acceptable, and does not strike us as baffling or mysterious. Police are instructed to employ not violence, but necessary and reasonable force, as are ordinary citizens in the protection of their persons and property. The shackling and occasional gagging of prisoners at the bar, their involuntary journeys to places of confinement, all the other punishments inflicted on them in the name of justice, entail either the application or threat of force, but we do not ordinarily call this violence. Sometimes we do speak of violence on the part of agents of the criminal justice system, but that is when the force they apply is excessive or in the wrong form, in light of current laws or mores. Slapping an unresisting prisoner in the face is violence; cracking a struggling prisoner's skull with a truncheon may not be. The boundary between force and violence, when applied by agents of justice, is not determined by its intrinsic form or absolute degree; *force* is called violence when it is normatively unacceptable. But legitimate violence—the sort that is not called violence—is not confined to the criminal justice system. It pervades and undergirds every sector of the institutional order: the family, commerce, education, politics. Every citizen, but especially those who, like parents, occupy positions of authority in established institutions, may, under certain circumstances, employ violence legitimately or may lawfully invoke third parties to exercise violence in their behalf. The probability that they will in fact do so ordinarily suffices to deter people from providing them with the occasion to do so. Therefore, violence in these institutional spheres ordinarily takes the form of a muted threat rather than naked force, but that does not make it any less real.

I am not suggesting that there is no difference between the legitimate and the illegitimate threat or application of force, any more than that there is no difference between the legitimate and illegitimate appropriation of another's property. The fact that force is legally or morally proscribed is something that people who contemplate using it must take into account. How they deal with such considerations enters into the problem of explanation. But the way to approach the study of violence is not to mark off its illegitimate from its legitimate forms and to focus our attention on the latter. It is to bracket this distinction, to set it aside—for the moment—and to consider, in general terms, the uses of violence in human affairs. We will then be in a better position to appreciate how multifarious these are, how mundane, how commonplace, and later, when we return to the distinction, how human and unremarkable are most of its illegitimate forms.

What are some of the uses of violence? One is to hurt people in return for some injury they have done to the honor or reputation of some person or collectivity. We hurt them, by some deprivation proportionate to the offense, for violation of some code in which we have a large investment and thereby communicate, in a dramatic fashion, our own attachment to that code. This is no place to go into the underlying psychology of the retributive sentiments, of the ways in which inflicting suffering on others somehow restores a sense of balance to an offended conscience or makes whole a wounded identity. But we go to war, we punish criminals, and we used to fight duels for reasons like these.

We also employ force for more instrumental reasons, to accomplish practical ends: to break up illegal gatherings, to remove people from buildings, to place people under arrest, to compel people to do our will, or to deter them from obstructing it.

Many sports, ranging from the medieval tourney to the modern boxing match and hockey game, are social games in which people win and lose and make a name for themselves by the artful display of violence. This violence, so far as it is contained within certain normative limits—which does not preclude that its effects may be lethal—may be integral, expected, legitimate, and relished by its audiences, whom we may think of as connoisseurs and amateurs of specialized forms of violence.

Violence may be used to establish, assert, and restore relationships, especially relationships of dominance, where these relationships have been threatened by challenges, by failure to exhibit appropriate deference, by assertions of autonomy incompatible with the demands of the relationship. Policemen, parents, judges jealous of the sanctity of the courtroom, all employ force or the threat of force, more or less legitimately (and sometimes illegitimately), to affirm and compel respect for such relationships.

There are also uses of violence that arise from the fact that it is risky. Recourse to violence may be motivated in part by the meaning it carries of willingness to expose one's self to danger, a meaning similar to that of the fireman's intrepidity in the face of a nonhuman danger. When this meaning is incorporated into the definition of male identity, it becomes a constituent of the machismo complex. Willingness to expose one's self to danger in behalf of a friend, a principle, an ally, or any other cause also carries the social meaning of sacrifice. How can I better persuade you of the utter earnestness and selflessness of my claims than by giving up or at least being prepared to hazard something of great value and irreplaceable, especially life and limb? If this is true of soldiers and policeman, it may be equally true of revolutionaries, terrorists, and rioters. Violence that is carried out secretly and anonymously with the manifest intention of achieving an object at no danger to one's self does not carry this meaning and cannot serve this purpose.

This list is not exhaustive, but it is enough for our purposes. These reasons for resorting to violence do not strike us as remarkable, perverse, or pathological. They do not suggest warped personalities or atavistic instincts. Nor do they distinguish the legitimate from the illegitimate uses of violence, the sorts of violence that we think of as social problems. Illegitimate violence is also used to communicate or validate claims about the sort of person one is, to demonstrate attachment to a cause or collectivity, to be successful in games where we keep score by noting and appreciating the artful use of violence, to accomplish a limitless variety of practical ends, and to shore up social relationships. There are also other uses of violence that may fall mostly on the illegitimate side of the normative line, but that is because the constituted authorities who legislate legitimacy or pass judgment on behalf of conventional society seldom need to employ violence for these purposes. For example, violence may be used to call attention in a dramatic way to one's helplessness and desperation, to grievances and injustice. The respectable and powerful do not often have the occasion to send such messages, and if they do, they have other ways of doing it.

This suggests a second major consideration in the study of violence: that, whatever its uses, there are usually other conceivable ways of accomplishing the same object, and 'that whether one goes about things in a violent or peaceful way is often the result of some calculus, sometimes intuitive and instantaneous, sometimes cool and deliberate, of the relative availability and of the costs and benefits of violence and its alternatives. The calculus is often mistaken and leads to unexpected and unwanted results but this is not peculiarly true of violence; it is true of human action generally.

The alternatives to violence are not necessarily less painful, cruel, or destructive than violence itself: for example, the deprivation of wealth and livelihood, humiliation, rejection, isolation, the destruction of reputation and dignity, both inside and outside the criminal justice system. If our intention is to hurt, these "peaceful" and often legitimate alternatives, if available at low cost and at minimal risk, may be more attractive and perhaps more effective than violence. This is not meant as a sour commentary on men's motives. It is meant to emphasize—again—that the motivation to violence may not be all that special, and that, in order to understand why people do or do not act violently, we must see them in a context of opportunities and alternatives.

To speak of opportunities and alternatives is not necessarily to speak of nonviolent ways of inflicting pain just for the sake of inflicting pain. Violence is used to coerce, to deter, to bargain, to compel others to listen, to make them pay their debts, to satisfy a grievance. These objectives may be accomplished in an infinite variety of ways, but their availability depends on the system of social arrangements, where one is located in such a system, and on one's personal endowment and resources. It may be used symbolically to assert or validate a claim to being a certain sort of person or to standing in a certain relationship to another. How useful it is for such purposes depends on the meanings attached to violence in a particular cultural setting, and on alternative modes of behavior that might carry the same meaning, for example, the behavioral vocabulary for expressing manhood or denying another's manhood, for expressing autonomy or equality or fealty.

I have been speaking of illegitimate violence from the perspective of respectable and conventional society. It scarcely needs to be emphasized that the conventional and respectable have no monopoly on moral sentiments; one man's callous contempt for human life may be another man's sacred duty. I am not suggesting that most violence of the illegal sort proceeds from a stern but unconventional morality. Neither, however, would I argue that behavior that conforms to law is motivated mostly by respect for the law or even morality, conventional or otherwise. In general, the legal status of an act does not tell us very much about the moral status of the reasons for it. We may, however, safely say that, among the reasons for "man's inhumanity to man" is man's humanity; that is, he kills or maims not because of a primitive passion for violence but, more often, because he has been so well socialized, because he has been taught to value his honor or freedom or good name or some principle or social tie so highly that he is willing to shed blood and to risk shedding his own in its behalf. Neither illegitimate violence nor violence generally is like a disease with its own special virus or bacterium. If we wish to understand violence, we must be prepared to consider the full range of human motives.

The modern state claims a monopoly of the legitimate use of force. This must be understood to include the right to authorize the use of force by people in positions of authority in other institutional sectors, for example, by parents and schoolmasters. This means that the legitimate uses of force are restricted to defense of the established institutional order and closely regulated by the constituted authorities. For the most part, however, it is used reluctantly. After all, it is messy; its outcome is often unpredictable; it may be as dangerous to the user as to the object; and it alienates even as it subdues. People in authority generally prefer to accomplish the purposes of their offices by other means. They are typically educated, sophisticated, and strategically located. They have access to a variety of personal and organizational resources. They are well equipped for persuasion, bargaining, and negotiation. It is understandable why they should find the unauthorized, that is, the illegitimate, use of force detestable and unacceptable. But that in itself does not explain why they also find it bestial, primitive, senseless, and pathological. They do not see their own violence in this light, however genuinely they may regret it.

, The reason for the peculiar horror toward the illegitimate use of violence lies, I think, in its universal availability. It is the resource that is available to almost any human being, however weak, impoverished, friendless, or unconnected he may be. If he is willing to run the risk and take the consequences, it is almost impossible, short of destroying or totally immobilizing him, to render him incapable of violence. We cannot say this of any other resource: wealth, position, intelligence, information, skill, connections. It can be accomplished, and its effects can be deadly, with the most exiguous of means and with the least preparation and premeditation. It is the one recourse, the one currency, of those who have nothing else: the slave, the lackey, the buck private, the tenant, the field hand, the convict. This universal availability makes it a source of universal uncertainty, anxiety, and dread. This is the principal reason for the special odium that attaches to the illegitimate use of violence, the inability to consider it dispassionately, and the reluctance to acknowledge its commonalities with the institutionally sanctified application of force.

Violence and Interaction Process

The concern with explaining acts of violence usually takes the form of some variant of the question, "Why would anybody want to do a thing like that?" The question focuses our attention on "the mind of" the murderer or assailant. It is an appropriate focus if we are engaged in assessing responsibility. But it is not the same thing as asking, "Why did it happen?" Consider the following quotation, which is Wolfgang's summary of a case from his study of homicide in Philadelphia:

Two friends became involved in an argument in a taproom over the nationality of the offender, an Italian, with uncomplimentary remarks being made by the victim about "dagos." This led to the accusation by the victim that the offender had stolen money from him. After they left the taproom, the victim threatened the offender with a broken beer bottle, whereupon the offender broke a piece of wood from a nearby fruit stand and beat the victim severely about the head.[1]

If the victim had been a bit more nimble or his skull a bit thicker or "the offender" a bit more drunk and unsteady or the piece of wood a bit flimsier, if there had been another friend along or if a bystander had intervened or if they had arrived at the taproom as it was closing, the outcome might have been different. The roles of offender and victim might have been reversed or there might have been no homicide at all.

There are two main implications: First, in any violent incident, there are numerous events and circumstances that, had they been different, might have altered the outcome. All such events and circumstances are part of the explanation. Second, violent incidents, however impulsive they may be, do not happen all at once. The history of the incident is the history of an interaction process. The intention and the capacity for violence do not pop out, like a candy bar out of a vending machine. They take shape over time. The course of events, at any stage, can move off in different directions, depending upon innumerable contingencies. Furthermore, those contingencies—the events and circumstances that shape the course—do not operate simultaneously. One event calls forth, inhibits, or deflects another; it invites, provokes, abets, tempts, counsels, soothes, or turns away wrath. The scene or setting, the quality of relationships, the structure of opportunities, the meanings of events, prospective costs and benefits, change constantly. Every violent episode, whether it is an altercation between two friends, a mugging, or a riot is the product of such an interaction history.

If this is the way violence happens, it is not remarkable that it is so difficult to predict who will be violent. In prisons, individuals with certain characteristics may have a somewhat higher probability of being involved in a violent incident than others, but predictions based on those characteristics will be wrong more often than not. As we have seen, violence is useful in too many ways—for example, to avenge or prevent injustice, to dramatize one's loyalty to a group—to be closely connected to any particular kind of personality. Besides, the occurrence of violence depends upon too many contingencies other than the personalities or backgrounds of the dramatis personae.

Words like contingency are simply meant to convey the idea of "if-ness:" if p, then we may expect things to move in this direction; if q, then in that direction. It does not mean that things happen in random, chaotic, and totally unpredictable ways. On the contrary, the bringing together of a set of circumstances that sets an interaction process moving in a certain direction and the occurrence of contingencies that kept it moving in that direction are anything but random relative to the organization of the larger system in which the process is embedded. More specifically, violence occurs more frequently in some prisons than others, in some sectors, in some subpopulations, in connection with some transactions and relationships, at some stages in the history of a prison, because the occurrence and distribution of interaction processes of any particular kind depend on the social organization of the prison. *Social organization* means such things as the ways in which the prison is related to its environment, the composition of its population, the division of labor, the structure of authority, the ways in which people and resources are located and moved about within the prison, the ways in which information is transmitted, stored, and recovered, the arrangements for coordinating and keeping track of people, activities, and things, the allocation of responsibility, the distribution of gratifications and deprivations, and so on. The remainder of this chapter deals with some of the ways in which the social organization of the prison affects the local scenes and interaction processes that bear upon the production of violence.

The Pangs of Imprisonment and the Causes of Violence

Explanations of prison violence often take the form of indignant recitals of the deprivations and injustices of life in prison. To recite these inventories of evils identifies the speaker as humane, liberal, and compassionate. But it is not the same as explaining violence. It is not that these recitals are exaggerated. Sometimes they are; sometimes they are understatements. At best, being in prison is a harsh and painful experience, but it is not always obvious why this should provoke violence. In fact, it is not always obvious that it does. It appears, on the basis of presently available information, that there is not much violence—at any rate, not much homicide—in the prisons of Western Europe.[2] One might speculate that prisons there are much more benign insitutions than those in this country. It is also true that those same countries have lower rates of violent crimes in general than we do; it may be that the relative absence of homicides in prisons may have more to do with the character of the populations and the culture they bring with them to the prison than with the character of the prison regimen. In our own country it is not even clear that there is more overt violence in prisons than there is in the communities where the inmates come from. Indeed, one wonders why there is not more violence in prisons; there seems to be so much to be violent about. It may be that the latent violence of management, that is, readiness on the part of staff to employ violence to enforce its regime, contains inmate violence more than it incites it. It is not apparent that the institutions with the least inmate violence are the least repressive. One always thinks of the cowed and abject populations of some of the Nazi prison camps. It may be that certain kinds of violence—notably, violence associated with mass protest and riots—do not typically occur in the most depressed prisons but in those where the repression is less total. One thinks of an observation that has been frequently made of revolutions: that they are typically produced not by the most oppressed segments of the populations but by those who have tasted some freedom, have some resources, and cherish some realistic hope that by rebelling they may improve their lot. In fact, one theory of prison riots is that marginal improvements in the conditions of prison life generate expectations that rise more rapidly than prison administrations are prepared or able to satisfy, increasing inmate militancy, and ultimately outbreaks of violence to force concessions or to dramatize the inmates' plight to publics outside the prison walls. In any case, inventories of deprivation are not enough. One must show how deprivation is translated into violence.

Some violence responds directly to the deprivation and its immediate source, the people who run the prison. It is meant as protest, as revenge, or as a form of pressure to compel change. But most inmate violence is not directed against staff but against other inmates.[3] An easy explanation is provided by the frustration–aggression theory: those who suffer strike out against the most vulnerable and least dangerous targets. There is probably *something* to this, but the frustration–aggression theory has taken a severe critical battering. To translate the deprivations of prison life into inmate-inmate violence we must show how they affect the conditions and contingencies that shape interaction and relationships among inmates. For example, the scarcity of commodities that are abundant and cheap in the free community may be felt and resented as a deprivation, but it also transforms the commodities into things that people will fight over. To be locked in a confined space with people one would not have voluntarily chosen as intimates is a deprivation; it also creates opportunities for inmates to goad other inmates to fury or to badger them till they strike back in self-defense, and at the same time it reduces the probability that a third party will intervene at a critical stage to prevent the violence from coming to a head. It is important that we distinguish between the fact that something is directly experienced as a deprivation and the fact that it helps to generate interaction processes that are likely to culminate in violence. It may turn out that, under certain circumstances, the granting of freedoms hitherto denied is experienced as a reduction of oppression and deprivation; at the same time it may open the prison to influences from outside the prison that may *increase* the probability of violence. Two examples: (1) It is at least conceivable that permitting unlimited, uncensored correspondence and visitation may help gangs inside the prison to maintain ties with the larger gangs in the community of which the prison gangs are detachments, so to speak, and thereby to maintain gang cohesion and intergang rivalry within the prison. (2) The same increase of the permeability of the boundary between the prison and the world without the prison may promote the solidarity and militancy of ideological groupings within the prison and the probability of antistaff violence. In neither case is violence guaranteed; it always depends upon too many other contingencies. Deprivation and gratification, whether inside or outside the prison, do not automatically and inexorably increase and decrease, respectively, the likelihood of violence.

Prison Populations and Violence

The nature of a prison is partly a function of the kinds of people who get sent there. Because this chapter is not meant to be a comprehensive overview of the sociology of prison violence, I allude only to a few aspects of this large subject. Of the characteristics that inmates bring with them to the prison, three seem to be of particular relevance to the matter of violence:

First is age: Young people seem to be more prone to violence than older people, both inside and outside the prison. This has probably more to do with a lack of investments and commitments that might be jeopardized by getting involved in violence than with some excess of biological drive. The young are less firmly established in occuptional careers; they have fewer family responsibilities; in all probability they are less secure in their reputations for undoubted virility; they have spent less of their lives in prison and are less prepared to submit to discipline, to do their own time and avoid trouble in order to put the prison experience behind them. For all these reasons, they are less responsive to institutional controls. It is still uncertain, however, how much they "contribute to the variance" in prison violence. Unfortunately, we must say the same for most of the other circumstances that we have reason to believe have *some* bearing on prison violence.

Second are the subcultural attitudes and meanings that inmates carry with them into the prison. A good bit has been written about "the subculture of violence,"[4] but the subject is still shrouded in controversy. In particular, it is argued that, although some racial, ethnic, and socioeconomic categories may be statistically more prone to violence, that violence is to be attributed rather to the press of circumstances than to some hypothetical subculture. The two notions are not, however, incompatible. Subcultures are socially transmitted and collectively maintained life-styles informed by distinctive beliefs, values, and focal concerns. They do not, however, arise mysteriously, by some kind of spontaneous generation, so to speak, and then perdure indefinitely by sheer inertia. They are themselves adaptations to the typical, recurrent, and shared experiences of people similarly circumstanced. As these circumstances change, the subcultures change. But they do not extinguish as rapidly as the circumstances that gave rise to them. Having become incorporated into the personalities of their members and integral elements of an organized and coherent life scheme, they do not mutate any more readily than any other beliefs, values, and focal concerns. The fact remains, however, that a subculture is a construct devised by the social scientist to make sense of data. To demonstrate its validity is no easy matter. The degree to which behavioral differences arise from differences in subcultures versus differences in immediate pressures and opportunities is still a meaningful and important issue.

I question the existence of a unitary subculture of violence but I believe there are a number of cultural ideas or themes that are likely, under certain circumstances, to conduce to violence; that they have a certain affinity for one another and a tendency to cluster; that they are nonetheless somewhat distinct and need not always go together; and that they occur disproportionately in prison populations and figure importantly in some of the configurations that give rise to violence. The populations of which I speak may include the prison staffs, especially the lower ranking custodial officers, as well as inmates. Some of these ideas or themes are the following:

The Machismo Complex. The boundaries of this notion are somewhat elusive. Certainly it exists in several variants. The central idea, however, is that of male honor, the sacredness of one's reputation as a man and one's personal responsibility for vindicating slurs upon that reputation. It is not the slur but the failure to expunge it by physical combat that destroys one's manhood, which is the core of his identity, and makes him contemptible. To be macho, then, is to be vulnerable to threats to identity that other men might shrug off, and to be denied alternative, nonviolent means of dealing with such threats. If one is insecure in his sense of manhood, he might even goad someone into saying something that can then be constructed as an attack on one's honor warranting an act of retaliation that vindicates his manhood. Machismo, imported into the prison, may provide occasions for violence that are only tenuously connected with the deprivations of prison life.

Preference for Private Justice. Most of us, if we are the victims of criminal or civil wrongs, turn naturally to the police and the courts for justice. We do not think we should "take the law into our own hands" and by and large we would prefer not to. In many other societies the prevailing attitude and practice is some form of self-help or private vengeance. This private practice of violence as the culturally preferred instrument of justice is not identical with machismo or "crimes of passion." DiGennaro concludes, from examination of judicial sentences for homicide in Sardinia, that:

Few homicides in Sardinia are committed as a result of passionate feelings caused by jealousy, or committed to protect women or their "honor." . . . The prevailing motive for homicide is linked to quarrels with an economic origin. . . . The majority of the problems that constitute the motive causing the crime could have been resolved by requesting the intervention of the judiciary: . . . No attempt is made prior to the crime to utilize the formal judicial system. In all the cases examined the offender, before resorting to violence, never asked for, or had the intention of asking for, the intervention of a judge . . . violence is not used as a means of obtaining the object in question, but rather is used as a means of punishing a person presumed guilty of a tort.[5]

Such a cultural attitude is itself an outgrowth of historical experience. One element of that experience may be subjection to a political and judicial authority that is remote, indifferent, capricious, and governed by interests opposed to those of the group in question. Such an authority is felt to be alien and unresponsive, difficult or dangerous to approach, and incapable of delivering justice. To obtain justice, one must administer it oneself. This does not by definition imply violence, but the range of sanctions available to private persons is narrow. Violence, as noted above, is one sanction that is universally available.

These and other structural sources of the reluctance to avail oneself of the formal agencies of justice do not only distinguish entire national or ethnic communities, they may also operate to create a sense of alienation or distrust of legally constituted authority in subcategories of the same population, and to generate subcultural preferences for the use of violence as an instrument of private justice. The prison itself, as a social system, may operate in similar manner on its inmate population, thus superimposing on the subcultures that its inmates bring with them to the prison proclivities to violence that are part of an autochthonous inmate subculture.

Superior Strength as a Criterion of Maleness and an Ordering Principle of Social Relationships. *Strength* means the ability to employ force to impose one's will upon others. *Machismo,* as defined (in keeping with its derivation from a Mediterranean tradition of honor) emphasizes the male's obligation to resort to combat to defend his honor and that of those—for example, female kin—for whom he has some responsibility. It does not, per se, equate manhood with the ability to subdue and dominate others by force. In our society, this theme is most explicit and pronounced in the lower levels of the class system. It is easy to exaggerate its importance; in the context of lower class life it is but one theme among many. However, it is a crucial item in the identities of a great many people and in the dynamics of many social games and relationships. It is particularly manifest in boys' gangs, where it plays an important role in ordering relationships within the gang and also among gangs. I believe that it is an element in a good deal of predatory violence of the sort that is sometimes called "mindless," because it is not necessarily constrained by considerations of fairness or directed to any manifest objective other than domination and the assertion of strength. It is evident in heterosexual relationships—in its extreme form in rape—where the name of the game is imposing one's will upon the female object—the very antithesis of willing and mutual surrender in a "meaningful relationship." It is particularly striking in homosexual relationships and above all in homosexual rape, where it is most clear that one's maleness depends not on the fact that one's partner is a man or a woman but on whether one takes the dominant and "active" or the submissive and "passive" role. Homosexual rape and less blatant forms of sexual coercion in prisons are probably less a matter of the displacement of frustrated sexual desire (which is, of course, real enough) than of demonstrating masculinity through one form of physical aggression in which the victim loses his claim to masculinity.

Third is the importation into prison of *relationships* that are productive of violence on the outside and continue to produce violence on the inside, such as the persistence within the prison of gang memberships and intergang relationships that originate outside the prison. This phenomenon has only recently been documented, notably in California and Illinois prisons, and it may be that it is limited to only a relatively few prisons. If this phenomenon—the persistent solidarity of the street gang and its continued preoccuption with reputation and intergang conflict—is as recent as it appears to be, its explanation poses some interesting questions. Certainly conflict-oriented gangs and the presence in prison of sizeable contingents of gang members are not new. It is not obvious why gangs should flourish in prison—after all, the prison is not the street—or why gang cohension, discipline, and leadership have only recently become salient features of the social organization of some prisons. I have already suggested that perhaps the increased openness of prisons to communication from without may account for continuity between the parent gang and its detachments in prison. It may be that, since these gangs are typically ethnic gangs, the phenomenon has something to do with the changing role of ethnicity in American life. In any case, the subject is not exhausted by noting that gangs are now an important part of the life of a number of prisons.

This is not to say that prisons are violent places because they contain violent people. I do not believe that there are people who, whatever their personalities or their cultural orientations, contain a certain quantum of violence that is bound to find expression in whatever milieu they find themselves. Violence is always a product of a specific configuration of circumstances, of an interaction process, and these configurations are in turn shaped by the organization of the larger system context. Still, we cannot blink at the fact that violence, licit and illicit, is endemic in the society from which the prisoners and their keepers are drawn. If prisons are productive of violence, it is partly because of the nature of the human material that is exposed to the socially structured situations of prison life.

Structural Sources of Prison Violence

Whatever one says on the subject of the social structure of prisons, however, it is only more or less true of any particular prison, because it is as easy and as misleading to stereotype prisons as to stereotype criminals. I note some of the important qualifications to my generalizations, but space does not permit the attention to variation that a proper treatment of the subject would require. I identify here a number of properties of prisons as organizations, and then I consider some of their implications for violence.

First is the structure of power and therefore of accountability. There is scarcely any other kind of organization where the bulk of the membership has so little to say about the conditions under which they live. The main charge to the prison staff from those who control its resources is containment. There is a great deal of talk about rehabilitation and humane administration but the former is at best exceedingly difficult to evaluate and the latter, even in prisons that are not situated in remote rural settings, is largely invisible to the publics to which the administration is answerable. In any case, the priorities of these publics are containment and order. Within the limitations of the budget the administration has considerable latitude but on all levels of staff the main charges still provide the decisive criterion for assessing adequacy of performance. Because failure of the administration to render a satisfactory account in these terms can be so disastrous to them and to the security and tenure of the staff, control flows downward and accountability upward in a quasi-military way. Within the staff, however, there is some accountability laterally and downwards. Because staff members are free men, because they have some alternative livelihoods available to them, because they cannot be clapped in solitary, and because they may be organized in unions, they have some bargaining power and some considerable voice in shaping the routines of their occupational life.

Inmates, too, are not devoid of power. It is a common observation that the staff's span of responsibility is always larger than its span of control. Whatever the staff's objectives, they can always be frustrated by the ingenuity of the subject population. In the traditional prison the means for accomplishing the staff's goals have been enlarged by enlisting the services of inmate leaders who in exchange have been granted privileges and amenities, which they, in turn, may use as resources to buttress their leadership and restrain inmate behavior that might threaten or embarrass the staff, such as attacks on staff members, escapes, and prison disturbances. By and large, however, most inmates have little bargaining power, little ability to call staff to account, few constituencies that can compel attention to their interests. In recent years this traditional symbiotic alliance between staff and inmate leadership has deteriorated in many prisons, for a variety of reasons and with a variety of consequences that we cannot go into here. In the main, however, these changes do not require drastic alteration of our generalization. To be a prisoner is to live by the rules and orders of one's keepers.

2) Second, these characteristics of prisons must be considered together with the fact that they are typically large-scale bureaucratic organizations. Such organizations are subject to strong pressures to routinization, that is, to predictable conformity to standardized procedures. Standardization implies the simplification of reality—of persons and situations—by inattention to their richness and complexity and by classifying them, for purposes of record keeping and intraorganizational communication, on the basis of a few characteristics deemed important for the purposes of the organization. In prisons these purposes emphasize, as we have seen, containment and order. One kind of pressure for standardization is the need to coordinate the work of large numbers of people who are not in face-to-face contact with one another. This coordination must therefore rely heavily on written records, messages, and reports. To attend to the idiosyncratic richness of the unsimplified reality in the manner of, say, family members or members of a small office staff would garner more information than the communication system could carry. A second source of pressure for standardization is the staff's interest in lightening its intellectual, moral, and emotional burdens. Each inmate is a unique person, with his own problems, chafing and suffering in his own way. To empathize deeply with each inmate, to try to sense his distinctive needs and problems, to be aware of him as a whole person and respond accordingly as one would to a friend or member of one's family, to try to communicate all this to other persons who have responsibility for the same inmates, is a stressful and exhausting kind of involvement. We find this kind of involvement in the lives of others under special conditions, usually involving mutual dependence and reciprocal accountability. In the prison these conditions are at a minimum. The result is reinforcement of the tendency to impersonality, affective detachment, and the simplification of reality. The reality that survives this screening is highly sensitive to those things of which staff must take

cognizance in making their accounts to their superiors. Not very much, however, of what matters most to inmates penetrates this screen and intrudes upon this reality.

3) Third, fiction, biographical reminiscences, and scholarly accounts describe the distance, the "we--they" relationship, and the undercurrents of conflict between officers and enlisted men in military organizations, to which prisons bear a certain resemblance. Despite this, they speak of "our" company and "our" regiment, of a more inclusive collectivity and identity that they share. This sense of community grows out of the fact that, as members of the same organization, they share a set of common tasks, in which they all have an important, even a vital, stake. This provides some basis for mutual identification, mutual concern, and mutual responsibility. Across ranks and within ranks, members cannot be indifferent to one another. They cannot stand altogether aloof, refuse to become involved in what the others are doing and in what is happening to them, and do their own time. This means, on the one hand, that members are available to one another as resources for coping with their problems and, on the other hand, as sources of social intervention and control that are more potent than the authority that flows down the chain of command. Prisons, by contrast, are probably uniquely lacking in the sense of an overriding common task and of community between the superordinate and subordinate ranks. There is not even much solidarity and mutual responsibility within the subordinate rank except, to a limited degree, for that which is called out by common opposition to the keepers. Violence, we have seen, has many uses: to obtain justice or, if you will, revenge; to secure payment of debts; to validate claims to being a certain sort of person; and so on. But there is hardly any situation in which violence is the only possible outcome. To the degree to which the interests of others are threatened by recourse to violence, they have an incentive not only to help provide alternative solutions to problems, but also to be sensitive to the earlier stages of interaction processes, when they are most easily deflected or reversed, and to intervene accordingly.

We have seen that the lack of accountability downwards, the routinization of staff operations, and the lack of community between staff and inmates reduce the effectiveness of staff both as resources for inmates and as agents of control, and that the lack of community within the inmate population does the same. This lack of community is in turn reinforced by the fact that inmates "want out" and, given the accounting system by which "The Man" keeps score, the inmate can do himself little good and might do himself a lot of harm by "getting involved." If, for example, an inmate is being harassed or exploited by other inmates, the prudent man will mind his own business. Unable to turn to his fellows for protection and support, and reluctant to call upon staff to take action against his persecutors, the troubled inmate may have no choice but to yield or attack. To respond by attack does not require that he be an aggressive or characterologically "violent" person. He may end by being branded as the aggressor, but he is himself the victim of a system that has provided him with a very narrow range of socially structured choices.

It is exceedingly important that we do not exaggerate the differences between the prison and the "normal" community outside. The "Kitty Genovese phenomenon" was not named after a prison incident. We do not have to invent a special psychology of the inmate mind to explain the silent witness who turns his back on trouble.

Like everything else I have said, these remarks have to be qualified. The inmate community may not be a solidary brotherhood, but it may contain groupings that do provide for their members the sense, the substance, the protection, and support of a brotherhood. We have mentioned gangs. We must also mention religious groups like the Muslims and radical and revolutionary groups. They have an obvious potential for conflict and violence but, because of their influence over their members and the apprehension they may inspire in nonmembers, they also have a capacity for disciplining, containing, and deterring violence. This is a complex subject that we do not know too much about, but we do know that it cannot be disposed of by stereotypes and glib generalizations.

A fourth important feature of the prison is that it is a world in which physical movement and social interaction are largely determined by staff decisions, leaving inmates a relatively small range of free choice. This choice is often less free in the open community than we like to think, but the difference in degree is nevertheless clear. In the open community, relationships that are likely to become abrasive are, on the whole, easier to terminate without loss of face or at unacceptable cost. It is no accident that, of the violence that does occur there, so much is between inmates. One reason is that family members and other intimates are so closely tied to one another through interdependence, joint responsibility, and external commitments that they are relatively unfree to move apart, to avoid one another, and to escape the circle of tension and mounting acerbity in which they are trapped.[6] Prisons, too, are traps. One of the very important methods of "conflict resolution" is avoidance.[7] Like any other method of conflict resolution, it depends on an appropriate "opportunity structure." In a prison, these opportunities are at a minimum. The back-against-the-wall situation is a systematic product of the physical and social ecology of the prison. Where disputants or the victims of exploitation cannot "leave the field" and do not choose to submit, there is a strong likelihood of a violent resolution.

A fifth feature of the prison concerns an unanticipated consequence of the deprivations of prison life. There is no point to enumerating them; they involve food, sex, cigarettes, money, clothing, work assignments, and other objects of value. Denial of access to these goods is painful and frustrating. Prisoners, being human, try, within the range of movement open to them, to make life more tolerable and interesting. Unimpressed by the administration's rationale for these deprivations, they devise illegitimate ways of obtaining them: traffic in contraband, clandestine sex, the illicit purchase and exchange of favors. Some of this activity would be illegal on the outside. Much of it would not, but in the prison they are available only as *illicit* goods. This has the consequence that, if they give rise to conflict and disputes as commerce (as we call it on the outside) and hustles (as we call it on the inside) invariably do, they cannot be settled by invoking the services of legally constituted authority. To do so one would ordinarily have to reveal his involvement in illicit activity and to expose himself to punishment. It is not different, in this respect, from disputes arising out of illicit activities on the outside. Organized crime does not typically turn to the law for mediation or for protection of life and property, unless the law itself has been corrupted. It has its own ways of securing justice, revenge, discipline, the collection of debts, and the enforcement of contracts, and these often take the form of violence or the threat of violence. Within the prison, likewise, the "criminalization" of activities for which the demand nonetheless persists has the consequence of insuring the unauthorized use of force, that is, of violence.

Implications for Policy

One direction one can take is to try to reduce the opportunities for violence. As far as inmates are concerned, this means the organization of space and the regulation of movement, association, and activities so that visibility is maximized, opportunities for illicit collusion minimized, and access to weaponry and materials that can be converted to weapons effectively denied. This makes sense up to a certain point, but it has serious limitations and may be self-defeating.

I have emphasized that, of all human resources, violence is the one that is most universally available. The presence at hand of guns and shivs itself suggests and prompts their use. But the heel of a shoe can also be a dangerous weapon, especially if there is someone in it. Naked fists can kill. Short of locking people up in perpetual solitary, it is difficult to prevent all encounters that might erupt in violence. Chapter 11 reports that a study of the first 11 months of the lockdown in the California system, beginning in December 1973, revealed no overall statistically significant reduction in violent incidents and that most of the assaults, which were confined to two of the institutions, tended to occur more often in lockup units than in general population situations.

We may have a problem here of how to reduce the opportunity for violence without increasing the incentive. It is possible to enhance the effectiveness of surveillance and control by more thoughtful attention to architectural design without necessarily restricting freedom of movement. Indeed, it is possible in this way to increase the inmates' own comfort and sense of security and, at the same time, reduce the obtrusive presence of guards. But only up to a point.

1976

To press this strategy very far would entail the annihilation of privacy and the humiliation and frustration of a goldfish-bowl existence. Eliminating all industries and work assignments that provide opportunities to fashion metals into weapons would severely narrow the range of useful, meaningful, and motivated work. In short, heavy reliance on this strategy would aggravate the general barrenness and impoverishment of prison life and the consequent sense of deprivation and bitterness that may ultimately feed back into violence. Furthermore, it would tend to emphasize the role of staff as keepers, the opposition between the management goal of control and the inmates' interest in choice, variety, autonomy, and self-expression. This, in turn, would intensify the social distance between staff and inmates, the avoidance of staff and inmates, and the reluctance that already exists to use staff as resources for problem solving.

Apart from all these practical considerations, there is the simple question of humaneness, of how great a price one is willing to exact of inmates in order to expunge the possibility of violence and disorder.

We can move in the opposite direction: to increase freedom of movement and association, to create private places for individuals and groups, to multiply opportunities and choices of all kinds. But this does not insure that prisons will be peaceable places. All legitimate opportunities—that is, opportunities to satisfy one's interests in socially acceptable ways—are also illegitimate opportunities. Every resource—freedom of movement, of access to persons, places, information, and materials—can be turned to illegitimate ends. Private places, not open to surveillance and intrusion, can be dangerous places. Freedom of association can be used by some to form combinations and conspiracies to exploit and coerce others. The opportunity to work—in leathercraft, sculpture, or pipefitting—with sharp and pointed tools is the opportunity to pocket weapons. The freedom to form therapy groups, social clubs, and ethnic societies is the freedom to form gangs. Every social group and setting must contend with the dilemma: how to provide the freedom and discretionary choice necessary for individual fulfillment and for the efficient use of resources for the common good and at the same time to insure that they will be used as intended. The prison is no exception. However cynical we may be about the arbitrariness of the net cast by the criminal justice system, we must acknowledge that prisons contain a lot of people morally prepared and by experience equipped to take advantage of opportunities to dominate, oppress, and exploit others. The problem of the prison—to construct a system of governance that reconciles freedom with order and security—is also the problem of civil society.

It seems to me that all measures for coping with this dilemma entail very basic changes in the organization of prisons. First are those measures that are designed to enhance the ability of staff to provide protection and redress to members and to make them more useful as resources for the solution of all kinds of inmate problems, including problems with other inmates and with staff themselves. These include ombudsmen, grievance procedures, staff–inmate councils and tribunals, mediation and arbitration procedures, possibly prisoners' unions and collective bargaining. All of these imply some sort of institutionalized alternatives to self-help and to recourse to violence and disturbances to compel attention. Such formal structures are important, but they are not as important as fundamental changes in the general spirit or climate of the institution. The formal changes are not likely to be effective unless inmate cynicism and distrust of both the will and the ability of management to respond to inmate needs is overcome. Management must be seen to be as genuinely concerned with the dignity and welfare of the inmate as a whole person as it is with the dignity and welfare of staff. If the claims of management are to be convincing, they must be backed up by a demonstrated readiness to make enormous exertions on behalf of inmates. The bureaucratic style of gathering and transmitting information, which is also a way of throwing away information, must yield to a different kind of communications structure, which is open to any information that bears upon the needs and problems of inmates and gets that information, at any time of night or day, to someone who is able to do something about it. Staff must be as prepared to disrupt their routines, to do extraordinary things, when the victim of an accident or an attack is an inmate as when the victim is a colleague. They must be visibly responsive to inmates *as constituents.* Inmates, fully aware that staff have responsibility for custody, must nonetheless see staff as instruments for the solution of the problems they bring with them to prison and the problems that grow out of living with others under the trying conditions of confinement. This is asking a great deal—more, perhaps, than is realistically attainable. But I an not just reiterating that if we do good unto others they will, in turn, be nice to us. Inmate grounds for not trusting staff, and therefore for not providing them with the information and cooperation they need in order to protect inmates from one another, are well founded. It takes special and dramatic pains to dispel this distrust.

When I speak of a change in the general climate or spirit of the institution, I mean that the change must be embraced by the top management, and that responsiveness to and respect for inmates become important criteria by which staff judge staff. Training is important, but the most important part of training is being at work in a place where manifest commitment to service and justice to the inmate routinely informs all workaday decision making. One gets the point. For some sense of what all this means in a real prison—the problems, the stress and strain, the disappointments, and the promise—read George Sumner's account of his experience at Soledad in Chapter 12.

A second class of measures deals with ways of building responsibility, problem solving, conflict resolution, and social control into the texture of inmate-inmate relationships. This means the creation of genuine communities in which inmates feel responsible for the welfare of the collectivity. I find it difficult to envisage such communities except on a small scale: very small institutions or relatively independent units within larger institutions. Smallness is critical because every inmate must be able to participate *directly* in designing, together with his fellows, the regime under which he will live. It must be realistically possible for a group of people, acting together, to hammer out a set of rules and procedures for governance, and the consequences of their own decisions must be immediately visible in their daily lives. For the regime to be responsive directly to the special needs of each member it is necessary that the members know one another well and therefore that they interact daily on a face-to-face basis. If they are to feel that the justice that they receive at the hands of their associates is fair, they must be able to meet together in a forum whose members have reason to trust that the others have the necessary knowledge, competence, and good will. For the regime to adapt quickly to the changing circumstances of the group or of particular individuals, it must be flexible; to be flexible, it must be possible for information to be shared quickly and to be quickly acted upon. I speak, in short, of communities where not only violence but injustice in any form is everyone's business, where each is accountable to all of the others, and where the result is measurable to members in terms of a less solitary, more secure, and more satisfying life.

To create such communities—we have some basis in experience for thinking that they are not altogether utopian[8]—also makes considerable demands on staff accustomed to the culture and organization of traditional institutions. A community is empty and meaningless if it has no real power to change the lives of its members. It must, of course, also recognize that it is a community within a prison, and accept that there must be limits to its autonomy; working out and adjusting the boundaries of that autonomy is itself a task for negotiation between inmates and management. But management must be prepared to yield a substantial measure of the power it has always taken for granted to those who were and still are generally regarded as neither deserving nor capable of exercising it.

I am not greatly sanguine about the prospect of changes like these on a very large scale, for reasons hinted at earlier. All of the changes suggested here entail drastic revision of the patterns of accountability. The established patterns of accountability are related to the linkage between the prison and society. Where the milieu from which the prison derives its resources and to which management is ultimately accountable places paramount emphasis upon containment and seldom attends to what goes on in prison, except when there is a riot, escape, or homicide, there is little incentive for management to relax its effort to maintain control through a military–bureaucratic chain of command, and there is a strong incentive on the part of inmates to create disturbances to compel the attention of the outside world to their situation. It is interesting and, in a way, saddening that in our society the external pressure to make management accountable comes not from the legislatures and the governors—the people most directly responsible to the public and in control of the purse—but from the courts. Most people are not that much interested in prisons.

Notes

1. Marvin Wolfgang, *Patterns in Criminal Homicide* (New York: Wiley, 1966), p. 227.

2. Peter C. Buffum, "Prison Killings and Death Penalty Legislation," *The Prison Journal,* vol. 53 (Spring-Summer 1973), pp. 49–57.

3. See, for example, The Task Force to Study Violence, *Report and Recommendations* (State of California: Department of Corrections, May 1974), p. 1.

4. Marvin E. Wolfgang and Franco Ferracuti, *The Subculture of Violence: Towards an Integrated Theory in Criminology* (London: Tavistock, 1967).

5. Giuseppe Di Gennaro, "Some Legal Considerations on the Sentencing of Sardinian Homicide Offenders," in Franco Ferracuti, Renato Lazzari, and Marvin E. Wolfgang, eds., *Violence in Sardinia* (Rome: Mario Bulzoni—Editore 1970), p. 63.

6. William J. Goode, "Violence between Intimates," in *Crimes of Violence: A Staff Report Submitted to the National Commission on the Causes and Prevention of Violence* (Washington, D.C.: U.S. Government Printing Office: 1969), volume 13, pp. 941–77.

7. William L. F. Felstiner, "Avoidance as Dispute-Processing: An Elaboration," *Law and Society Review,* vol. 9 (Summer 1975), pp. 695–706.

8. Lawrence Kohlberg, Kelsey Kauffman, Peter Scharf, and Joseph Hickey, *The Just Community Approach to Corrections, A Manual, Part I* (State of Connecticut Department of Correction, 1974).

2

The Beast Behind the Wall
John P. Conrad

Consistency is a hobgoblin for twentieth century criminologists. What we thought even ten years ago, if recalled today, too often seems obsolescent, if ·not downright embarrassing.

Before preparing this Chapter, I reread a paper on the apposite topic, *Violence in Prison,*[1] which I contributed to *The Annals* in March 1966, to see how much I could still defend. At that time I was chief of research, California Department of Corrections, and my data were Californian. There is an obvious complacency in the article, which found expression in the thought that "it [was] highly probable that there [were] a number of urban settings in which life and limb [were] more in jeopardy than in our most hazardous prison." Then I had the data to support this point, but it could not be made today.

The melancholy part of the article consisted of an enumeration of the reasons why prisons in this country ought to be places of violence. The argument still seems intact: prisons ought to be violent places, given the society from which prisoners come and the circumstances of their incarceration. But I thought then that a well-trained and disciplined staff, addressing itself to the creation of a community of inmates and staff, could contain the violence, reducing it to a tolerable minimum. It seemed that our California prisons were well on the way to the achievement of this goal; our efforts to humanize incarceration were reaping an invaluable reward. I went on to the inane suggestion that our plans to create a "special security prison" might well complete a system in which violence would be exceptional indeed; most of my colleagues in California were also of that opinion. At that time, we were working hard on the design of such a facility, hoping to minimize its oppressiveness through the application of the principles of small group organization and liberal use of incentives to participate constructively in the correctional community, if not merely to conform.

Ten years have passed and obviously neither California prisons nor the prisoners in them are the same. The changes have not been limited to California. In the same article I also reported on the virtual nonexistence of violence in the prisons of Sweden. I discussed the systematic effort of Swedish prison administrators to reduce the repressiveness of custody through furloughs, well-paid work, conjugal visits, and the building of small facilities emphasizing a modicum of comfort and convenience amid the required austerity.

There have been changes in Sweden, too. Two years ago I made another visit to that country, which coincided with a spectacular prisoners' strike aimed at changing a system that the strike leaders denounced as arbitrary and

23

dehumanizing. Although Swedish prisons are far from the squalidly dangerous places that prevail in this country, there are violent men confined in them and violent incidents occur. A kind of militance has developed in which radical intellectuals and prison inmates have elevated the submerged opposition of staff and inmates into overt conflict. This movement has been well described by Thomas Mathiesen in his recent account of the KRUM organization, *The Politics of Abolition.*[2]

Among penological connoisseurs, Dutch prisons have been widely admired. They are small, there are few of them, sentences are short, and their administrators make enlightened use of rehabilitative techniques and programs. The low crime rates of the Netherlands make an excellent point of departure for those who wish to show that a minimally punitive criminal law does not necessarily increase the volume of crime. So the world was startled last summer by a violent confrontation between terrorist prisoners at an institution at Scheveningen and a staff that could not accede to demands made for the release of certain comrades. The confrontation ended with the explosive intervention of the Dutch marines, far from characteristic of the placid conditions of Dutch prisons in previous years.

An even more recent incident in Italy provides still another illustration of the intensely political character of prison violence that has emerged in Europe as well as in this country. Judge Giuseppe di Gennaro, a member of the highest court in Italy, was kidnapped in Rome by a group calling itself the Armed Nuclei of the Proletariat. The judge was kept for five days in a damp cellar, handcuffed and blindfolded. Although his leftist sympathies are internationally known, he was derided as a servant of the establishment. The strange aspect to the incident was that the Armed Nuclei were able to conduct negotiations for their objective in synchronized timing with the inmate captors of a guard at the prison at Viterbo, who had been taken in a well-planned affair involving guns, explosives, and radio transmitters. The abductors of the judge demanded that their inmate associates at Viterbo should be defended by lawyers of their choosing and that they should be transferred from Viterbo to another prison. All these concessions were made, whereupon Judge di Gennaro was freed.

It is probably idle to speculate on the motives of the perpetrators of such an incident when their identities are so little understood and the details of the episode are still known only fragmentarily. Still, we can discern several new and disturbing elements in the nature of prison violence: First, in at least some of the advanced countries of Europe, prison violence reflects the politicization of prisoner life. The process in this country clearly expresses the racist conflicts endemic in American life; in Europe we seem to be witnessing a revolutionary attack on the institutions of social control. Second, as a concomitant to the political quality of conflict, the technological escalation of the confrontation puts the nature of violence into a context far different and far more dangerous than the simple predatory attacks on fellow prisoners that used to consitute most of the assaultive behavior taking place. It is a relatively simple matter to control the predatory conduct of a small gang, which, in its thievery and intimidation, manages to make a lot of enemies among other inmates. It is quite another thing to deal with violence that is directed at the staff by men who can represent their cause as one that is carried out in behalf of all inmates and at the same time engages revolutionary support outside the walls. The apparatus required for the control of semiliterate thugs concerned with sex, cigarettes, and candybars is not adequate for the control of guerilla operations aimed at the disruption of the entire criminal justice system.

These speculations expose me to the possibility of deflation by events in a world that has never been so unpredictable. The special turbulence of the late sixties has subsided, at least in this country the movements that inspired the politicization of the prisons have disintegrated. Nevertheless, the makings of a principle can be discerned: Violence in prison tends to reflect violence on the streets. Where street violence is the instrument of street crime, there will be analogs in prison to the muggings and rapes that prevail outside. Where violence expresses the conflictual aspirations of ethnic gangs, there will be gang violence in prisons. Where there is violence that expresses political activism, (no matter how crude the politics), there will be political violence in prison. We are a violent society; our violence is increasing on the streets, and we can expect it to increase in the prisons.

Vulnerability of Prisons

I do not foresee the coming disintegration of the entire criminal justice system. It seems likely to me that many years will pass before most American prisons and jails are seriously threatened by political attacks on their stability. Nevertheless, there are some institutions that are under this kind of threat now and that are likely to continue to be vulnerable for many years. These are prisons that are close to centers of revolutionary activity and regarded by revolutionary leaders as useful targets. This is the place to consider what features make these prisons such likely objectives for revolutionary attack.

First, where a convincing discrepancy between the injustice of the system and claims of social justice can be demonstrated, the revolutionary cause can at the same time place the system on a moral defensive and also enlist the sympathetic support of large elements of the general public. This is especially true when the prison can be shown to be an instrument of racial injustice; the cause of the racial minority in prison can be argued to be the cause of that minority everywhere. But in Norway, where there are no minorities to speak of, it has been quite possible to make a case out of the social injustice of the prison system by calling attention to the unfairness of the vagrancy statutes under which many working class Norwegians were confined. Even if we succeed in eliminating the glaring elements of racism in our administration of the prisons, we will still have to deal with the justice or injustice of other and more arguable policies and practices.

2) A second feature that creates vulnerability is the ineptitude of prison administrators. The record of Attica is the paradigm case, but it is a paradigm that represents most prison systems. Attica was and is far too large even for the control of unsophisticated thugs, and so are dozens of other maximum custody American prisons. The conduct of a conspiracy in such a setting is simple and many prisoners have always been able to get away with antisocial activities simply because the staff is organized only to maintain a modus vivendi with the inmates. But where purposeful and intelligent criminals operate under these capricious controls, their success will be far more damaging to the system than an escape or the introduction of some contraband. The evidence will not support the notion that the Attica tragedy was the consequence of a radical conspiracy, Russell Oswald to the contrary notwithstanding. It rapidly became a political event, and intelligent leadership on the inmate side exploited the mistakes of a maladroit staff. These mistakes culminated in a callous confrontation in which indifference to life was displayed on both sides. The state won a Pyrrhic victory; American prisons cannot survive many more such episodes.

3) A third feature that makes the prison an attractive target of opportunity is its sheer unpopularity as an institution. There is a short life of prison reformers among American wardens, admired for their deviancy from the norms for their role. Osborne, Lawes, Duffy, and Scudder—perhaps there have been a few others—managed to achieve a certain celebrity by making humane changes in deteriorating situations. Most of their colleagues have been content with the apologetic rhetoric of the correctional establishment, which has never mobilized wide public support. Locking people in cages, no matter how necessary it may be to do so, is a dirty business. Those whose occupation it is will be grudgingly accepted at best, and easily attacked by those who find it to their interest to do so.

Reducing Prison Violence

What can be done to reduce the appalling potentiality of prison violence? The solutions are well known and all too familiar. The fact that they have yet to be adopted attests to the indifference of the American people. Apparently we really do not care enough to do what has to be done and what actually has been done in countries far less affluent and confronted with far less urgent situations. Nevertheless, these measures must be taken if we are to avert more disasters:

First, we simply cannot afford any longer to maintain the megaprison. The Law Enforcement Assistance Administration introduced in Part E of the

Omnibus Crime Control and Safe Streets Act the concept of the prison of 400 as the maximum size eligible for support for construction from public funds. This is a standard in European prisons where confrontations do occur, but seldom with the disastrous quality so common in American prison riots. The megaprison of 1,000 to 5,000 or more inmates constitutes a standing invitation to sudden and explosive violence. Accountants can easily show that prisoners are cheaper to keep when they are kept by the thousands, but everyone else knows that this kind of ant-hill housing is an intolerable degradation of the most debased human being.

Second, we have to attend to the ethnic origins of prison staffs. Gresham Sykes used to speak of the solidary opposition between staff and inmates as constituting a model for corruption on both sides. That concept flowered in the days when most inmates in most prisons were white, and the minorities were really minorities in most prison populations. Those days are gone, and the solidary opposition between inmates and staff has taken on the characteristics of the prevailing racial hostilities outside. We will not solve this problem by waiting for affirmative action on the civil service lists to take effect, but we had better find some way of eliminating the situations where an armed band of white guards is herding a predominantly black mass of prisoners. The black guards will still have the solidary opposition model to live with, but they will come to their tasks with some understanding and concern for fellow blacks rather than the fears and misunderstandings that so often characterize our interracial relations.

Third, we must become serious about training and the consequences of its absence. One way of looking at the troubles of the American prison is to consider the heritage of decades of nontraining. It is only in the most recent years that any staff in any American prisons have been systematically prepared for their jobs. Essentially the prison is operated on principles that have evolved from the expedients adopted by unlettered men to deal with emergencies for which they were unprepared. A man can learn something in this way, and the survival of the prison proves the point. But there is a tradition of needlessly bad human relations between guards and prisoners, which has to be unlearned and replaced with understanding. The supervisory and managerial functions are poorly handled at best, probably because there is so little certainty as to what ought to be done and how it should be carried out. The future will confront prison staff from top to bottom with unprecedented problems, the outlines of which we can vaguely discern as ominous and comprising a greatly increased potential for hostility and violence. At all levels staff should be learning firm but humane measures for controlling violence when it occurs. There is much to be learned from the Attica episode, but only if it is first recognized as the tragic fiasco it was. There should be continuing efforts to build some sense of community and concern. We cannot be sure that the group counseling movement of the sixties accomplished anything else, but it certainly contributed to the creation of the bonds from which community is built. Efforts should be renewed to use the counseling structure as a vehicle for problem-solving exchange of concerns and ideas about the community in which both sides are desperately involved.

Fourth, we must redouble the effort to eliminate injustice from the whole system of criminal justice, but particularly in the prison. Highest on these agenda should be the elimination of the indeterminate sentence, and its adminis-tration by parole boards. The concept of the flat term, as expounded by David Fogel, will need some correction in detail, but in its general principle it is an overdue reform. The meaningless processes that pass for parole decision making, the invalid criteria for deciding readiness for release, and the cruel ambiguity in which we maintain prisoners now constitute a system that has no real counter-part anywhere else—although I regret to report that the English have been attempting to create their own version of this American malpractice.

But there are other injustices that must be remedied. Prisoners who violate institutional rules should be dealt with and sometimes severely, but they should also get the due process that is the essence of justice. Under the prodding of the courts we have begun to make steps in this direction, but there is much more to do and little excuse for not doing it. Rules must be reviewed to see that they continue to make sense. Penalties must be humanely and reasonably adminis-tered; the horrifying conditions that prevail in some isolation units should be seen as simply un-American, as characteristic of some totalitarian country.

The injustice of work for derisory pay at a few cents an hour, or no pay at all, should be obvious, even though it will not be easy to correct. Most cor-rectional administrators agree, I think, on the desirability of a fair day's pay for a fair day's work, but I seldom hear them call for it in public. Their assumption is that this is an idea whose time has not yet come, but it will not come soon unless informed leadership takes action.

Finally, we must find administrators with foresight, men and women who can think ahead with compassion and concern for the people in their charge. By its nature, the prison, like the society in which it is embedded, will always be fraught with conflict. Many of the confrontations among people who are never entirely rational will always be unpredictable and even by hindsight will be seen as unavoidable. But the warden who wants to prevent violence must be an activist. He must say as little as possible about the philosophy of prison reform and instead must be seen as incessantly doing what he can to clean his prison up.

Some years ago when I was visiting a certain very large prison a staff member remarked to me that there was a good deal of unrest behind the walls: "It's like living with a gigantic and unpredictable beast," he said. I thought of Cicero's aphorism: "The Roman Senators are all good men, but the Roman Senate is a wicked beast." These are the days when we think in terms of systems and systems analysis, often to good advantage, but whether we think of beasts or systems we shall inevitably lose if we cannot find the men. There is indeed a beast behind the wall, but he can be tamed if we keep the men in sight.

Notes

1. John P. Conrad, "Violence in Prison," *Annals,* 364 (March 1966), 113-19.
2. Thomas Mathiesen, *The Politics of Abolition* (Oslo, Norway: Universitets-forlaget, 1974).

3

Biological Substrates of Violence
Kenneth E. Moyer

Aggression is not a unitary construct. There are a number of different kinds of aggressive behavior.[1] This means it is not going to be possible to construct a single model that will fit all of them in detail. But we can talk about the mechanisms or the kinds of mechanisms that are common to some if not most of the different kinds of aggressive behavior.

The basic premise of this model is that there are in the brains of animals and man neural systems that when fired in the presence of a relevant target result in aggressive or destructive behavior toward that target. There is now abundant evidence to support that premise.

Some of the most fundamental work on this area has been done by John Flynn at Yale. Flynn has worked with cats and, as some of you may know, has enlarged on techniques that were developed in the early 1940s. It is possible to implant an electrode in specific areas deep in an animal's brain. The electrode can then be attached to a plug that is cemented to the skull. The plug can then be attached to a stimulation source and it is possible to stimulate the depths of the brain of an animal that is awake and free to move around. When the experiment is finished for the day, the subject can be returned to its home cage none the worse for wear.

The cats used by Flynn are friendly and will not attack a rat. They may, in fact, live with a rat for months and not molest it in any way. If an electrode implanted in the cat's lateral hypothalamus is stimulated, it will ignore the experimenter standing there, but it will immediately attack and kill an available rat. The kill will be quite precise resulting from a bite in the cervical region of the spinal chord. This is the typical predatory behavior of the feline. However, if the electrode is located in the medial hypothalmus, and the animal is stimulated in the presence of the rat, it will ignore the rat, turn and attack the experimenter. The attack on the experimenter will be highly directed. It is not similar to the random attacks of a decerebrate animal. This cat appears as though it intends to do the experimeter harm, and, in fact, it will.[2]

There are a large number of similar experiments. Some have been done in my laboratory.[3] One particularly interesting experiment that illustrates a number of things was done by Robinson, Alexander, and Bowne.[4] They took a small Rhesus monkey and implanted an electrode in the anterior hypothalmus. They

---

This chapter is based on material from the author's book *The Psychobiology of Aggression,* to be published by Harper and Row.

then put the animal in the usual primate chair, activated the electrode, and showed that the monkey did not become aggressive towards inanimate objects, nor did it become aggressive towards the experimenter. It was then put in a cage with another monkey that was larger and dominant to the experimental animal and with the dominant monkey's female consort. When stimulated in this situation the experimental monkey viciously and immediately attacked the dominant monkey. It did not attack the female. It attacked only the dominant male monkey. This appeared to be a valid primate attack because the dominant monkey reacted by counterattacking just as viciously as it usually would if attacked by a submissive animal. This scenario was repeated a number of times and although it is quite unusual, Robinson et al. found that the dominance relationship changed. The stimulation induced attacks were so vicious that the formerly dominant animal ultimately became submissive to the experimental monkey. The behavior of the female was interesting. Initially she sided with the dominant animal, and as the fortunes of war began to shift a little bit she became neutral. Then finally when the dominance relationship was changed she sided with the experimental monkey and attacked the formerly dominant one. This experiment shows first that the particular brain stimulation used resulted in one specific kind of aggression, which I have called "inter-male," that is, the specific tendency for one male to attack another. Second, this experiment demonstrates that aggressive behavior is stimulus bound. In the absence of the *relevant* stimulus, that monkey, even though stimulated time and again, showed no irritability or increased tendency to attack other targets.

It is important not to generalize too quickly from one species to another. One must be particularly cautious in generalizing from animals to man. However, we now have good evidence that man, for all of his encephalization, has not escaped from the neural determinants of his aggressive behavior. There are now several hundred people who have electrodes implanted in their brains, which are attached to small sockets cemented to the skull. These patients can be brought in to the laboratory, plugged in, and precise areas deep in the brain can be electrically stimulated.

A case reported by King is particularly instructive.[5] This patient was a very mild-mannered woman who was a generally submissive, kindly, friendly person. An electrode was implanted in the area of her brain called the amygdala. Dr. King stimulated this patient in the amygdala with a current of four milliamperes and there was no observable change in her behavior. (One cannot tell when one's brain is stimulated, there are no receptors that can indicate brain stimulation; thus, she was unaware of any stimulation.) When the amperage was increased to five milliamperes, she became hostile and aggressive. She said things such as, "Take my blood pressure. Take it now." Then she said, "If you're going to hold me you'd better get five more men." Whereupon she stood up and started to strike the experimenter. He then wisely turned down the current.

It was possible to turn this woman's anger on and off with a simple flick of the switch because the electrode was located in a part of the neural system for hostility. She indicated having felt anger. She also reported being concerned about the fact that she was angry. She did not report pain or other discomfort. She was simply turned on angry.

There are a number of pathological processes that can occur in the brain, which result in the activation of the neural systems for aggression in humans. Brain tumors, if they are in the areas of the brain such as the hypothalmus, the septum, or the amygdala, can result in the manifestation of increasing amounts of hostility. A relatively rare kind of epilepsy can also involve the activation of the hostility systems. Individuals afflicted with this disease show periods of excessive aggressive behavior with little or no provocation.[6]

In addition to the neural systems for aggression, there are also neural systems for the inhibition or the blockage of those systems. There is considerable experimental evidence for this. Bernstein and I[7] showed several years ago that if you remove the olfactory bulbs from a rat you turn a peaceful laboratory rat into a vicious animal that will attack other rats, mice, or the experimenter. The bulbectomized rat is highly irritable. Wheatley[8] showed back in the forties that if the medial hypothalmus of the cat is lesioned, a tame cat is turned into a wild cat, and very quickly. Apparently these suppressor systems inhibit the activity in the neural systems for aggression. There is, of course, much additional evidence to support these findings.

It is a fortunate fact that in neither man nor animal is aggression very frequent. It is relatively uncommon. Thus, in order to understand the physiology of aggression, we must understand what it is that turns on these neural systems and what it is that turns them off. Perhaps one of the best ways to think about this is in terms of thresholds for the systems. In certain circumstances the threshold for the firing of the neural systems for aggression is very high. In that case it takes a great deal of provocation to activate systems. There are other circumstances in which the thresold is very low and relatively little provocation will result in the activation of the neural systems with the result that the individual has an increased tendency to behave aggressively.

Some of the variables that influence the thresholds for the neural systems for aggression appear to be hereditary. For example, we have shown in my laboratory that some strains of rats behave aggressively towards mice in significantly greater numbers than do others.[9] This has also been shown in any number of other laboratories. It is possible, as Lagerspetz[10] has shown, to take a large population of mice and select from them aggressive animals and nonaggressive animals. Within a relatively few generations, if the very aggressive animals are mated, it is possible to develop a highly aggressive strain in which the mice will attack immediately when they are put together. If the nonaggressive animals are bred, a strain can be developed that will not fight no matter what you do to them. Dr. Wolpy at Earlham College tells me that he is raising an extremely aggressive strain of rabbits. These rabbits will attack other rabbits, or the experimenter. If some of these animals get out on the Indiana countryside there are going to be some surprised hunting dogs.

We obviously do not have any comparable data on man. The problem is much too complex for the geneticists to deal with. However, if this model has any validity and if there are specific neural systems for different kinds of aggressive behavior, it must be that different thresholds for aggression are inherited. Neurological differences must be inherited in the same way that differences in the shapes of noses are.

Another significant variable that contributes to differences in the threshold level is blood chemistry. It has been known for centuries that one can take the raging bull and convert it into a gentle steer by the operation of castration, which reduces the level of testosterone in the blood stream. The formal work on this problem was done in 1947 by Beeman,[11] and has been repeatedly confirmed in many laboratories. Dr. Beeman worked with a strain of mice that would fight on being put together. She castrated the animals of the experimental group prior to puberty. When those mice were put together they did not fight at all. The control group showed the usual amount of aggression characteristic of that strain. She then carried the experiment a step further and implanted pellets of testosterone subcutaneously in castrated mice. When the testosterone became effective they fought at the same level as the control animals had. She then surgically removed the pellets of testosterone whereupon the mice once again became docile. It was possible to manipulate the aggressive behavior of these mice simply by manipulating the testosterone level.

There are a variety of other blood chemistry changes that influence the thresholds for aggression. For example, we know that frustration and stress are inportant variables in inducing aggressive behavior, particularly if the frustration and stress are prolonged. This likely is because the stressors change the hormonal status and thus change the thresholds for the neural systems for aggression. Although we do not yet have experimental evidence to support this conjecture, there are a number of people working on the problem.

It is also true, as many women have found, that there is a period during the week before the menstruation when a significant percentage of women feel irritable, hostile, and are easily aroused to anger.[12] Those who have had inadequate training in impulse control sometimes behave and act on those impulses. In fact, one study that was conducted on 249 female prison inmates showed that 62 percent of the crimes of violence were committed in the premenstrual week, whereas only 2 percent of the crimes of violence were committed in the postmenstrual week.[13]

Lest anyone believe that women's rights should in some way be restricted because of their periodic tendency to violence, let me point out that from mouse to man, with very few exceptions, the male is the more aggressive sex.

Statistics show that the homicide rate is 5 times as great for the male and something like 20 times as great for armed robbery. As Broom and Selznick said, "Compared with females, males have a greater excess of crimes in all nations, all communities within nations, all age groups, all periods of history for which we have statistics, and for all types of crime except those related to the female sex, such as abortion."[14]

Learning has a powerful influence on aggressive behavior, just as it does on other behaviors. It is possible, by manipulating the contingencies of reinforcement, to teach an animal to eat until it becomes obese. It is also possible to manipulate the contingencies of reinforcement so that an animal will starve to death in the presence of food. We should expect no less of an influence on aggressive behavior.

As learning and the internal impulses to aggressive behavior interact, one can learn to inhibit internal impulses to aggression. Also, one can learn to express aggression in the absence of any emotional internal impulse to aggressive behavior. Man of course learns better and faster than any other animal.

If, in fact, there are neural systems for aggressive behavior, it should be possible directly to intervene, cut out, or lesion these neural systems, and reduce the amounts of aggression. It can be done. One can take the wildcat Rufus Rufus, which will attack with the slightest provocation, and convert it to a pettable pussy cat by burning out a very small part of the brain called the amygdala. After the operation it will never be violent again.[15]

The same thing can be done with the wild Norway rat, one of the few animals that will attack without apparent provocation. If a bilateral amygdalectomy is done on a wild Norway rat, as soon as it comes out of the anesthestic, it will have an amygdalectomy hangover for awhile, but it will never bite again. You can pick it up and carry it around in your lab coat pocket.[16]

There are wild men just as there are wild cats, men who are so violent that they are a constant threat to themselves and to everyone around them. These are individuals who must be kept in the back wards either under constant sedation or under constant restraint, frequently in isolation, with no furniture, because they are so violent they will destroy anything that comes close to them.

There are a number of surgeons now who have done exactly the same operation on man as described above for the cat and the rat, that is, a complete or partial bilateral amygdalectomy. Narabayashi and his colleagues in Japan, for example, indicate that they get 85 percent success in the reduction of violent behavior after a bilateral amygdalectomy.[17] Heimburger claims that he gets a 92 percent increase in docility in these extremely violent patients through the same operation.[18] Not only was it possible to release those individuals into the open wards, that is, take them out of isolation, but two of his patients have been released into society and are making at least a reasonable adjustment.

There are a variety of other areas in the brain where lesions can be made that result in a reduction in the amount of aggressive behavior. It should be emphasized that this finding is of tremendous theoretical importance. However, this is not a viable, useful, therapeutic technique. There are several reasons for this: One is that these operations are obviously not 100 percent successful. The claims of Narabayashi and Heimburger are higher than most. When an operation is not successful the individual is brain damaged without reason. Brain damage is, of course, irreparable. There is no regeneration of nerve cells in the brain. I cannot think of any prisoner situation in which this would be a desirable technique. It should be a therapy of absolute last resort.

If there are suppressor systems in the brain it should be possible to activate them directly and reduce aggressive behavior. An experiment by Delgado is particularly instructive.[19] He implanted an electrode in the area of a monkey's brain called the caudate nucleus. He selected the Boss monkey as his subject. (Boss monkeys can be extremely mean. The dominate the rest of the colony; they push the other monkeys around and take first sex, first food, and first anything else they want, and they keep the rest of the colony under control.) The electrode was brought out to a radio, which was bolted to the monkey's skull. The radio was connected by a very tiny relay to a battery, which the monkey wore on its back in a battery pack. Thus, when the radio was activated by a transmitter the relay closed and resulted in the stimulation of the monkey's brain. It was then possible for Delgado to stand outside the cage and stimulate the caudate nucleus of the monkey's brain by pressing a button on a transistorized radio transmitter similar to the type you use to open your garage door. The monkey then had complete freedom in the colony and was untrammeled by wires. With periodic stimulation of the caudate nucleus, the Boss monkey calmed down, ceased threatening, and became very nonaggressive. This was not an arrest reaction, that is, the monkey was quite capable of functioning in other ways. He simply lost his aggressiveness. When this became apparent in the colony a couple of young smart-alec monkeys soon infringed on the Boss' territory and on his territorial preogatives. They began to take over and push the Boss monkey around. When Delgado stopped pressing the button the Boss monkey soon got things "whipped back into shape."

Delgado took this experiment one step further. He put the transmitter inside the cage next to the food bin. One small monkey, who was short on brawn but long on brains, learned to stand next to the button and watch the Boss monkey. Every time the Boss would start to fluff up and become aggressive or threaten, the little monkey would push the button and calm him down.

Exactly the same procedure can be used on man. Heath reported on a patient who had an implant in an area of the brain called the septum.[20] It was possible to bring this patient in, paranoid, raging, swearing, threatening, struggling, sit him down in a chair, and stimulate his brain. Again, the patient did not know his brain had been stimulated. He immediately relaxed, became docile, and assumed a positive attitude. When the electrode is in the area of the septum, the patient may tell you a dirty joke or reveal plans to seduce the waitress down at the corner bar. There are other suppressor areas, however, that do not activate sexually toned responses.

It would be possible to run the wire from that electrode down the back of this patient's neck to a battery pack that he could wear on his belt. You could then give him an "antihostility button" and whenever he began to feel very mean he could press the button, calm himself down, and bring himself back into the civilized world.

The technology has already been developed. Heath developed it as a therapeutic device for an individual with narcolepsy.[21] Narcolepsy is a disorder in which the individual falls asleep at inappropriate times. I have had many students afflicted with this disorder. This particular patient suggested that his narcolepsy was very troublesome because it interferred with his profession. He was a night club entertainer and would sometimes fall asleep in the middle of his act. What Heath did was to implant an electrode in the arousal system of the brain. He brought the wire down to a transistorized stimulation unit and gave the patient an "on button." Whenever he started to drift off to sleep the patient could press his "on button" and turn himself back on. He had a type of narcolepsy in which he sometimes fell asleep before he could get to the button. His friends soon learned, however, that when he did that they could reach over and press his "on button" and bring him back into the conversation.

I pointed out that Delgado had his monkey hooked up to a radio. There is no reason why exactly the same type of therapeutic technique could not be used on humans. At least four people that I know have been under radio control of one sort or another.[22] An electrode could be placed in a suppressor area of the brain just as Delgado did with the Boss monkey. It could be brought out to a radio, which is bolted to the subject's head. His brain could then be activated by a transmitter and the patient could then range as widely as the area that the transmitter will reach.

There are problems with this approach. Since the radio has to be bolted to the skull, it means that the bolts have to go through the scalp. This is a constant possible source of irritation, and a source of infection. There are also psychological problems. People tend to report that they feel conspicuous with radios on their heads. However, one woman fashioned a wig so that she was able to cover her radio adequately.[23]

Even those problems are being solved due to the recent microminiaturization in electronics. It is now possible to take the radio, the power to operate it, and a radio transmitter and put them all into a unit that is about the size and the shape of a half a dollar. The electrode can be put in place, attached to this unit and the unit can be implanted under the skin anywhere. As soon as the individual's hair grows back he looks like anyone else. In fact, it is technologically possible right now that the individual sitting next to you is under radio control and you would not know it unless he parted his hair wrong this morning.

The suppression of aggression by electrical stimulation is of tremendous theoretical importance. However, like brain lesions, it is not yet a reasonable or useful therapeutic technique. One of the reasons that it is not is because of a phenomenon discovered in animals called kindling. In the parts of the nervous system where these kinds of implants must be made, under certain conditions of stimulation, the cells being stimulated begin to fire spontaneously. It is not yet known why. Not only do they fire spontaneously, but they tend to recruit other cells until the recruitment is so great that the motor system is involved and the individual goes into behavioral convulsions. Although this has never been reported on people it has been reported on animals, and should certainly give us pause until more is known about the phenomenon.[24] Also, there is at least one case on record in which it is claimed that the subject became addicted to the stimulation of his amygdala, which suppressed his aggressive behavior.[25] Some of the changes produced in the brain during electrical stimulation may not be reversible. At this stage of development, brain stimulation certainly does not appear to be a practical method for controlling aggression.

There are other methods however. It is possible to control certain kinds of aggressive behavior by manipulating the endocrine system. The woman, for example, who suffers from periodic hyper-irritability every month, has a physician who either is not aware of the problem or does not keep up on the literature. There are a variety of therapeutic measures now that can be taken to alleviate that problem.

There are also people who show a kind of aggressive behavior, known as sex-related aggression. These are the violent individuals for whom the object of aggression is the same as the object for sexual behavior. These are the individuals who commit the brutal sexual murders. There is now reasonable evidence to suggest that in the not-too-distant future we will have a variety of endocrine substances that can be implanted with a depot implant under the skin where the material is released slowly and will suppress this kind of aggressive behavior.[26] There are also antiandrogens, such as cyproterone[27] and a synthetic progesterone, medroxyprogesterone. There is now experimental evidence that both of these might be useful in blocking sex-related aggression.[28]

Also, there is now a whole armementarium of antihostility drugs. These drugs are not specific antihostility agents but have hostility reduction as a significant part of their total pattern of action.[29]

For the individual who is in solitary confinement, in the back ward, under sedation and restraint, most men would agree that he cannot be made much worse. He should have available to him the fruits of this kind of research. That seems to be a relatively unmixed blessing.

What are the implications for normals? I once had a neighbor who met all the usual criteria for normality. Certainly she could not and should not have been put away. But, she had a very low threshold for aggressive behavior. She worried about it. She had extreme anxiety over it. She made frequent resolutions that she was not going to behave in that way. In spite of her considerable concern, she still found that she was screaming at her husband and slapping her children without cause. Again, most men would agree that this woman, if she wishes, should have available to her some of the antihostility drugs, which would help her to control this unwanted behavioral tendency. Certainly it will be a more peaceful world when each of us, if we choose, can control our unwanted and irrational aggressive behavior.

We should examine the other edge of the double-edge sword of progress. Knowledge is accelerating at an ever-increasing rate. We cannot stop it. We can only hope to use it wisely when it comes. Airplanes are now being built that are longer than the entire initial flight of the Wright brothers. If we have a comparable increase in our understanding of the physiological substrates of aggressive behavior, and there is every reason to believe that we will, what kinds of control will be available to us 50 or 70 years from now?

In may laboratory at Carnegie-Mellon University we have squirrel monkeys, which, when untamed, are extremely mean. If you put your hand in the cage to pet them, they will bite it viciously and repeatedly. We can only handle them with heavy gauntlet gloves. Judy Gibbons and I showed some time ago that we can take a few thousandths of a gram of diazepam and put it in the milk that we give the monkeys to drink. They apparently cannot taste it, nor could I when I tried it. As soon as the drug becomes effective, these animals become docile. They become friendly. They are not knocked out. They simply lose their aggression. We can reach in and pick them up with our bare hands, cuddle them to our shoulders, and walk around the laboratory with them.

The milk you drank this morning was homogenized, irradiated, and had Vitamin D added. Will the milk you drink tomorrow morning also have an antihostility drug added? If it does, will that make for a more peaceful population? And if it does, will it be worth it? The absolute physiological control of certain kinds of aggressive behavior in individuals is here right now. The absolute physiological control of large groups of people is not here — yet.

Notes

1. K. E. Moyer, "Kinds of Aggression and Their Physiological Bases," *Communications in Behavioral Biology,* 2 (1968), 65–87.

2. M. D. Egger and J. P. Flynn, "Effect of Electrial Stimulation of the Amygdala on Hypothalamically Elicited Attack Behavior in Cats," *Journal of Neurophysiology,* 26 (1963), 705-20.

3. R. J. Bandler, "Facilitation of Aggressive Behavior in the Rat by Direct Cholinergic Stimulation of the Hypothalamus," *Nature,* 224 (1969), 1035-36; "Cholinergic Synapses in the Lateral Hypothalamus for the Control of Predatory Aggression in the Rat," *Brain Research,* 20 (1970), 409-24.

4. B. W. Robinson, M. Alexander, and G. Bowne, "Dominance Reversal Resulting From Aggressive Responses Evoked by Brain Telestimulation," *Physiology and Behavior,* 4 (1969), 749-52.

5. H. E. King, "Psychological Effects of Excitation in the Limbic System," *Electrical Stimulation of the Brain,* D. E. Sheer, ed. (Austin: University of Texas Press, 1961), 477-86.

6. H. Gastaut, "Interpretation of the Symptons of Psychomotor Epilepsy in Relation to Physiologic Data on Rhinencephalic Function," *Epilepsia,* 3 (1954), 84-88.

7. H. Bernstein and K. E. Moyer, "Aggressive Behavior in the Rat: Effects of Isolation and Olfactory Bulb Lesions," *Brain Research,* 20 (1970), 75-84.

8. M. D. Wheatley, "The Hypothalamus and Affective Behavior in Cats," *Archives of Neurology and Psychiatry,* 52 (1944), 296-316.

9. R. Bandler and K. E. Moyer, "Animals Spontaneously Attacked by Rats," *Communications in Behavioral Biology,* 5 (1970), 177-82.

10. K. Lagerspetz, "Studies on the Aggressive Behavior of Mice," *Annales Academiae Scientiarum Fennicae,* Series B (1964), 1-131.

11. E. A. Beeman, "The Effect of Male Hormone on Aggressive Behavior in Mice," *Physiological Zoology,* 20 (1947), 373-405.

12. K. Dalton, "Menstruation and Acute Psychiatric Illness," *British Medical Journal,* 1 (1959), 148-49; "School Girls' Misbehavior and Menstruation," *British Medical Journal,* 2 (1960), 1647; "Menstruation and Crime," *British Medical Journal,* 3 (1961), 1752-53; *The Premenstrual Syndrome* (Springfield, Ill.: Charles C. Thomas, 1964).

13. J. H. Morton, H. Addition, R. G. Addison, L. Hunt, and J. J. Sullivan, "A Clinical Study of Premenstrual Tension," *American Journal of Obstetrics and Gynecology,* 65 (1953), 1182-91.

14. L. Broom and P. Selznick, *Sociology: A Text With Adapted Readings,* (New York: Harper & Row, 1957).

15. L. Schreiner and A. Kling, "Behavioral Changes Following Rhinencephalic Injury in Cats," *Journal of Neurophysiology,* 16 (1953), 643-58.

16. J. W. Woods, "Taming of the Wild Norway Rat by Rhinencephalic Lesions," *Nature,* 178 (1956), 869.

17. H. Narabayashi, T. Nagao, Y. Saito, M. Yoshida, and M. Nagahata, "Stereotaxis Amygdalotomy for Behavior Disorders," *Archives of Neurology,* 9 (1963), 1-16.

18. R. F. Heimburger, C. C. Whitlock, and J. E. Kalsbeck, "Stereotaxi Amygdalatomy for Epilepsy with Aggressive Behavior," *Journal of the American Medical Asosciation,* 198 (1966), 165-69.

19. J. M. R. Delgado, "Cerebral Heterostimulation in *a Monkey Colony,"* Science, 141 (1963), 161-63.

20. R. G. Heath, "Electrical Self-stimulation of the Brain in Man," *American Journal of Psychiatry,* 120 (1963), 571-77.

21. R. G. Heath, "Behavioral Changes Following Destructive Lesions in the Subcortical Structure of the Forebrain in Cats," *Studies in Schizophrenia,* R. G. Heath, ed. (Cambridge: Harvard University Press, 1954), 83-84.

22. J. M. R. Delgado, V. Mark, W. Sweet, F. Ervin, G. Weiss, Y-Rita-Bach, and R. Hagiwara, "Intracerebral Radio Stimulation and Recording in Completely Free Patients," *Journal of Nervous and Mental Diseases,* 147 (1968), 329-40.

23. ―――., *Physical Control of the Mind* (New York: Harper and Row, 1969).

24. G. V. Goddard, "Long Term Alteration Following Amygdaloid Stimulation," *The Neurobiology of the Amygdala,* E. Eleftheriou, ed. (New York: Plenum, 1972), 581-96.

25. V. H. Mark, F. R. Ervin, W. H. Sweet, "Deep Temporal Lobe Stimulation in Man," *The Neurobiology of the Amygdala,* B. E. Eleftheriou, ed. (New York: Plenum, 1972), 485-507.

26. T. L. Chatz, "Management of Male Adolescent Sex Offenders," *International Journal of Offender Therapy,* 16, No. 2 (1972), 109-15.

27. U. Laschet, L. Laschet, H. R. Fetzner, H. U. Glaesel, G. Mall, and M. Naab, "Results in the Treatment of Hyper or Abnormal Sexuality of Men with Antiandrogens," *Acta Endrocrinologica* (6th Acta Endocrinological Congress), Supplement 119, (1967), 54; U. Laschet, "Antiandrogen in the Treatment of Sex Offenders Mode of Action and Therapeutic Outcome," *Contemporary Sexual Behavior: Critical Issues in the 1970s,* J. Zubin and J. Money, eds. (Baltimore: Johns Hopkins University Press, 1973), 311-19.

28. D. Blumer and C. Migeon, "Treatment of Impulsive Behavior Disorders in Males with Medroxy-progesterone Acetate," Paper presented at the Annual Meeting of the American Psychiatric Association, May 1973.

29. K. E. Moyer, *The Physiology of Hostility* (Chicago: Markham, 1971).

4

A Psychological View of Prison Violence
Hans Toch

Nothing could be more timely than a book on this subject at this time, because we are talking against a backdrop where we have a conspiracy of the right and the left to make prison a more violent place.

Outside Pressures

The left has saddled us with a model of "diversion" and decarceration in which one is willing to stipulate that a mythical 5 percent residual (which might become 50 percent in reality) ought to be in prison. This means that prisons would become repositories of more homogeneously state-raised, serious, chronic offenders with more patterned histories of violence in the community, and these inmates would be seen as appropriately warehoused rather than treated. That obviously creates institutions in which we will see violence (and other problems) among men about whom the originators of the strategy do not seem to have terribly many concerns.

We see a companion move on the right: Not only are we facing mandatory sentences for repeat offenders, but we are facing legislative efforts to enhance the eligibility for incarceration among preteen offenders with histories of violence. This again would make prison a new and different sort of place—the sort of place none of us is going to enjoy running.

We are seeing pressures that are creating institutions that have predominantly young and sophisticated offenders, who everyone agrees are extremely unsavory and unamenable to intervention. We see that rising crime rates expedite processing and exacerbate bitterness among our clients. We also face staff in institutions whose resources are being stretched to the breaking point, who become increasingly alienated themselves.

The mythical "5 percent" is worrisome on other counts. For one, we become willing to stipulate the validity of classification systems, which might irreversibly and arbitrarily classify persons as falling under the "5 percent" heading, in the face of the fact that science lags quite a bit behind classification practice. We are willing to ignore the fact that we cannot predict future violence, while we must pretend that we can. We are forced, in order to survive, to exercise

---

These informal remarks, and the subsequent discussion, followed the dinner that was the opening event of the conference.

control options in institutions that aggravate rather than ameliorate the violence problem, because all of us know that violence feeds on violence—in the sense that when we react to violence, or when the clients of our system react to it, we create climates of fear, suspicion, and retaliation that do nothing to make one's life easier. We are being deprived of flexibility to work with inmates by the fact that release dates are becoming increasingly arbitrarily fixed.

Trends in Prison Violence

This book appears against the backdrop of very concrete trends in the violence picture in prisons. Institutions are becoming more different from each other in the types of violence they feature than they were ten years ago. There seems to be more violence among equal contenders or groups than there was ten years ago. Ethnicity seems to play an increasingly substantial part in the violence picture, but was only beginning to ten years ago. (One even wonders about the wisdom of resegregating prisons.) Inmate background seems to be becoming more related to institutional conduct than it used to be (although not enough to predict). There is more violent talk today in prison yards than there used to be. Here we have the issue of presumed militance, which must be untangled from violence. Civil rights issues have become increasingly raised in relation to the management of special groups of offenders. Institutional programming is becoming more restricted in response to violence and the need to control it, to the point where we may be producing malignant cysts of violence in places like readjustment centers.

Aggressive Overtures Against Young Inmates

We know some of the descriptive or external characteristics of victims and aggressors in institutions. We know that many aggressors are sophisticated, urban black inmates. Many of the victims are young, much less sophisticated whites. We know that many victims are from nonurban areas, and that they tend to be slightly built and boyish looking.

What do we know about the phenomenon itself—about the transaction between the victim and the aggressor? We know relatively little. We do not even know what the base rates are. We know that the Philadelphia exposé does not apply to prison settings. It may not even apply to the typical detention settings. In prison, it is safe to say, actual rapes are relatively infrequent, although we have reason for assuming that they are more frequent than the incidents that come to our attention.

What is very prevalent in prison is the problem of exploitively aggressive sexually tainted overtures with threats of rape, where the threat of rape is clearly at issue for the victim, who may develop a great deal of despair relating to his physical safety, and to his adequacy as a man and as a functioning human being. It is this second area that poses a number of challenges. We can work at making people physically safer in prison, but can we also deal with the problem of reducing victim status, and of neutralizing long-term self-doubts? Can we build immunity in men to the aggressive overture of others? Can we give inmates a less fear-conditioned view of prison life and of life generally? Can we provide socially protective settings as well as safer ones? Can we protect men without stigmatizing them further? Can we build up a support system for the man who does not have any? Can we—and this may be a pipe dream—build some sense of community into the inmate culture to reduce the no-man's land that surrounds the victims of exploitation?

These questions arise out of a set of assumptions about what happens in incidents in terms of the victim's role in them. First, the victim is not only equipped with physical stigmata, he is not only attractive to the aggressor in looks, but he is also equipped with deficits in interpersonal skills and resources, which he displays as the incidents unfold. The aggressor's games become more serious and more determined when the victim clumsily responds to the initial overtures, when the victim shows fear and resourcelessness.

Second, the victim is socially vulnerable. That is, not only is the world of the state-raised youth alien and strange to him, but he is not supported by peers who can equalize the illusion of power that is central to the self-assured, subculturally supported aggressor. Third, the victim operates in a situation in which other people tell him that his options are fight or flight. There is no point in fooling ourselves about the fact that it is only inmates and not staff who provide the monotonously standard advice to the inmate that the only way to keep from getting assaulted is to attack the potential aggressor and to demonstrate through fighting that "you are a man." This presumption that men handle their problems physically, that the only countermove to threat is deterrence, is an endemic assumption in our system. It is one of those premises that creates a backdrop of norms that makes violence-reduction efforts in prison very difficult.

Fourth, the victim is in a double-bind, in that the options we provide him entail a loss of status if he avails himself of them. He may see himself faced with the choice of being perceived as a sex object or as a rat, if he comes to staff. Or he may seek refuge in special subsettings in which the presumption solidifies that he is inadequate. It is interesting that every large prison does contain ameliorative subsettings. It contains tiers, wards, work places, in which people can seek refuge if they are vulnerable. But these are also places that are not particularly high-status places.

Prison Niches

In one New York prison for youthful offenders there is a very effective tier of this kind. It is known as the "Weak Company" among staff, and is known as the

"Homo Company" among inmates. It does the job, and must get credit for what is a considerable service. People keep afloat, who might otherwise go under, but they do so at a price. There are people who pay tremendously desperate prices for peace of mind and safety in prison. There are people who segregate themselves. They are locked up 23 hours a day in solitary, with no programs whatsoever. They are cheerfully willing to pay that price, because they are terribly panic stricken and scared, because they respond to the violence that surrounds them if they get out of their protective cells.

These are trade-offs. They raise the issue, are there other program possibilities in which less of a sacrifice has to be made by the victim or potential victim?

Impact of the Manliness Myth

There is a strong emphasis in prisons and in the subcultures from which both staff and inmates derive on the importance of manliness. The victim, the typical victim of strong vs. weak prison incidents, is bound to have a long-term residue of his experience in terms of his "unmanly" conception of self. If we simply supply staff support to such people, we run the risk of further buttressing their dependency and helping to undermine their self-esteem.

The same holds if we give them the sort of ego-alien advice that we tend to give. We tell people to fight who are not built in that fashion. That is, they do not conceive of themselves as fighters. It not only does us or them no good to counsel combativeness, it does a great deal of harm, in the shape of grotesque twistings and turnings that these people have to undergo as a result. I have met men who have felt compelled (until I got to know them well) to display a tremendous amount of pretense about how they had this history of kicking their potential aggressors in the testicles and then bloodying their noses. I knew very well from the records that this was a pitiful deception and self-deception, reflecting not so much the person's self-conception, but the sort of silly game he was impelled to play to meet our prescriptions.

The Inmate Aggressor

All of our prevailing views of inmate aggressors—of men who threaten rape—have validity to them. Part of the problem is sexual deprivation. Part of the problem is attitudes related to ethnicity. Part of the problem is the motivation to display power and to gain status in a situation where a man feels emasculated. Accendency–submission is a very strong theme. Aggressors take a depersonalized view of their victims, in which their own need satisfaction is the only point at issue. But one can see these forces making a joint contribution to the aggressor's role in relation to the victim.

Sexual aggression in prison is defined as heterosexual conduct by the aggressors. They at least try to see it that way, although some of them have trouble. What this probably means is that prison aggressors relate to their victims in a way that is not terribly much different from the way they relate to their women, or to other objects of need-satisfaction outside prison. One of my associates, Dan Lockwood, had a conversation with one inmate, who had a history of being involved in all kinds of gang rapes. This spanned about ten years in various institutions. We asked him, "What was your first contact with homosexual activity?" He said, "Well, about three years ago," which was the date the man met his first prison queen, or became personally acquainted with her. That was what *he* defined as homosexual conduct. It never occurred to him to see the other seven years as homosexual conduct. They were lower preference sexual contacts.

There is a real continuity here between outside prison and in prison, in terms of people who engage their inmate victims much in the way they engage women outside. You may have a sort of pimp syndrome here—a set of overtures, offers that a man feels cannot be refused. One may even be able to track very close parallels to concrete incidents in the outside world involving women, or even involving victims of crime.

The victim is judged after the preliminary definition of his target potential, which is made in terms of attractiveness cues. The victim is judged for his conformity or lack of conformity to criteria of maleness. The main reason why blacks may aggress more against whites is that some blacks may be more apt to define some whites as not behaving like men, or not behaving as they conceive men to behave. They are less apt to see most blacks as falling under this same heading. Interpersonal tests are posed, which are partly designed to gauge the masculinity of the potential victim in terms of criteria such as those discussed by Al Cohen in his book on gang boys. The ascendancy–submission theme is involved as a parameter of male–femaleness, and need satisfaction becomes an implicit male prerogative, while the depersonalization of the victim becomes a corollary of the victim's perceived femaleness.

Reducing Systemic Supports for Violence

The prognosis, program-wise, is dim. As long as we have inmates and staff who share the working-class conception of maleness, we may have men forced into displays of power and physical prowess that lead to violence. We will be in bad shape until we can make it respectable for the strong to go to the aid of the weak, and to show concern for their peers without violating subcultural norms. We must build a reward system for *positive* interaction in prison—for human service roles among inmates and staff.

One of the most direct paths to reducing violence in penal institutions is the creation of a more positive human services climate. It is one of those situations where the most effective path to the goal may be one that on the face of it looks pretty indirect. But I think what happens is that by virtue of the negative stance of the total institution we reinforce violence among inmates and staff. We need the sort of situation that enables inmates to start feeling that it is not all right to sit there unconcerned or stand there laughing while someone is raping someone else in the shower. We need to create a situation where coming to the aid of another man, either formally or informally, can be seen as compatible with one's self-conception as a manly and worthy person.

Playing the Other Man's Game

From the aggressor's vantage point, his medium is his message, and his game is largely an end it itself. The aggressor, in the tradition of Walter Miller's value of smartness, entertains himself at the expense of his victim. He gains status from his verbal ascendancy, both in his own eyes and among his peers. He gains status from his ability to affect the victim. This means that the more seriously he is taken—the more the victim is visibly affected and damaged—the more likely it is that the aggressor's cycle continues and escalates. The more the victim reacts, the more easily the aggressor can define himself as a man who can manipulate and outsmart other people, which gains him his status.

The same holds between inmates and staff. When staff react to inmates' verbal games by taking them very literally and reacting to them, they are unwittingly feeding escalation. I assume there is much militant talk in prison, but much verbal behavior would remain no more than verbal behavior if threats were not taken literally and converted into the assumption that self-elected spokesmen are potentially revolutionaries and a danger to the prison as an institution. Any time a self-styled revolutionary is taken seriously, we reinforce the role he plays through his status-seeking verbalization. We provide payoff in a direction opposite to the one we want.

We can create management problems of considerable magnitude by taking inmates literally, including happily self-segregated inmates who manipulate us by invoking disciplinary procedures into permanent solidification of undeserved status. In New York State we have inmates who have been in segregation continuously from the time they came into prison. They are out for two days, and then they come back in. They spend 90 percent of their time being disciplined. I know a correctional official who has said to such inmates, "Look fella, what would it take, what must I do for you so you'll stay out? Some game is being played between you and us. It doesn't do you any good, and it doesn't do us any good. We don't want you segregated. What would it take, what sort of assignment would you want? Where would you like to be? What sort of program?" As a result of such negotiations, my friend has gotten some people out of segregation where they have spent much of their prison stay. They seem to be doing quite well outside. But prior to this juncture, disciplinary personnel and custodial staff had been blindly playing into the inmate's games, on the inmate's terms.

I remember a very skilled psychiatrist, a prison superintendent, who went into a segregation wing where we had notorious inmate militants. The guards did not want to let him in, and they said, "These people will kill you." He went in anyway, and talked to the inmates. "Well," he said, "they talk tough. But why don't you let me take a few of these people and put them into my Diagnostic and Treatment Center, which is a therapeutic community." He transferred some of the inmates into a standard group-centered sort of tier. The presumed incorrigible militants not only did very well but became substantial members of that small program. They have also since been released and have not done any worse than anyone else. They kept on talking tough, but there is no harm in talk.

What I am saying is not applicable to men who play the revolutionary game physically in the real world. The real militant is your black army type who comes into prison from membership in a make-believe military organization or underground movement. He is likely to persevere in his phantasy, and it is real. But there are few such men.

Self-inflicted Violence

A third area of prison violence, which is diametrically opposite to the one I've described, but very much in tune with the theme I am trying to develop here, is self-inflicted injury. For the very reasons we oversell some violence, we undersell this one. That is, we undersell the depth of motive that is involved in self-inflicted injury, which incidentally is a large-scale phenomenon in prison. Both inmate and staff subcultures conspire to downgrade this type of violence. Staff tends to classify self-violence as attention-getting and manipulative, while inmates see it as an unmanly and weak thing to do *unless* it is blatantly manipulative. Even the inmate who does this sort of thing has to define it as manipulation—as superficial—unless you explore further, to get at the depth of his despair.

We define this sort of violence as of administrative concern primarily in terms of completed suicide, that is, in terms of preventive measures. It is also at times viewed as a problem of mental illness, meaning that we dump it in the laps of the specialized professionals.

Invariably, as we have talked with these people, their extremity, and the subcultural and personal taboos that they must overcome are very real. The casualness of the act is a pretense, almost in every case. The least frequent motive we find involved in such violence relates to situational coping, but even here, we have people who get themselves in deeper because they try harder, because their adjustment problems are just more substantial to begin with. That is, we have inmates here who are just not prepared to assimilate the full range of prison experience. We cannot make the working assumptions that our efforts to minimize stress in prison, which are real and well-deserved of praise, are adequate for all inmates.

We had a unit in a New York State institution designed for the "emotionally handicapped" inmate, for inmates who had a tough time in the yard. There was a reduction in special programs, and they took these inmates and distributed them among prisons. It took about a week and most of the inmates found their way into another special program, elsewhere. The same inmates. Ninety percent of them have a history of self-injury. They are people who cannot survive in the yard. Yet, if it were not for special programs, that is exactly where they would find themselves.

Most inmates who injure themselves have problems that relate more in depth to them as continuing people. The problems have to do with their careers—with issues of interpersonal relations and self-esteem. In attending to these people, one cannot define one's task merely as ameliorating suffering. One must think of resocialization and reintegration, which is, after all, presumably the nature of our game.

Crisis management, mobilized by seeing crisis in self-inflicted violence, could be an area in which treatment, loosely defined, can have tremendous payoff. Crisis management, incidentally, affords us the opportunity to exand the role of custodial officers into a human service role, and to use inmates in human service capacity. In New York State there is a program in which inmates are used as inmate counselors. That is, inmates are acting in formal counseling roles. In the same program, they had correctional officers involved in treatment. They were running groups. They had caseloads. There is a model here for what we can do for victims—both of their own violence and of other people's violence—in terms of expanded roles for correctional officers and inmates.

A third category of self-inflicted violence does call for more clinical services. This involves problems of collapsing defenses, and it shows us people face to face with their own feelings and impulses. We have men here who sense urges and feelings in themselves, which they cannot assimilate, and which move them to panic, explosion, or confusion. Again, prisons are ill-designed to accommodate these people. I am not talking here about psychotics in full-bloom, but about their second cousins, which exist in larger numbers than we suspect. When a man is afraid of everything around him, an isolation cell is the last place he should be. Yet, that is where we put him "for his own protection," when he shows indexes of his concern. A man who is attuned to the violence potential within himself and in others has understandable difficulties in prisons, which are settings where there is a lot of conflict. Such people require special subsettings in prison, therapeutic milieus—if you will—in which professional assistance is available without a man having to demonstrate that he is a classic schizophrenic.

Collective Violence

I presume that collective violence means riots. In what respects is a riot violent? When we talk about violence with respect to riots, we think first of all of the property destruction that is the equivalent of what happens in the free-world riot. We may also be talking about the first act of the first inmate who starts the snowball rolling—who liberates the human waves from the dike by attacking the first guard. We are talking about the private violence that occurs under the cover of anarchy, under the cover of riots, such as retributive incidents and sexual victimization. We are also talking of the formal violence used to end the riot, if it is employed. (There has been too much machismo in correctional reactions to the issues of negotiation. You all know of those in official positions saying things such as, "one must never give in.") There is the sort of collective violence we see in the loss of control of custodial officers in the wake of a riot, which is situationally induced. To be fair again, one must stress that the past-riot conduct of custodial officers is unrepresentative. It is just as unrepresentative as the conduct of police officers who face a mob for 16 hours in the heat, who are verbally abused and have things thrown at them, and who (surprise!) finally lose control.

Explanations of riots are not explanations of violence in riots. Persons involved in any type of violence in a riot are a smaller number, and are drawn from a more restricted range than the number of riot participants. There are special motives for violence, which are separable from motives for rioting. The dynamics of various types of violence in riots and the dynamics of riots are discriminatively different from each other.

In reference to Attica, we know that an assault took place to end the riot and to recapture the hostages that resulted in a great deal of bloodshed. We conventionally assume that this assault and the strategy involved led to the bloodshed. A friend of mine has pointed out that if every officer in the phalanx converging on the hostages had held his ground as scheduled, and if one inmate had not panicked in response to unscheduled deviations from the projected strategy, no fatalities might have occurred. In other words, privately motivated, isolated individuals on each side could (and possibly did) convert a limited response into a massacre. What this suggests to me is that whether violence is collective, organizational, or group centered, it can benefit from a close review of the roles played by individual participants acting under the impetus of private motives and immediate pressures from their intimates and subcultural confreres.

Discussion

Irwin: There are several areas that I would like to discuss; one is homosexual rape. I think that the incidence of it is exaggerated. I don't want to diminish the problem—it is a horrible type of violence, one that catches our feeling intensely. But it therefore renders us susceptible to overreaction. I also think that it is almost insolvable. There are some things you can do to reduce it, to protect persons, but they all have their price.

Homosexual rape was really a temporal phenomena. We saw a period during the 1960s when the naive, white youth fell into the correctional system and was too often the victim of the more sophisticated (in terms of the system) black. There was also the black–white hostility at that time. The black who really harbored a deep resentment toward middle-class whites. When the "hippies" first started hitting the jails (for marijuana and other drug offenses)— and jail was where this occurred much more often than the prison — they often found themselves victims of this kind of activity. However, it is my impression that this period has passed. The persons in that segment of the prisoner world have become more sophisticated. The white drug takers continue to go to prison but they have wised up, and they know the game; they are much less prone to fall into the interactional system that leads to aggressive rape.

Toch: I stipulate the relative infrequency of rape, but what horrifies me is the prevalance of overtures. We have started to do a couple of random samples of prisons, in order to get a glance at the people who come to our attention as victims. The thing that is abolutely horrifying is that we are having a tough time finding inmates who haven't at some stage been terrorized by other inmates. We are even finding a fairly sizeable proportion in whom those effects are still very much alive.

Irwin: The broader problem is an ongoing process of *verbal* assault on one's manhood in prison. The theme of the prison version of the "Dozens," is pervasive. It used to be the game of the prisons until they became so violent that groups just didn't talk with each other; this was the major way of relating. In the street with the "Dozens" a person tries to pick out the most sensitive point, like one's family. But in prison it is one's manhood. The game goes back and forth constantly, the most boring and degrading kind of game. The person who loses is the one who weakens and gets angry. The inference is that he is really a latent homosexual and can't take the game. The effect of this after years and years is weird. But there are some obvious structural answers. It's definitely related to overuse of imprisonment, particularly in the case of juveniles. States such as California raise a large segment of youths who have spent their whole lives in foster homes, reformatories, and youth centers, and then they come to the adult prison. Because of this they are really very poorly equipped heterosexually. Their whole life is prison sex, long sentences, and the lack of contact with the female world. All three factors could be adjusted without any severe

53

consequences to our criminal justice system. Recommendations for change should be designed to make prisons more permeable, with shorter sentences, and an end to the overextended youth prison system.

Ellis: If you assume that heterosexual instigation doesn't stop when a person goes to prison, then the problem becomes how he is going to use up this energy. Nocturnal emissions and solitary masturbation are two ways; homosexual relationships constitute a third. I did my research in three North Carolina maximum security units. In the North Carolina prison system, most homosexual relationships are consensual so perhaps this is not really a problem. However, there are great risks to homosexual relationships. Unlike nocturnal emissions and solitary masturbation, homosexuality has implications for one's interactional pattern. It brings in hazardous modes of relationship with others. All sorts of things are going on because of the attempts to secure partners.

Second, I have a running battle in my own mind between functional and diffusion attempts to explain what is going on in prison, including aggressive behavior. I don't believe either model itself is sufficient. Probably more would be gained by integrating them.

Nagel: We apparently equate violence in prison with homosexuality in some way or another. At a time when prison administrators are worried about all sorts of violence not directly related to homosexual activity, when every administrator in the country is beginning to either build or thinking of building maximum-security prisons, we should not be concentrating so much on homosexuality in prisons.

Toch: In 1963 the California Department's Task Force broke down violent inmate vs. inmate incidents in prison, and the largest area at that time was violence that had its origin in homosexual relationships. That certainly doesn't seem true anymore in California and it may not be true elsewhere.

The reason why it's important to raise this topic is because somehow in the low-level violence that occurs in prison there is the relationship between aggressors and victims in which you have relatively pure victims and relatively pure aggressors. It's heavily permeated by that kind of contact.

It may very well be that in some instances you're dealing with an individual who is trying to take someone else's commissary items away from him or who is trying to bully him in some other fashion. But some of the prototypical behavior has to do with assault on someone's conceptions and self-conceptions of manliness.

John Irwin said something crucial when he talked about the issue of the state-raised youth and his view of the world in manly terms. The important aspect of that situation isn't the sexual contact, it's the issue of violence as it relates to a person's ability to maintain his self-esteem against those kinds of assaults.

If we head towards a maxi-maxi prison world in which all you get are the 5 percent of very hardened offenders, and the traditional victim is no longer available, then possibly this area of violence becomes academic.

Ellis: I agree about the emphasis on incidents that are sexually related. We have two ways to approach this: We should at least give some view of the participant's model of the process and its problems, and should not be exclusively concerned with what an administrator, from his observer's point of view, feels his problems are. For the participant, homosexually related aggressive behavior is a problem, and it causes a lot of problems. That in itself should be reason enough to examine it.

Megargee: Thus far the emphasis on homosexuality as a focal point of violence has been from the viewpoint of the world-be homosexual aggressor attacking the victim. But there are two other ways that violence can result from homosexual encounters: One is the terrorized victim who may respond with violence. The second is between two would-be aggressors who fight over the favors of a potential victim. The violence is not simply the classical rape situation, but also the victim's reaction, or that of the two potential aggressors.

Park: In a place like San Quentin, this person-to-person homosexual thing is not very important because the whole place is so tense and the thing is defined in group terms.

Megargee: What we are now involved in is a matter of group identification. What might have been an isolated incident before now gets the whole institution uptight. You get polarization—these things escalate. Formerly people would concentrate on doing their own time; an incident now becomes a political issue; an argument or fight between two individuals may provoke a major racial confrontation.

Frank: One thing helps, at least analytically, separate the sexual from the aggressive; that is to look at some of the aggressive behavior, which may be the case with a sexual assault, as a special case of a more general business of primate dominance and submission. When you look at it that way, it is very important for the prisoners to be submissive to staff. But that has created some of the aggression of the prisoners who are required to supply a certain amount of submissive behavior towards staff. They in turn demand submission from others.

Jacobs: There are two issues before us: to describe prison violence and to try to account for it. With respect to description of prison violence, Professor Toch pointed out the two kinds of violence most unique to prison—homosexual rape and riot. There is garden variety violence in the prison as well. Over time the frequency of these various types of violence may well have changed.

To account for the distribution of prison violence longitudinally and cross sectionally is another matter. No doubt the social meaning of the identical acts of prison violence does not remain constant. A sexual attack of one person against another might have meant one thing 20 years ago and another today. This should force us to specify the social context in which prison violence occurs. No doubt there are variations among prisons in different states and even in the same state. For example, whether rape is inter- or intraracial and what kind of racial situation exists in the prison where it occurs is a crucial issue.

Toch: That point holds in terms of trends and it also holds in terms of the specificity of institutions. An administrator such as Jim Park should be very much at home, in terms of his experience, at another San Quentin with its retaliatory gang situation. He might not be quite as at home, say, in Folsom, in which the violence picture still is relatively traditional, similar to what it was ten years ago. He might not even be at home in another California prison where you have more of an organized crime type of situation, except between Mexican organizations. Or he might not be at home in another California institution with relatively little violence. We are getting into a situation where the generality of what we used to be able to say just isn't there anymore.

As we cover New York State, for instance, the spectrum of what occurs in one institution is markedly different from another. That even relates to this issue of dominance–submission.

I can point to one institution for youthful offenders, for instance, where the bulk of the inmates have a continual concern that revolves around being very irritated at the paternalistic behavior of their guards; this is their running sore. This is an institution created for middle-class white youths and it's now inhabited by sophisticated urban youths. The guards still deal with those kids as if they were dealing with middle-class white youths and treating them by this dominance–submission issue. You go into another institution and the guards might be very concordant with the stance of the inmates. So it's getting to be a rough business in terms of generalizing.

Wilsnack: It seems obvious that the act of violence may not have an inherent or fixed meaning but rather tht the definition of even an individual act of violence, such as self-inflicted injury, is the result of a social process. In *some* cases, injuring one's self may be defined as a highly privatized way of escaping the situation. However, in Lansing Prison, Kansas in 1969, you had a hard-line commissioner coming in whose expected appointment precipitated a riot. He came in, established a new administrative detention facility, and this was followed by over 300 cases of self-inflicted injury involving roughly 100 inmates, with many multiple cases. Clearly the individual acts of self-inflicted injury were perceived as protest actions rather than as escape actions. The definition of the particular act is not necessarily a private individual decision, but has to do with how the inmates collectively arrive at saying, "We're participating in this kind of homosexual behavior," or "We're participating in this kind of self-destructive behavior." Each individual doesn't get to give his own private meaning to his action; he has to take account of what it means to the inmate population in general.

Toch: One thing hit a very responsive chord, with regard to violence—not self-injury. Take the example of some men in prison whom administrators would have classified as being the toughest nuts they have. When you walk into that segregation unit, there he is. Everyone tells you, "Watch out! He'll throw feces at you. Don't walk into that cage, for God's sake!" I had the distinct impression after talking to some of these fellows that their violence was not very dissimilar to what you're describing, in the sense that some of the time the violence had the purpose of getting them into segregation because they couldn't take the problems out in the yard. Violence was the respectable way of getting out of that yard. One couldn't very well go to a counselor and say, "Look, get me out!" The other boys wouldn't like that. An inmate knew that if he really acted up he could gain two points: (a) He would get himself out of there, which is what he wanted, and (b) he built his reputation. Staff don't want themselves used; they want to call the shots. But sometimes inmates actually do use staff in order to get staff to respond to them in a way that will pay off to them in ways that staff don't realize.

Nagel: I sat in a court hearing with two of the most intractable inmates from Clinton Prison who were contesting in Federal Court the humanity of the super-super segregation unit there. These two individuals, who had not been allowed out of that super-super segregation unit for 19 months, were taken to Albany County jail where they sat for 5 weeks in a dormitory without one bit of trouble, where they sat in a courtroom without handcuffs for 9 days, and at the end of the hearing the judge said, "I do not understand why they can't handle you up at Clinton because I've never had two witnesses in front of me who were more gentlemen." We have been looking at violence as something related to the characteristics of the inmates themselves, without taking into consideration the interaction between the inmates and the environment in which they live. Whether the violence is the chicken or the egg I don't know; it might just be the chicken.

Cohen: One theme in this discussion is the notion that in the past, homosexual rape has not been understood because it was perceived as a sexual rather than a power thing. Although sex is obviously involved here, in a way it plays a minor role. Its principal significance is as an indicator or marker of dominance and submission. That's the motivation that is underlying and is the motivation that underlies responses to it. Its significance is not the homosexuality but the homosexual aggression, in terms of the meaning that power, dominance, and submission has for people.

Two kinds of interpretations are suggested here: one, in terms of primitive, species characteristics — primate dominant–submission relationships; the other, in terms of cultural patterns, particularly in terms of social class and culture where sexual relationships between men and women are to a large degree defined and motivated by a concern with dominance and submission and the expression of power—specifically that power which is expressive and symbolic of masculinity. This is reflected in the incongruities between lower class and middle-class conceptions of homosexuality and suggests the possibility that homosexuality as such doesn't really have much meaning in some lower class cultural settings. The meaning of homosexual relationships in prison is a demonstration of a person's masculinity by asserting in a forceful way his dominance over another person. The question them becomes, "Why in prison?" or "Why on the particular scale that we have it?"

Here I see a confluence of the two notions of the diffusionist and the functionalist positions, the notion that something is a product either of the circumstances inside the prison or something that people bring with them to the prison from the outside culture. What they bring with them from the outside culture is this definition of the meaning of homosexual aggression or sexual aggression in general.

Then you have to ask, "What is it now about the prison that encourages this particular form of demonstrating machismo?" There are a couple of things: One is the notion that within a prison with this highly disciplined life many opportunities for demonstrating and establishing masculinity—for vindicating one's claims to masculinity—are denied and homosexual aggression becomes not so much an avenue for sexual frustration as a matter for expressing the frustration of the demonstrating of one's manhood.

The other thing is that inmates are actually compelled by the nature of prison (and they themselves may be ambivalent about this) to assume submissive relationships with respect to staff. This in turn constitutes, in a sense, an insult to their masculinity. Perhaps an insult wouldn't be felt quite so deeply by inmates from another social class, but from the cultures they come from, it is particularly insulting and may express itself in turn in the form of sexual aggression—the only objects being available are their own biological sex, so we call it homosexual.

Part II

Explaining Violence

5

Explaining Collective Violence in Prisons: Problems and Possibilities

Richard W. Wilsnack

The basic problem with theories of collective violence in prisons is that there are no theories. There are many conclusions and generalizations about prison violence, and some of these may help us understand particular incidents or may serve as starting points for theories. However, no one has yet offered a general explanation of collective violence in prisons that applies unambiguously to observable events, and that has been tested systematically against history or the experience of a large number of prisons. In fact, there is a scarcity of comparative or numerical information about prison disturbances that could be used to test a theory.[1] Furthermore, the best available data tell more about which individuals participate in unrest than about the characteristics or preconditions of the unrest itself.[2] At least until there are better data and hypotheses about how and why collective violence occurs in prisons, interpretation of such violence is at the mercy of whoever can speak loudest or with the most influence.

In the absence of theories, current explanations of collective prison violence have some peculiar characteristics. First, it is common to generalize from single cases. For example, detailed reports on the Attica rebellion repeatedly claim that its characteristics are not unique,[3] yet no one has shown in a thorough and precise way *how much* the events at Attica represent conditions or processes in all American prisons. Second, authors and authorities often give the greatest emphasis to those causes of prison unrest they find most comfortable to believe. People with a politicized view of imprisonment are likely to emphasize ideological causes;[4] people who administer penal systems often say more about outside causes of unrest than about the effects of administrative practices inside.[5] Finally, prison unrest is frequently discussed as though it were a single category of events. It is difficult to find, anywhere in the literature, a distinction between prison disturbances that are violent and those that are not, or between protests that involve seizure of power and those that do not.[6]

Nevertheless, there are many ideas available that might help to explain the origins of violent prison disturbances. The task is to assemble and reshape these ideas so they can be either used in theory construction or else carefully disproved. This chapter attempts to make four contributions to the task: First, major hypotheses and explanatory themes in the literature on prison disturbances are summarized and evaluated. Second, additional hypotheses are drawn from relevant studies of collective violence in other institutional settings (mental hospitals, college campuses, and urban ghettoes). Third, many of the hypotheses are tested against conditions and events at a sample of state prisons during the period 1971–73. Finally, findings from the state prisons suggest a theoretical framework that may help to explain both riots and nonriot resistance as distinct forms of collective disturbances in prisons.

Interpretations of Prison Riots

A recurring theme in the literature on prison disturbances is that prison riots result partly from excessive and intolerable stress and deprivation imposed by the prison environment.[7] As Tannenbaum summarized this idea:

If . . . there is a great deal of unecessary irritation, if the environment is irrating, then no amount of discipline or cruelty will save the institution from internal violence. . . . The pressure becomes so great that the prisoners break out in unexpected fury. . . .[8]

A serious weakness of this idea is that our prisons in general are constantly and highly stressful and depriving places, but riots occur infrequently and in relatively few institutions. However, the value of thinking about stress and deprivation is that if many prison environments push inmates close to their limits of tolerance, then seemingly minor changes in other conditions, or minor increases in stress, can have a major effect on the outbreak of collective violence. We are sensitized to take a closer look at conditions such as overcrowding, idleness, physical hardships, maximum-security environments, tightened-security procedures, and official violence.

A second theme in explanations of prison riots has been that riots follow disorganization in the social structure of the prison. Some writers have emphasized the effects of distintegration or power loss in the informal inmate social order. Hartung and Floch, and also Sykes, indicate that an important effect of prison reforms can be to weaken informal inmate leadership, thereby unleashing aggressive, pathological inmates who are prone to act violently. In addition, Cressey argues (and Hartung and Floch imply) that established inmate leaders may *use* rioting to cripple reforms that threaten them and to remove competitors from leadership. McCleery also suggests that rioting may be a consequence of a power struggle among inmates.[9] Other discussions of prison violence give more emphasis to instability and uncertainty in the relations between inmates and staff. Ohlin and more recently McCleery and Mattick have proposed that prison riots may follow from problems such as the disruption of informal arrangements for exchange, negotiation, and power sharing between inmates and staff; a general breakdown of the patterns of inmate behavior expected and rewarded by the staff; and the failure of administrators to provide a clear definition of a changing situation.[10] The two types of disorganization, among the inmates and between inmates and staff, should stem from events such as reform programs, rule changes, administrative changes, and conflicts among staff or among inmate factions.

A third idea of what makes rioting more likely has been suggested particularly by persons directly involved in the management of prisons.[11] This is the inability of correctional personnel to respond effectively to strains on inmates before the strains result in a riot. The effects of this condition should appear where prison staffs have a high rate of turnover and where staff members are undermanned, underpaid, or undertrained.

A fourth approach to explaining prison riots is the idea that a riot may be a way of communicating grievances to an audience outside the walls. Flynn, Hannum[12], and Schrag all comment briefly on the possibility that the riots, at least in their latter stages, [are] interpreted by the inmates as a mechanism for bringing public pressure to bear on correctional policy....[13] The idea of the prison riot as communication is underdeveloped; no one has demonstrated that certain messages are consistently directed to certain audiences. However, we are alerted to look at the relations between inmates and officials or groups outside the correctional system. Davidson suggests that a precondition for unrest may be the absolute power of administrators over inmate communications with the outside world.[14]

Behind any idea of rioting as communication lurk two controversies: The older controversy is about how much the participation in collective violence is voluntary and deliberate. Some interpretations of prison riots assume that much active participation is either careless or coerced and manipulated by leaders.[15] This assumption violates the common-sense notion that inmates must know the riot will end eventually and participation will be punished; it also contradicts the widely held belief that mass participation in prison violence is not engineered and coordinated from the start.[16] If it is possible that hundreds of inmates will not automatically join in a losing battle, then we should learn more about their own rationales for rioting. Unfortunately, thus far we have heard the views of only the most articulate and outspoken participants in the most politicized violence.

Inmates interpreting their violence as part of a political struggle have stimulated a new controversy about how much collective violence in prisons has changed. Inmate political rhetoric and the emergence of ideological cadres among inmates have led some people to conclude that collective prison violence in the 1970s is very different from what has happend before.[17] What presumably distinguishes the disturbances of the seventies is the inmates' demands for power, their use of publicity, and their expansion of the conflict and participation beyond the walls and the correctional system. However, it is not yet clear how deep the changes are. Accounts of rioting in past decades show that publicity and demands for power over administrative positions and policy have been occurring for a long time.[18] But there is no systematic review of recent disturbances to show whether publicity, power demands, and outside involvement are present more consistently or make up a larger part of the activity. There are no comparative data on the subtler question of whether power demands are becoming broader in scope, for example, with calls for amnesty replacing calls for no reprisals, or demands for policy-making powers replacing demands for specific changes in specific policies. Again, where facts are missing, opinions hold sway.

The various attempts to explain collective violence in prisons may not be contradictory, and different conditions identified by different authors may occur not in isolation but in combination. Attica had not only environmental hardship, but also administrative conflict and staff inadequacies, and its inmates publicized their grievances and emphasized their ties to the outside world. The same patterns were present in the Jackson, Michigan riot of 1952.[19] There may be some interaction among several conditions that increases the chances of violence. Moreover, it is possible that the specific analyses of prison disturbances have not identified all the important causal factors.

Collective Violence in Other Settings

Our understanding of prison violence does not have to come only from prisons, if events there are similar to violent episodes in other institutional settings. In particular, it may be worthwhile to review evidence and hypotheses about collective violence in other situations where the everyday lives of a large number of clients are directly dependent on and controlled by a small, closed set of administrators, who in turn are responsible to a public outside their relationship to the clients.[a] There may be clues to the origins of prison violence in studies of unrest in mental hospitals, on college campuses, and in urban ghettoes.[b]

Reviews of collective behavior in mental hospitals, for instance, suggest that disturbances there are preceded by failure in the attempts of inmates to communicate with or rely on administrative personnel. The ideas about what leads to

[a]This description resembles the concept of total institutions used in Erving Goffman, *Asylums* (Garden City: Doubleday Anchor, 1961), and in Samuel E. Wallace, ed., *Total Institutions* (Brunswick, N.J.: Transaction Books, 1971). However, analysis of total institutions appears to emphasize restriction and control of communications between inmates and outsiders. The characteristic emphasized here is that administrators are responsible more to outsiders than to their immediate clients. A related idea of involuntary clientship has been developed by David Garson in "The Disruption of Prison Administration," *Law and Society Review* 6 (May 1972): 531–61.

[b]It would also be valuable to look at mutinies in military units, if more than individual case studies were available. See, for example, Richard M. Watt, *Dare Call It Treason* (New York: Simon and Schuster, 1963); Richard Hough, *The Potemkin Mutiny* (London: Hamish Hamilton, 1960); and Neil Sheehan, *The Arnheiter Affair* (New York: Random House, 1971). One comparative analysis of mutinies concludes that they differ from strikes not only by involving seizure of power, but also by occurring among clients who were previously totally powerless. See Cornelis J. Lammers, "Strikes and Mutinies: A Comparative Study of Organizational Conflicts Between Rulers and Ruled," *Administrative Science Quarterly* 41 (1969):448–72.

this failure seem to echo and reinforce the prison literature: staff overload, high rates of staff turnover, and withdrawal of staff from contact with patients (inmates) under conditions of administrative conflict and uncertainty.[20]

In studies of campus unrest and ghetto riots, the almost universal conclusion is that the likelihood of a serious disturbance increases with the size of the client population.[21] There are also a few studies indicating that the degree of violence in disturbances is related to population size.[22] However, interpretations of *how* population size affects the incidence of violence or unrest are poorly developed. Basically, one can choose a simple or a complex interpretation. The simple view argues that larger populations are more likely to provide the necessary "critical mass" of *individuals* willing and able to participate in a disturbance,[23] or perhaps a necessary frequency of hostile interpersonal contacts between clients and administrators.[24] The more complex view is that population size is a single indicator for a combination of *conditions* that leads to disturbances. Population size may be a proxy for intensified contact and sharing of experiences among clients,[c] reduced opportunities for clients to have effective contact with administrators,[25] and reduced client concern about what administrators can do to them or for them (since the client's relations with the administration are likely to be more limited, impersonal, and anonymous). There may be some truth to both the simple and complex interpretations, but no one has directly examined how population size influences disturbances. There is further uncertainty because many researchers do not allow for the possibility that what makes a violent disturbance occur may not be the same as what determines how intense the violence becomes, or what determines how frequently disturbances occur in one location.

Many other characteristics of collective violence in our cities and universities are probably unique to those environments,[d] but a few patterns may have broader relevance. For example, some studies find there are more campus

---

[c]This might help to explain the positive relation of population *density* to ghetto rioting, which shows up in the analysis of Bryan T. Downes, "Social and Political Characteristics of Riot Cities: A Comparative Study," *Social Science Quarterly* 49 (December 1968): 504–20; Bryan T. Downes, "A Critical Reexamination of the Social and Political Characteristics of Riot Cities," *Social Science Quarterly* 51 (September 1970): 349–60; John G. White, "Riots and Theory Building," in *Riots and Rebellion: Civil Violence in the Urban Community*, ed. Louis H. Masotti and Don R. Bowen (Beverly Hills: Sage Publications, 1968), pp. 157–65; Jerome L. McElroy and Larry D. Singell, "Riot and Nonriot Cities: An Examination of Structural Contours," *Urban Affairs Quarterly* 8, no. 3 (March 1973): 281–302; and William R. Morgan and Terry N. Clark, "The Causes of Racial Disorders: A Grievance-Level Explanation," *American Sociological Review* 38, no. 5 (October 1973): 611–24. Joe R. Feagin and Harlan Hahn, in *Ghetto Revolts: The Politics of Violence in American Cities* (New York: MacMillan, 1973), p. 32, draw a similar inference.

[d]Obviously, one must be cautious about applying conclusions from campuses and ghettoes to prisons because of differences in the situations. For example, students and ghetto residents commonly have more opportunities to move out of a bad situation than inmates, and a wider choice of voluntary activity than inmates. Consequently, collective violence in the ghetto or on the campus may be chosen from a wider range of options, or it may involve individuals who have lost their options in ways much less constant and predictable than by imprisonment.

disturbances where student bodies are heterogeneous and less cohesive.[26] This suggests a refinement of the inmate disorganization theme: violent prison disturbances may be more likely where all kinds of inmates are housed together and little organization has developed among them. Another hypothesis about campus unrest is that it occurs where faculty, the line personnel, are less involved with either students or the institution.[27] A parallel hypothesis for prisons might be that collective violence will be more common where the line personnel, the guards, are indifferent or hostile toward both the inmates and the higher administration.

A perplexing finding from research on ghetto riots is that riots were more likely or more violent where blacks were less deprived of some, but not all, social resources.[28] If collective violence erupts where clients are *partially* better off, this is another reason to study the effects of prison reforms in greater detail. It is even more important to consider the various possible reasons why collective violence should erupt among clients receiving a few more benefits. Intensified feelings of injustice, caused by a gap between what clients receive and what they feel they deserve, seem likely to be present constantly in prisons and unlikely to distinguish those institutions that produce riots from those that do not.[29] A second and more plausible interpretation is that disturbances are more likely where increased client (i.e., inmate) resources threaten the power of line administrators (i.e., guards), leading to more frequent hostile confrontations, which eventually provoke collective violence.[30] A third interpretation is that violence stems from the clients' recognition of their powerlessness: when events or changes, such as marginal improvements of benefits, show clients they do not have *control* over their benefits, nor the power to force satisfactory improvements, within the existing administrative arrangements.[e] The third interpretation directs attention to what happens when inmates share, lack, or lose power, apart from whatever reforms may be involved.

By this point, there seems to be an overabundance of general and specific conditions that might help to explain collective violence in prisons. Reports on prison riots suggest that environmental stress, social disorganization and conflict, staff deficiencies, and inmates' desire to communicate with audiences outside are important preconditions. Studies of collective violence in other institutional settings indicate that the size and heterogeneity of the client population, the disengagement and isolation of line personnel, and changes in clients' perceived resources or power may be influential. However, all that can be offered thus far is a shopping list of explanatory variables. What is needed is a theoretical framework, which can select and combine some of the variables

---

[e]This interpretation is consistent with the analysis of ghetto rioting by Feagin and Hahn in *Ghetto Revolts,* pp. 43–44 and 53–54; it also fits the apparent effects of symbolic administrative power-sharing and flexibility on campus unrest, in Peter Blau and Ellen L. Slaughter, "Institutional Conditions and Student Demonstrations," *Social Problems* 18, no. 4 (Spring 1971): 475–87.

in a more useful way. A recent small-scale study by Ohlin and myself takes two steps toward developing such a framework.[f] First, bivariate analyses identify certain conditions that are most likely to be related to the outbreak of prison disturbances. Second, these conditions can be combined in a plausible and testable interpretation of how and where disturbances occur.

The Prison Survey

Ohlin and I wanted to learn whether any particular conditions in prisons had simple, direct relationships to prison riots. There were no systematic data available to answer even such elementary questions. Therefore, we designed a questionnaire concerning the recent histories of state prisons, where major riots had typically occurred. The sample of prisons to be studied included the largest state penal institution for adult male felons, with medium or maximum security, in each of the 50 states plus the District of Columbia (51 prisons in all).

The questionnaire covered events and conditions during an 18-month period, in most cases between January 1971 and June 1972. Based on literature reviewed above and an analysis of case studies, the questions dealt with several categories of preconditions, the characteristics of any collective disturbances, and the aftermaths of disturbances. Each question asked whether a specific event or change had occurred or not occurred during the 18-month period. Additional information indicated whether conditions existed before, during, or after a disturbance.

The questionnaire allowed for a possible distinction between riots and other forms of collective resistance to authority, such as work stoppages and hunger strikes. On the basis of past accounts, a riot can be identified as a seizure by inmates of prison territory where they can move freely but staff cannot, plus a presentation of demands that affect more inmates than those actively participating in the disturbance. Nonriot resistance involves similar demands without seizure of territory; the demands are usually backed up by a refusal of inmates to engage in some officially sanctioned activity. Questions based on these descriptions appeared to avoid any confusion with mass escapes or brawls among inmates.

Although some information for the questionnaires was obtained outside the correctional systems, the detailed knowledge required for most responses had to come, directly or indirectly, from a variety of correctional officials. Three factors may have affected the reliability of the results. Replies did not all come from persons in the same administrative position. Often there were insufficient

[f]The research summarized here has been sponsored and supported by the Research Council of the National Council on Crime and Delinquency, with additional assistance and support from the Center for Criminal Justice, Harvard Law School.

responses to a small portion of the 160 questions. Much of the information asked for was potentially embarrassing or ideologically important to wardens or higher officials.

To encourage reliable responses that would be unaffected by the respondent's position, we asked for simple replies about specific public events, that is, events which potentially could be checked against media accounts. (For example, one question asked, "Have there been official statements or reports confirming that the prison or some of its facilities are overcrowded or overused?") The responses on sensitive topics did not appear to conceal much. Three riots were reported that actually could not have been learned about through the major news media. Two-thirds of the prisons (55% of those with no collective disturbances) reported four or more different signs of unrest among individuals: lists of grievances, lawsuits, assaults on inmates or on staff members, self-inflicted injuries, suicide, murder, or arson.

However, since responses were not always complete, it was possible that information about certain kinds of prisons could be systematically left out. If information were missing mostly for prisons that had riots, that might conceal preconditions for rioting; if information were missing mostly for prisons with no rioting, then apparent preconditions for riots might be spurious. Fortunately, comparisons among three categories of prisons—those that had riots, those that had nonriot resistance, and those that apparently had no collective disturbances—showed no significant differences in the amount of missing data ($p > 0.2$ in all three comparisons).

It was also possible that at prisons which had already experienced disturbances, officials would openly admit all the conditions that made unrest unavoidable. In contrast, at apparently undisturbed prisons, officials might deny or be unaware of any ways in which trouble was brewing. The misleading result would be that prisons with prior disturbances would report many preconditions, while undisturbed prisons would report few. We were able to check this possibility indirectly, by calculating a ratio of the number of "safe" public events reported (e.g., administrative changes, public and political activities, new coverage) to the number of more "sensitive" internal problems reported (e.g., staff conflicts, staff deficiencies, violence among inmates). The hypothesized response bias should make the ratio exceptionally high for prisons with no collective disturbances. However, the data showed no significant differences between the ratios for prisons with no disturbances and the ratios for prisons with rioting or with other forms of collective resistance to authority (p's > 0.2).

We were able to obtain usable data on 48 of the 51 prisons chosen for our sample.[g] Since we found no indications of major response biases within the sample, we have analyzed the data on the assumption that they accurately

---

[g]We were unable to obtain sufficient information about prisons in Alabama, Kansas, and Mississippi.

reflect characteristics of the set of prisons studied. Given this assumption, the data permit tests of some general predictions from the literature, at least for one type of institution during one period of time. Furthermore, while the findings cannot simply be generalized to apply to other prisons and other times, they can suggest a testable theoretical interpretation of how prison disturbances originate.

Results of the Survey

The data show two general patterns: First, it appears that nothing automatically produces collective violence in prison, at least within an 18-month time period. No single precondition nor combination of preconditions covered in our questionnaire was always followed by a prison disturbance. We can identify conditions that may be necessary to collective violence, or that may help it occur, but none that makes such violence a certainty.[h]

Second, there appear to be important differences between rioting and non-riot forms of resistance to authority in prison. Certain preconditions were characteristic of prisons that experienced rioting. Other, different preconditions characterized prisons where inmates engaged in collective resistance (such as strikes) but did not riot. The clearest findings from the data are summarized briefly in Table 5-1.

The data offer some support for the idea that collective violence is provoked by the stress and deprivation that inmates experience. Both rioting and nonriot resistance occurred more often in maximum-security facilities where inmates were overcrowded and idle. Two-thirds of the prisons having disturbances had at least two of these conditions beforehand. Furthermore, 83 percent of the institutions that had at least two of the preconditions later experienced disturbances (contrasted with 43% of the less depriving institutions). The overcrowding and idleness may intensify contact and sharing of grievances among the inmates. Also, two-thirds of the institutions with depriving conditions had heterogeneous populations: inmates with different offenses, records, and ages were housed together. Unrest may be particularly likely at end-of-the-road, maximum-security prisons where troublesome inmates are sent regardless of their offenses or history.

Some changes in the prisons did not have the effects one would expect from the literature. Neither potentially depriving procedures for tightening security nor potentially disorganizing reforms had any clear positive relationship to rioting or nonriot resistance. There is also only slight support for the

---

[h]There are several possible reasons, besides imprecision or unreliability of the questionnaire, why we were unable to find preconditions that were always followed by disturbances. Some necessary conditions may have been left out, the time period (18 months or less) might have been too short, methods of temporarily suppressing unrest may have been ignored, or perhaps some precipitants of collective resistance are unpredictable.

Table 5-1
Preconditions of Prison Disturbances

Preconditions	Criterion	Related Consequences (Proportion of Cases Having the Preconditions)
Environmental deprivation 　Maximum security 　Overcrowding 　Idleness	2 of 3 present	Collective resistance (both riot and nonriot) $(20/30)^a$
Inmate disintegration 　Increased assaults among inmates 　Assault on a prison official 　Heterogeneous population	2 of 3 present	Rioting $(9/12)^a$
Administrative instability 　Major changes or absences in the administration 　Staff conflict	Both present	Rioting $(9/12)^b$
External pressure 　Legislative action 　Influence by citizen groups	Both present	Rioting $(12/12)^a$
Publicity 　Major newspaper coverage 　VIP visitors 　Critical articles in prison paper	2 of 3 present	Rioting $(10/12)^b$
Levels of preconditions 　Inmates: deprivation or disintegration 　Administrators: changes or conflicts 　Outsiders: pressure or publicity	Conditions present at all 3 levels	Rioting $(9/12)^a$
Inmate changes 　Offenses 　Ethnicity	Either present	Nonriot resistance $(10/18)^c$
Inmate organizational resources 　More than 1,000 inmates 　Separatist cadres	Both present	Nonriot resistance $(10/17)^b$
Staff weaknesses 　No training program 　Waivers of tests or diplomas 　Staff less than 25% of inmate population	2 of 3 present	Nonriot resistance $(11/16)^b$

Note: The complete sample contained 12 prisons that had rioting, 18 prisons that had only nonriot resistance, and 18 prisons that reported no collective resistance to authority. In some analyses, a few prisons were excluded because it was uncertain whether preconditions had preceded the disturbances in these prisons.

[a] $p < 0.01$, Chi-square test, $dF = 1$

[b] $p < 0.05$, Chi-square test, $dF = 1$

[c] $p < 0.10$, Chi-square test, $dF = 1$

supposed effects of political changes. Inmates had presented grievances or requests to administrators in 76 percent of the prisons that later had collective resistance, compared with 59 percent of the prisons that had none. Separatist groups such as the Muslims or Panthers were reported in 70 percent of the prisons experiencing resistance, but in 50 percent of the prisons without collective resistance. Neither of these two differences was statistically significant by the chi-square test ($p > 0.10$).[i]

However, there is evidence for the general idea that collective violence occurs amid disorganization and conflict in the inmate population and in the prison administration. Indicators of social disintegration among inmates were increased assaults among inmates, inmate assault on a prison official, and a heterogeneous inmate population (in terms of ages, offenses, and careers). At least two of these indicators were present in three-fourths of the prisons that later experienced rioting. Three-fourths of the prisons with riots had also experienced major administrative changes (in organization or personnel) or prolonged absences of key administrators, combined with public evidence of conflict within the prison staff. Less than 40 percent of the prisons that did not have riots reported these characteristics of the inmates or of the prison administration.

There is less support for the idea that riots happen because of shortcomings of correctional personnel. Less than 40 percent of the prisons that had rioting lacked training programs for guards, or allowed waivers of diplomas and tests for job candidates, or had custodial staffs less than one-fourth the size of the inmate population. However, at 67 percent of the prisons with riots, the salaries of guards were officially admitted to be low, and turnover of personnel was greater than 20 percent per year. These possible indicators of staff discontent were reported in only 39 percent of the other institutions ($\chi^2 = 2.80$, $dF = 1$, $p < 0.01$).

There are two findings relevant to the idea of rioting as communication. First, outside the walls before a riot, there was an audience of people concerned about how the prison was being run. All riots were preceded by actions of both legislators and citizen groups to influence prison operation. Second, the problems of prisons that had riots had earlier gained publicity, through major newspaper coverage, visits of VIP's, and articles in the prison newspapers. Over 80

---

[i]Since the prisons are not a random sample, the significance of chi-square cannot have the precise meaning of inferential statistics. How far the results should generalize (e.g., to federal prisons, minimum-security prisons, or juvenile reformatories) is a substantive question, not just a statistical one. However, significance testing can suggest whether the way that prisons were assigned to categories in contingency tables could be the result of a random process rather than a systematic one (cf. Robert F. Winch and Donald T. Campbell, "Proof? No. Evidence? Yes. The Significance of Tests of Significance," *The American Sociologist* 4, no. 2 (May 1969): 140–43). Significance testing can enhance or reduce confidence in the relationships discussed here, even though the degree of proper trust in the results cannot be specified.

percent of the prisons with riots were publicized in at least two of these three ways, compared with 47 percent of the other prisons. It is also worth noting that in 11 of the 12 riots covered in this survey, rioters demanded to meet with the press.

To sum up, prison riots appear to develop from preconditions at three different levels: inmate deprivation and social disintegration, administrative conflict and instability, and pressure and publicity from outside the walls. Preconditions at all three levels were present in three-fourths of the prisons that had rioting, in less than half of the prisons that had only nonriot resistance, and in one-sixth of the prisons that had no collective resistance.

The conditions most common at prisons with only nonriot resistance, other than environmental deprivation, are not the same as the preconditions of rioting. The effects of social change and of population size suggested in the literature are related specifically to nonriot resistance. The prisons with strikes but not riots were most likely to report changes in the offenses or ethnicity of the inmate population during the preceding five years. In these prisons also inmates most often had the combined organizational resources of large populations plus leadership cadres from groups such as the Muslims or Panthers. Considering these preconditions, it appears that politically aware inmate organization was most likely to emerge in prisons that subsequently had only nonriot resistance, at least within the 18-month period studied.

At the same time, over 60 percent of the prisons with only nonriot resistance reported two or three of the following staff weaknesses: no training programs for guards, waivers of diplomas or tests for job candidates, and a custodial staff less than one-fourth the size of the inmate population. Less than 40 percent of the other prisons were as deficient.[j] Nevertheless, only 39 percent of the prisons with only nonriot resistance reported inmate assaults on staff at any time, while 57 percent of the other prisons reported such assaults, although the difference is not great enough to be statistically significant ($p < 0.10$). The pattern of inmate organizational resources combined with staff weaknesses without widespread violence against the prison staff suggests that collective resistance may be limited to nonriot forms in a context of inmate self-discipline and accommodation with the guards.

Toward a Theoretical Interpretation of Prison Disturbances

To integrate our data and some of the ideas reviewed earlier, we have drawn on the work of Lipsky.[31] He distinguishes between direct confrontation, in which a

---

[j]The percentages are conservative estimates, indicating the minimum contrast between the two groups of prisons if sufficient data had been provided by all prisons. However, information on the size of the current inmate population or the size of the current custodial staff was unavailable for four prisons with no collective resistance, two prisons with only nonriot resistance, and four prisons with rioting.

dissatisfied group has resources to negotiate directly with an adversary, and protest, in which a powerless group, unable to bargain for its demands directly with an opponent, tries to enlist the support of an influential third party, which can force the opponent to give in. Nonriot resistance resembles the direct confrontation, while rioting resembles protest.

Collective resistance of both kinds is most likely to occur in prisons where inmates must rely on their own resources to make life tolerable (e.g., maximum security, "end-of-the-road" institutions with too many prisoners) and where they are still actively defending their interests. In prisons where inmates are well-organized and in a position to withhold needed administrative resources (e.g., manpower, cooperation, and peacekeeping among themselves, needed particularly where staffing is inadequate), they may engage in nonriot resistance as a strategy of direct bargaining with prison administrators. Nonriot resistance may be especially likely if inmates believe administrators are willing and able to bargain, or that public opinion will compel administrators to negotiate, or that it is necessary to test inmate organization and administrative resources. However, in other prisons inmates may feel powerless, often because they are disorganized, and sometimes perhaps because administrators refuse to negotiate, or because administrators cannot deliver on promises. In these prisons, inmates may join in rioting, in initially disorganized collective violence, when they can realistically hope to gain the attention of a powerful audience outside the walls, an audience who can make desired administrative changes happen. Thus, one should expect any prison riot to include an attempt by inmates to gain leverage outside the prison system to bring about changes inside the system.[k]

However, for a riot to erupt there must be not only deprived and powerless inmates and attention from influential outsiders, but also uncertain and unstable administration. If the instability reduces the effectiveness of staff control, it may provide a rare opportunity for inmates to seize enough power and time to get their message out and to make the right people take it seriously. If the uncertainty reflects a power struggle between "friendly" and hostile administrators, inmates may riot from a sense of urgency, a feeling that if they sit still their enemies may win and a bad situation will become intolerably worse.

Prisons that have riots seem to differ from prisons that have collective resistance without any rioting. However, all the prisons surveyed that had riots also had some other form of collective resistance before or after the rioting. This suggests that the characteristics of prisons with only nonriot resistance are not essential for that kind of resistance but rather inhibit rioting or make it seem unnecessary. Furthermore, rioting and nonriot resistance may be linked together. In one direction, a riot that is "successful," in terms of unifying

[k]A discussion of the contrasts between strikes and mutinies, comparing internal vs. external conflict resolution and the role of third parties, with a perspective similar to ours, can be found in Lammers, "Strikes and Mutinies."

inmates and liberalizing administration, may be followed by nonriot resistance because the inmates now believe something can be gained from negotiations with administrators. In the other direction, rioting may be a response to failures of less violent or smaller scale protest. In the course of nonriot resistance, administrators may prove unwilling or unable to negotiate meaningfully, and inmate organization may prove inadequate. The powerlessness felt from these failures can set the stage for more desperate action. A further possibility is that conflicts of leadership among inmates may promote nonriot tests of strength against the administrators, and also may lead to failure, by undermining the staying power of inmate organization, thus tilting the situation toward eventual violence.

What Ohlin and I have tried to construct here is a theoretical interpretation of prison disturbances that fits together the data from the prison survey and many explanatory themes from the literature on collective violence in institutional settings. Hopefully, the ideas offered here are specific enough to be testable, and may provide some insight into the differences and relationships between violent and nonviolent collective resistance in prison. However, it is important to recognize that many major theoretical questions have been left untouched. The *processes* of rioting are left unexplained: the emergence of leadership, the formulation of demands, and the changes in how and why inmates participate. There is no discussion of "the demonstration effect,"[32] whereby rioting in any one prison may encourage inmates elsewhere to revolt, producing a "wave" of riots. There is also no discussion of official violence in prisons, nor of ways that inmate violence may get exploited for administrative purposes.[33] Finally, there are other forms of collective violence that need attention: gang warfare or feuding of the kind that has developed in San Quentin and Soledad prisons in California; anarchy such as developed in Walpole prison in Massachusetts; and the possibility of guerrilla warfare behind the walls. This review points out many theoretical problems and questions and suggests answers to only a few of them. However, at least it can be shown that our knowledge of collective violence in prison does not have to be as fragmentary and oversimplified as it has sometimes looked before.

Notes

1. Cf. William D. Leeke, "Collective Violence in Correctional Institutions," *American Journal of Corrections* 33, no. 3 (May–June 1971):12–16; G. David Garson, "The Disruption of Prison Administration: An Investigation of Alternative Theories of the Relationship among Administrators, Reformers, and Involuntary Social Service Clients," *Law and Society Review* 6 (May 1972):531–61.

2. For example, Benjamin S. Wood, et al., "Troublemaking Behavior in a Correctional Institution: Relationship to Inmates' Definition of The Situation,"

American Journal of Orthopsychiatry 36 (1966):795-802; W. Douglas Skelton, "Prison Riot: Assaulters vs. Defenders," *Archives of General Psychiatry* 21, no. 3 (September 1969):359-62; Edith E. Flynn, "From Conflict Theory to Conflict Resolution: Toward the Control of Collective Violence in Prisons (Paper delivered at the Annual Meeting of the American Sociological Association, New York, August 29, 1973).

3. Cf. Badillo and M. Haynes, *A Bill of No Rights: Attica and the American Prison System* (New York: Outerbridge and Lazard, 1972); New York State Special Commission on Attica, *Attica* (New York: Bantam Books, 1972); Russell G. Oswald, *Attica—My Story* (Garden City: Doubleday, 1972).

4. For example, Angela Davis, "Lessons: From Attica to Soledad," *New York Times,* 8 October 1971, p. 43; John Pallas and Bob Barber, "From Riot to Revolution," *Issues in Criminology* 7, no. 2 (Fall 1972):1-19; Steven V. Roberts, "Prisoners Feel a Mood of Protest," in *Prisons, Protest, and Politics,* ed. Burton M. Atkins and Henry R. Glick (Englewood Cliffs: Prentice-Hall, 1972), pp. 101-4.

5. For example, Fred T. Wilkinson, interview, "We're Reaping a Harvest of Permissiveness," *U.S. News and World Report,* 27 September 1971, p. 22; Vincent R. Mancusi, testimony in U. S. Congress, House, Select Committee on Crime, *American Prisons in Turmoil,* 92d Cong., 1st sess., 29 November 1971, pp. 12-15; D. Lowe, "The Problem of Social Upheaval in Penal Institutions," *Journal of California Law Enforcement* 8, no. 3 (1974):121-23. See also Clarence Schrag, "The Sociology of Prison Riots," Proceedings of the American Correctional Association, 19th Annual Congress, Denver, 1960, p. 137.

6. However, cf. Vernon Fox, "Why Prisoners Riot," *Federal Probation* 35, no. 1 (March 1971):10; Cornelis J. Lammers, "Strikes and Mutinies: A Comparative Study of Organizational Conflicts between Rulers and Ruled," *Administrative Science Quarterly* 14 (1969):558-72.

7. Cf. James V. Bennett, "Prisons at the Pivot," *The Prison Journal* 33, no. 1 (April 1953):4-5; American Correctional Association, *Causes, Preventive Measures, and Methods of Controlling Riots and Disturbances in Correctional Institutions* (Washington: American Correctional Association, 1970), pp. 1-3; Fox, "Why Prisoners Riot," p. 12.

8. Frank Tannenbaum, *Crime and the Community* (New York: Columbia University Press, 1951), pp. 337-38.

9. Frank E. Hartung and Maurice Floch, "A Social-Psychological Analysis of Prison Riots," *Journal of Criminal Law, Criminology, and Police Science* 47, no. 1 (May-June 1956):51-57; Gresham M. Sykes, *The Society of Captives* (Princeton: Princeton University Press, 1958); Donald R. Cressey, "A Confrontation of Violent Dynamics," *International Journal of Psychiatry* 10, no. 3 (September 1972):93-108; Richard H. McCleery, "The Governmental Process and Informal Social Control," in *The Prison: Studies in Institutional Organization and Change,* ed. Donald R. Cressey (New York: Holt, Rinehart, and

Winston, 1961), pp. 149-88. See also Fred Desroches, "Patterns in Prison Riots," *Canadian Journal of Criminology and Corrections* 16, no. 4 (1974): 332-51.

10. Lloyd E. Ohlin, *Sociology and the Field of Corrections* (New York: Russell Sage Foundation, 1956); Lloyd E. Ohlin and Eugene S. Zemans, "Progress at Menard," *The Prison Journal* 34, no. 1 (April 1954):9-12; Richard M. McCleery "Correctional Administration and Political Change," in *Prison within Society,* ed. Lawrence Hazelrigg (Garden City: Doubleday Anchor, 1969), pp. 113-49; Hans W. Mattick, "The Prosaic Sources of Prison Violence," Occasional Paper No. 3, Law School of the University of Chicago, 1972.

11. For example, Bennett, "Prisons at the Pivot," p. 4; Walter M. Wallack, "Citizen Responsibility for Prison Riots," *The Prison Journal* 33, no. 1 (April 1953):10-11; American Correctional Association, *Riots and Disturbances,* pp. 8-11.

12. Frank T. Flynn, "Behind the Prison Riots," *Social Service Review* 27 (1953):74; Robert R. Hannum, "An Experience with Inmate Attitudes and Grievances in a Prison Riot," *The Prison Journal* 33, no. 1 (April 1953):23-24.

13. Schrag, "The Sociology of Prison Riots," p. 144.

14. R. Theodore Davidson, *Chicano Prisoners: The Key to San Quentin* (New York: Holt, Rinehart, and Winston, 1974).

15. For example, Hartung and Floch, "A Social-Psychological Analysis of Prison Riots"; Sykes, *The Society of Captives;* Cressey, "A Confrontation of Violent Dynamics."

16. Cf. Fox, "Why Prisoners Riot," p. 10.

17. For example, Robert Martinson, "Collective Behavior at Attica," *Federal Probation* 36, no. 3 (September 1972):3-7; Pallas and Barber, "From Riot to Revolution."

18. For example, John Bartlow Martin, *Break Down the Walls* (New York: Ballantine Books, 1953); Peg and Walter McGraw, *Assignment: Prison Riots* (New York: Henry Holt, 1954); G. David Garson, "Force versus Restraint in Prison Riots," *Crime and Delinquency* 18, no. 4 (October 1972):411-21; Garson, "The Disruption of Prison Administration."

19. Cf. Martin, *Break Down the Walls.*

20. Cf. Norman K. Denzin, "Collective Behavior in Total Institutions: The Case of the Mental Hospital and the Prison," *Social Problems* 15, no. 3 (Winter 1968):353-65; Merton J. Kahne, "Suicides in Mental Hospitals: A Study of the Effects of Personnel and Patient Turnover," *Journal of Health and Social Behavior* 9, no. 3 (September 1968):255-66; John W. Meyer, "Collective Disturbances and Staff Organization on Psychiatric Wards: A Formalization," *Sociometry* 31 (1968):180-99.

21. For colleges and universities, Alan E. Bayer and Alexander W. Astin, "Violence and Disruption on the U.S. Campus, 1968-1969," *Educational Record* 50 (Fall 1969):337-50; Joseph W. Scott and Mohamed El-Assal,

"Multiversity, University Size, University Quality and Student Protest: An Empirical Study," *American Sociological Review* 34, no. 5 (October 1969): 702-9; Harold Hodgkinson, "Student Protest — An Institutional and National Profile," *The Teachers College Record* 71, no. 4 (May 1970):537-55; Peter Blau and Ellen L. Slaughter, "Institutional Conditions and Student Demonstrations," *Social Problems* 18, no. 4 (Spring 1971):475-87; for ghetto riots, Bryan T. Downes, "A Critical Reexamination of the Social and Political Characteristics of Riot Cities," *Social Science Quarterly* 51 (September 1970):349-60; Seymour Spilerman, "The Causes of Racial Disturbances: A Comparison of Alternative Explanations," *American Sociological Review* 35, no. 4 (August 1970):627-49; Robert M. Jiobu, "City Characteristics, Differential Stratification, and the Occurrence of Interracial Violence," *Social Science Quarterly* 52 (December 1971):508-20; Jerome L. McElroy and Larry D. Singell, "Riot and Nonriot Cities: An Examination of Structural Contours," *Urban Affairs Quarterly* 8, no. 3 (March 1973):281-302; William R. Morgan and Terry N. Clark, "The Causes of Racial Disorders: A Grievance-Level Explanation," *American Sociological Review* 38, no. 5 (October 1973):611-24.

22. For example, Bryan T. Downes, "Social and Political Characteristics of Riot Cities: A Comparative Study," *Social Science Quarterly* 49 (December 1968):504-20; Downes, "A Critical Reexamination"; Durward Long and Julian Foster, "Levels of Protest," in *Protest! Student Activism in America,* ed. Julian Foster and Durward Long (New York: William Morrow, 1970), pp. 81-101; Morgan and Clark, "The Causes of Racial Disorders."

23. Cf. Richard E. Peterson, *The Scope of Organized Student Protest in 1967-1968* (Princeton: Educational Testing Service, 1968); Spilerman, "The Causes of Racial Disturbances: A Comparison of Alternative Explanations"; Seymour Spilerman, "The Causes of Racial Disturbances: Tests of an Explanation," *American Sociological Review* 36, no. 3 (June 1971):427-42; Alexander W. Astin and Alan F. Bayer, "Antecedents and Consequents of Disruptive Campus Protests," *Measurement and Evaluation in Guidance* 4, no. 1 (April 1971):18-30; Kenneth Keviston and Michael Lerner, "Campus Characteristics and Campus Unrest," *The Annals* 395 (May 1971):39-53.

24. Cf. Morgan and Clark, "The Causes of Racial Disorders."

25. For campus disturbances, cf. Scott and El-Assal, "Multiversity, University Size, University Quality, and Student Protest"; and Blau and Slaughter, "Institutional Conditions and Student Demonstrations"; for urban rioting and constituents per councilman, see Stanley Lieberson and Arnold R. Silverman, "The Precipitants and Underlying Conditions of Race Riots," *American Sociological Review* 30, no. 6 (December 1965):887-98; Spilerman, "The Cases of Racial Disturbances: A Comparison of Alternative Explanations"; and McElroy and Singell, "Riot and Nonriot Cities: An Examination of Structural Contours."

26. Cf. Hodgkinson, "Student Protest — An Institutional and National Profile"; Masu Sasajima, Junius A. Davis, and Richard E. Peterson, "Organized

Student Protest and Institutional Climate," *American Educational Research Journal* 5 (May 1968):291–304.

27. Hodgkinson, "Student Protest — An Institutional and National Profile," pp. 547–48.

28. Cf. Downes, "Social and Political Characteristics of Riot Cities"; Spilerman, "The Causes of Racial Disturbances: A Comparison of Alternative Explanations"; Robert M. Jiobu, "City Characteristics and Racial Violence," *Social Science Quarterly* 55, no. 1 (March 1974):52–64; A. Bruce Dotson, "Social Planning and Urban Violence: An Extension of McElroy and Singell," *Urban Affairs Quarterly* 9, no. 3 (March 1974):283–301.

29. Cf. Morgan and Clark, "The Causes of Racial Disorders"; Dotson, "Social Planning and Urban Violence."

30. Cf. the idea of "competition" in Herbert J. Gans, "The Ghetto Rebellions and Urban Class Conflict," in *Urban Riots: Violence and Social Change*, ed. Robert H. Connery (New York: Academy of Political Science, Columbia University, 1968), pp. 42–51; and Dotson, "Social Planning and Urban Violence," pp. 287–88.

31. Michael Lipsky, "Protest as a Political Resource," *American Political Science Review* 62 (1968):1114–58.

32. See Thomas H. Greene, *Comparative Revolutionary Movements* (Englewood Cliffs: Prentice-Hall, 1974), pp. 116–18.

33. Cf. Erik Olin Wright, *The Politics of Punishment: A Critical Analysis of Prisons in America* (New York: Harper Colophon Books, 1973); Min S. Yee, *The Melancholy History of Soledad Prison* (New York: Harper's Magazine Press, 1973).

Prison Violence and Formal Organization

James B. Jacobs

While all the empirical data presented in this book indicate lower *rates*[a] of violence in prison than on the streets (especially if we compare prisons with the high crime rate districts from which offenders are drawn), it is still true that violent behavior is common in most prisons[b] and that it is very common in a few American prisons. While the most distinctive manifestation of prison violence is homosexual rape there are also garden variety assaults, knifings, and other types of attacks with improvised weapons. Attempts to account for the presence of prison violence usually point either to the violent backgrounds of the offenders today incarcerated in the state prisons or to the internal pressures of the maximum security environment that generate frustration, aggression, conflict and violence.

Throughout our society during the past decade violence, particularly gun attacks, has become much more frequent. There has been an increase in the rate and proportion of such attacks carried out by younger offenders. Violent criminal careers may be starting earlier. In any case violence that has become more prevalent on the streets has been imported into prison. Moreover, the expanded use of probation and the overall decline (recently reversed) in prison populations has meant that a greater percentage of felons committed to prison are there for violent offenses. Intense racial conflict has profoundly increased the potential for interpersonal violence in prison. Homosexual rape particularly seems to be characterized by its interracial expression.[c]

---

[a]While it might be objected that the frequency of prison violence is much greater than what comes to the attention of the authorities, there is no reason to believe that this is a greater problem in prison, where violence is more visible, than on the streets. On the other hand, there may well be *special problems* both in the reporting and recording of crime statistics in prison; it is a revealing commentary on the field that so little attention has been given to the systematic collection of such data.

[b]There is a real problem in defining and operationalizing the category "violence." Some psychologists are even ready to code angry words as violence. Using the records of Stateville's chief investigator, who is responsible for filing a report on all serious incidents in the prison, I have counted 24 acts of physical aggression resulting in serious injury between April 30, 1974 and May 1, 1975 for an average inmate population of approximately 1,600 (stabbings 8; attack with blunt weapon 9; physical assault 5; rape 2: total 24).

[c]Even where blacks composed a minority (25%) of the prison population Leo Carroll found that approximately 75 percent of the rapes involved black rapists and white victims. There were no reported instances of white rapists and black victims. "Race and Sexual Assault in A Maximum Security Prison," read at the Annual Meeting of the Society for Social Problems in Montreal, August 1974.

79

What all importation explanations of prison violence have in common is the location of the source of prison violence in the offender. Prison administrators who adhere to this view of prison violence are logically led to the traditional response of attempting to isolate the troublemakers and separate the races to the extent that is practically and legally possible.[d] To the extent that the courts have checked the staff's absolute recourse to coercive sanctions[e] and to the extent that the readiness to do violence has become far more prevalent among prisoners, the administrative strategy of maintaining control through punishment has lost much of the efficacy it once had.

A second set of independent variables offered to explain prison violence points to what has frequently been called the "pains of imprisonment":[f] crowding, sexual frustration, dehumanization, idleness, boredom, institutionalization, powerlessness, etc. It is said that the structural pressures and frustrations built into crowded maximum security living are so intense that even normal irritants of everyday life may overwhelm inhibitors and trigger acts of aggression. It is here, however, when discussing the frustration–aggression hypothesis that the word "aggression" is often used so loosely as to become coterminous with *all rule violations.*[g]

To the extent that the "pains of imprisonment" "cause" prison violence, prison administrators are essentially unable to *prevent* the violence. Minor reforms are possible, but significant abatement of the "pains of imprisonment" requires action beyond the prison walls, in the legislature and increasingly in the Department of Correction's central office. To eliminate many of the frustrations enumerated above would require top-level policy decisions and, more importantly, a commitment of resources (to construct miniprisons, vocational programs, viable industries, conjugal facilities) that appears politically unrealistic. This is not to say that administrative strategies aimed at ameliorating the pains of imprisonment are never implemented and never successful. The number of letters and visits is increased; new training sessions for guards are established,

---

[d]The serious policy issue of whether it would be better to recognize the harsh reality and run segregated prison facilities for whites, blacks, and Spanish-surnamed Americans rather than to try to create a harmonious model of racial integration in prison has never to my knowledge been seriously debated. cf: Washington v. Lee, 263 F. Supp. 327 (M.D. Ala. 1966). It has been seriously suggested by inmate members of all three races.

[e]The judicial opinions over the past five years curbing administrative discretion in prison are legion. See, for example, Wolff v. McDonnel, 94 S.Ct. 2963 (1974), where the U. S. Supreme Court held that prison inmates facing a loss of good time or confinement in segregation must be provided a rudimentary due process hearing.

[f]To the best of my knowledge the phrase belongs to Gresham Sykes. See *Society of Captives* (New York: Atheneum, 1966).

[g]Thus, many studies of violence code such a wide range of behaviors (from homicides, knifings, and rapes to cursing, threatening, and stealing) as violence that the analyses are severely jeopardized.

and some new "programs" are introduced. However, when such incremental reforms are initiated within the existing prison ecology without conceptual planning for security, frustration seems to be little affected and the concomitant weakening of control may lead to an acual increase in violence.[h]

A third set of independent variables rarely examined but meriting our close attention focuses on the quality of prison management. How well does the administration evaluate problem areas and move toward solutions? How well does the decision-making structure insure that policies once articulated are actually carried out and that accurate information is passed back up the chain of command? Too often in this field traditional and ritualistic organizations are unable to evaluate or respond to persistent or emergent problems. No doubt the inmates of the 1960s and 1970s posed new challenges (of which racial conflict is the most important) to the prisons. These challenges illuminated the ritualism of traditional regimes like that of Illinois' Stateville Penitentiary with which I am most familiar.[1] But not only the old "disciplinarians" were guilty of organizational myopia; so too were the new "rehabilitators" who came out of college programs with degrees in psychology, sociology, and social work. While inmates challenged the safety of fellow inmates and the staff, and while the courts demanded more rational and visible decision making, the reformers brought to the prisons diffuse philosophical commitments but few organizational strategies.

My comments are not meant to exorcise prison officials but rather to highlight the crucial importance of prison management in shaping the content and extent of prison violence.[i] My argument here is that maximum-security prisons are not as safe as they might be (although to be sure for many of their residents prisons are the safest environments they have ever lived in). Given the prison's geographical boundedness, the staff's near monopoly over fatal force and the *possibility* of almost total surveillance, we might expect that despite the violence proness of the inmates and the numerous frustrations inherent in maximum security imprisonment, the eruption of prison violence could in most cases be controlled. Why is this not the case?

While I have already pointed out that prison violence can (although not too successfully) be addressed by administrative interventions aimed at reducing the violence proneness of the inmates, by confining troublemakers and deterring the rest, or by ameliorating the structural sources of frustration, it is the

---

[h]Carroll notes, "It is my contention that humanitarian reforms of the prison social structure transformed the prison into an arena within which is acted out a pattern of racial conflict that has its roots deep within the socio-cultural history of American Society." See footnote c, *supra*, at p. 77.

[i]My own sensitivity to the significance of managerial capability as a variable within the prison setting was stimulated by David Brierton, Stateville's warden since December 1974. I owe him a great debt of gratitude for his insights and co-operation in my research.

management of the *opportunities* and *instrumentalities* of violence with which I am presently concerned. These are rather prosaic topics for academic commentators. Lofland writes as follows:

Social scientists have shown a strong tendency to underplay matters of hardware and places in accounts of deviant acts and deviance generally. A concern with hardware and place is traditionally identified with the police and other categories of persons — such as political conservatives — who are devalued and scorned in the social scientist's typically liberal world view. Liberal ideology aside, and viewing the matter on grounds of simple technical efficacy, the constriction of availability of hardware for those acts requiring any, seems reasonably to inhibit the possibility of their occurrence.[2]

A systematic study of the structure of opportunities and the distribution of instrumentalities leading to prison violence cannot be carried out without comprehensive data on the circumstances of prison violence. The first step in identifying the etiology of prison violence is to develop some viable mechanism of reporting *accurate* crime statistics within prisons. For the same reasons that crime victims on the streets do not report their victimization (e.g., fear, humiliation, alienation, belief that the authorities cannot or will not do anything) prisoners often do not report theirs. Some mechanism must be developed to encourage inmates to report instances of victimization. Two prerequisites will have to be assurances of anonymity and confidence that generating such information will make a difference. Possessing accurate prison crime statistics will enable us to identify the most frequent locations in the prison for violence, the most common times of day, the most likely pool of victims and offenders, and the most common types of weapons. Furthermore, *uniform* crime statistics would allow us to make some very telling comparisons between dangerous and safe prisons, as well as allowing us to evaluate what trade-offs (privacy, for example), are required to insure safety inside prisons.

Changes in the physical plant can have a crucial impact on opportunities for engaging in violence. During the regime of Warden Joseph Ragen (1936–61) Stateville Penitenary was reputed to have one of the strictest security systems in the United States. During this period the inmate dining room served 3,600 inmates in two sittings for each meal. When there was a threat of riot in the air, inmates might be fed in their cells for fear of collective violence erupting when the inmates congregated at the single dining room. The system worked well enough until the late 1960s and 1970s when instances of individual and collective violence (exacerbated by the presence of four powerful Chicago street gangs) increased and were followed by several month-long general lockups. It was not until 1974 that the main dining room was dismantled and inmates served their meals regularly in individual dining areas in each cell house. This single change greatly reduced the threat of prison-wide violence by placing the inmates at four-man tables in the cell houses where surveillance and security were much better.

Stateville Penitentiary, like many other American mega-prisons consists of a hodgepodge of buildings, alleys, tunnels, corridors, backrooms, blind spots, etc. Not until David Brierton assumed the wardenship in December 1974 had anyone begun to identify the most dangerous places and sought solutions by sealing them off, closing them up, fencing them in, breaking down walls, etc. A prison should be the ultimate exemplar of "defensible space."[3] It should be an irreducible and primary principle of prison administration that *every inmate is entitled to maximum feasible security from physical attack.*

Rapes do not occur in the warden's office or on the front lawn. They occur in closed offices, in back rooms, in dark cells with faulty locks, and in other poorly or even unsupervised areas. There should be no such areas in a prison. If they cannot be supervised by guards they should be supervised by closed circuit television. The only alternative is to seal up the area. Privacy values should, of course, be considered and protected but the evaluation of competing values needs to be made explicit. Is it "better" for inmates to be free from the intrusions of an electric eye if this means substantially increasing their vulnerability to rape? Unfortunately, as long as we have mega-prisons, we will be forced to make hard judgements.

Until the fall of 1974 first-line discipline at Stateville Penitentiary was carried out by placing the rule violator in special "isolation cells" sealed with a heavy security door that prevented the guards from seeing or hearing what was going on inside the cells where six to eight inmates were often crowded together. In all probability the disciplinary unit itself became the most frequent locale of rapes. A nongang member locked in an isolation cell for 15 days with five or six members of the Black Stone Nation or Devil's Disciples might be subject to a brutal experience of sexual assault.[4] The administrative response was an effort to insure that "sheeps" and "wolves" are not mixed in the same cells. Such intuitive judgements invariably involved misjudgements and the rapes continued until isolation was abolished and punishment was carried out in one-man cells. No doubt such situations have and continue to exist in prisons across the country. The chief "cause" of such brutalities is poor prison management.

As the Lofland quote makes clear, "hardware" is a low status subject for criminologists.[j] In prison where gun control is a reality, knives ("shivs" in prison argot) are the most lethal weapons. (At Stateville Penitentiary there were eight *reported* stabbings between April 30, 1974 and May 1, 1975.[k] During the same period there were nine batteries with a variety of blunt instruments that resulted in serious injury.) In recognition of the lethality of knives prisoners in every American prison I have been in are not allowed to use steel knives even for eating. But year after year shivs remain plentiful behind the walls. Where do

---

[j]Of course, the notable exception here is Professor Franklin Zimring whose outstanding research of gun violence has made academic study of the subject respectable.

[k]See note 2, at the conclusion of this chapter.

these shivs come from? This is not a subject upon which prison officials themselves are likely to shed much light. No doubt there are single instances where shivs have been ingeniously fashioned from a variety of incredibly unlikely objects, but it is my *impression* that most shivs are "manufactured" in prison industries or made from fragments loosened from metal beds. Can't the manufacturing process be interrupted?

The prevailing response to knifings and other violent crimes in prison, as is the case on the street, is an effort to identify the guilty individual. As on the street the guilty culprit is imprisoned in the prison's prison—segregation or some other form of special sequestration. Once having been identified, "tried," convicted, and confined, the crime is deemed to be solved. While this may be a laudable and necessary moral and deterrent response to intraprison violence it does not interrupt the processes that lead to the possession of deadly shivs and ultimately to serious violence.[1]

Reminiscent of the argument made by opponents of gun control, prison administrators claim that the attempt to eliminate prison violence by eliminating weapons is futile because "where there's a will there's a way." The pervasive belief that the prisoners are so ingenious that nothing can keep them from making a weapon if they are so inclined ("guns don't kill, people do") recalls Goffman's insightful observation that "normals" impute supernatural capabilities to deviants.[5]

Prison administrators, however, may overestimate both the ingenuity of their residents and the intensity of the commitment to violence. At least in a large proportion of cases it may well be the case that violence in prison is "situational" and is carried to its ultimate result only because of the unhappy concurrence of an opportunity and instrumentality of violence. To the extent that inmates are viewed as "explosive" and "violence prone," prevention of prison violence becomes defined as "impossible" and administrators fall back into fatalism about the periodic occurrence of a murder, rape, or assault. In any case where the situation is defined as pitting prison staff against an adversary with supernatural ingenuity, the former certainly cannot be held responsible for violence when it does occur. To the contrary, they may actually be congratulated for preventing more pervasive "outbreaks" of violence.

All this leads me to conclude that prison organizations are not security oriented. The relentless search for contraband carried out in the name of security, for example, is more directed toward maintenance of the traditional order than toward insuring maximum feasible safety for staff and residents. Anyone who has entered a maximum-security prison probably recalls that he

---

[1]A security issue similar to the shivs is suggested by the great debate that rages in prison over which "outsiders" should be allowed entrance. Those desiring entry (media, reformers, scholars, etc.) are screened in order to determine their *true motives*. Once they are deemed acceptable and given access supervision may be very lax, as when an attorney was reputed to have smuggled a gun to Soledad prisoner George Jackson.

has been asked to empty out his pockets and leave his chewing gum at the gate. But how many of us have been passed through metal detectors or thoroughly searched?

Prison "security" is highly *ritualistic* behind the walls of these closed insitutions. Even today litigation flourishes around whether inmates should be allowed to write letters to whom they please or to subscribe to this militant magazine or that racist tract. Administrators argue that such publications might inflame inmates to extreme behavior. There is no evidence for this conclusion although convoluted scenarios can readily be supplied; but no matter, prison censorship is viewed as a central tenet of prison security. Departments of corrections have vigorously appealed to appellate courts rulings that would permit prisoners to correspond with relatives not on their correspondence lists.[6] By contrast, no prison that I know of has a procedure whereby it can insure that the staff will not be poisoned in the staff dining room where the food is prepared and served by the prisoners. In response to my inquiries I have always been told that "they could if they wanted to but that kind of thing would not make any sense." Unlike the mail, the possibility of staff being poisoned has never been seen as a serious security issue.

All the prisons with which I am familiar use some sort of metal bunk with metal spring upon which a mattress is placed. From time immemorial inmates have methodically broken these beds down and sharpened pieces of loose metal into deadly weapons. On occasion they have also used the springs as projectiles, which are shot by rubberbands at guards and other inmates. Punishing the guilty individual after the knifing or slingshot attack does not, of course, intervene into the process, eliminate the problem, or reduce the probability of future injuries.

One way to intervene seriously is to interrupt the production of the shivs and projectiles by finding a substitute for the metal bed. Could a one-piece plastic unit be devised? While I am not in the business of designing prison furnishings it seems to me that a foam rubber slab would substitute admirably for the metal bed; it might even be more comfortable. Prison administrators have met this suggestion with incredulity, arguing that it is naive to think that "our inmates could be prevented from getting weapons so easily." But some experimentation in this area might be useful, perhaps leading to more precise identification of the dynamics of knife attacks. The example is offered more for its illustration of the types of analyses that are required rather than for the implementation of the substantive suggestion.

The metal beds are not the only regular raw materials from which weapons can be produced. The prison industries often provide a ready source of metal scrap as well as a wide array of tools with which shivs can be manufactured. Weapons can be hidden in the prisoners' clothing and shoes and passed easily out of the shops. The pressures involved in the normalization of day-to-day interactions between inmates and guards often make the "shakedown" an empty ritual.[7]

Perhaps prison industries producing metal products made sense during a period in American history when random violence was less frequent, when inmates were serving longer sentences, when the old cons had a high stake in the status quo, and when the administration's recourse to coercive sanctions was practically unchecked. They may also have made more sense during a period when they could be run profitably rather than in the red. What levels of violence and knife attacks would today convince administrators to close these industries?

More to the point, what levels of prison violence would stimulate a prison administration to evaluate rigorously the security challenges posed by its industries? Could scrap metals be more rigorously supervised and accounted for? Could all inmates entering and leaving the industries be passed through one or a series of metal detectors? When I have posed these questions the replies have once again clustered around the position that metal detectors do not work, that inmates could find a way to thwart them and that if there was a solution it would have been implemented years ago. Perhaps the situation is more tolerable for some when it is defined as "impossible."

Mine is not an advocacy for repression or a call for repeal of the humane and civilized court decisions of the past few years. Nor does this argument contradict those who advocate abandonment of the maximum-security mega-prisons or their wholesale reconstruction through massive injections of funding. I, of course, would welcome such reform. In case either of these suggestions became reality the problems of prison management would be different and would require different solution, but not different analysis.

The argument that has been made here reinforces the principle that the prison staff has a paramount responsibility to protect inmates from one another. In order to reduce violence and to make prisons safer places for both inmates and staff, management must be more sophisticated, rational, systematic, and thorough. Under the existing realities of overcrowding and strained resources the best chances for reducing violence are linked to diminishing the opportunities that enable one inmate to attack another.

The opportunities to be diminished are associated with both place and hardware. Our rationale closely parallels those that lie behind antigun laws and plans for illumination of dangerous city streets. Some strategies of intervention into the processes of intraprison violence may intrude upon privacy and other important values in order to enhance the effectiveness of surveillance. Unfortunately, such tough policy choices cannot be avoided; they are being made today although not explicitly. Where greater intrusions are made they should be carefully monitored so that they may not be perverted for other purposes. The kinds of trade-offs discussed in this chapter will create a setting for the inmate in which he can realistically breathe more easily.

Notes

1. James B. Jacobs, "Stateville: A Natural History of a Maximum Security Prison," Ph.D. dissertation, Department of Sociology, University of Chicago,

1975. See also: James B. Jacobs, "Street Gangs Behind Bars," *Social Problems* 21 (Winter 1974); "Participant Observation in Prison," *Urban Life and Culture,* 3 (July 1974); and Harold G. Retsky, "Prison Guard" *Urban Life,* 4 (April 1975); "The Stateville Counselors: Symbol of Reform in Search of a Role," *Social Service Review* (March 1976).

2. John Lofland, *Deviance and Identity* (Englewood Cliffs: Prentice-Hall, 1969), p. 71.

3. Oscar Newman, *Defensible Space: Crime Prevention Through Urban Design* (New York: The Macmillan Company, 1972).

4. Jacobs, "Street Gangs Behind Bars."

5. Erving Goffman, *Stigma: Notes on the Management of Spoiled Identity* (Englewood Cliffs: Prentice-Hall, 1973).

6. Morales v. Schmidt, 340 F. Supp. 544 (E.D. Wis. 1972); F.2d. (7th Cir. 1973).

7. Jacobs and Retsky, "Prison Guard," p. 20.

7

The Organization of Prison Violence
James W. L. Park

Rational discussion of violence in prisons must be accompanied by a clear understanding that such violence has causes within the correctional system and in the outside society. While, there is no doubt that frustrations inherent in prison life are responsible for some violence and that prisons often provide situations in which violence can easily occur, critics of the correctional system overemphasize these factors and ignore earlier sources of violence in the family and community experiences of the inmates. Note that some 71 percent of the inmates received in 1973 by the California prison system had a history of violence prior to their incarceration.

1976

Rather than creating unique kinds of hostility, the prison setting concentrates the tensions and anger that exists in a dilute form in the outside community: racial tensions, for example. In some cases, there may be a direct transfer of violence from the community into the prison and from the prison back into the community as in the activities of groups advocating violent solutions to social problems.

The outside society has influenced the climate of California institutions through an increased use of community-based programs, such as probation, that has reduced the percentage of convicted felons sent to prison from 30 percent to around 12 percent. As contrasted with ten years ago, the prisons now receive fewer property offenders, almost no check writers, more armed robbers, fewer skilled craftsmen, fewer genuine first offenders, and more "state raised" inmates.

The search for ways of reducing prison violence is not apt to be successful without an understanding that remedies for the basic causes of such violence are no more easily available than are solutions to the problem of violence in the outside society. The relatively small size of a prison makes easier only oppressive controls, not basic solutions.

Remedies

That violence inside and outside may have common sources is suggested by the fact that the rise in California prison violence during the past five years was matched by a similar increase in the community. Tensions between races and cultures are not apt to be alleviated in the prisons much before they are remedied in the outside society.

The Changing Nature of Violence

The nature of the violence problem in California prisons has changed dramatically in a short period. As recently as 1965, a major report on prison violence made no mention of the large, well-organized ethnic groups that have been the most serious source of prison violence in recent years, nor of the revolutionary ethic that has undergirded many assaults on employees.

The way in which violence is expressed has also changed. Confrontations involving large groups of inmates have been replaced by the hit–run tactics of guerrilla warfare. Assaults on employees prior to 1970 were typically the unplanned side effects of escapes or other incidents that prison staff were attempting to control. Since 1970 violence against staff has had an increasingly deliberate and ideological character.

In the early 1960s, the violence level in California prisons remained essentially constant and low enough to cause little concern. In the last half of the decade, violence began to increase, and by 1970, had begun to rise at an alarming rate as Table 7-1 demonstrates. Both staff and inmates were involved in increasing incidents of assault, and in a rising fatality rate. Departmental response was to increase controls, install alarm systems, and to segregate leaders of warring groups.

Efforts were made to identify sources of inmate discontent but alleviation of these problems did not appear to be an effective means of immediate violence reduction. Line employees felt strongly that their safety rested upon increased staffing and physical security measures.

Sources of Prison Violence

Prison violence can be categorized into four interrelated but independently identifiable areas according to a 1974 California department study of violence.

Table 7-1
Violence in California Prisons

| Calendar Year | Total Incidents Involving Inmates | | Incidents of Inmates Assaulted by Inmates | | Incidents of Employees Assaulted by Inmates | |
	Number	Rate per 100 Average Institution Population	Total	Fatal	Total	Fatal
1970	366	1.36	79	11	59	2
1971	465	2.00	124	17	67	7
1972	592	3.04	189	35	55	1
1973	777	3.67	197	19	84	1
1974	1,022	4.30	220	20	93	–

Violence as a Function of a Closed Prison Society

The violence of a closed prison society includes that associated with gambling, debts, homosexual behavior, crowded living conditions, poor institutional design, inability of employees to supervise properly, life-style and cultural–racial incompatibilities, time-setting policies, and the cumbersome way in which a bureaucracy attempts to meet human needs. Much of this violence is between individuals although predators may form small, relatively impermanent alliances for the purpose of exploiting other inmates.

Violence as a Function of Individual Emotional Disturbances

Although an insignificant source of violence in most institutions, individual emotional disturbance contributes significantly to the number of assaults at institutions handling psychiatrically disturbed inmates, and to a large number of nonfatal assaults on employees.

Violence as a Function of Revolutionary–Retaliatory
Ideology

The revolutionary–retaliatory ideology involves very small groups whose existence as well as membership may be unknown to prison staff until an incident occurs. These groups form and disband under different names and with different participants. Continuity is provided by a common ideology with emphasis on the rhetoric of revolutionary violence.

There may be encouragement from like-minded groups in the outside community who provide moral support, legal aid, free literature, and visitors for cooperative prisoners. Both inmates and employees have been victims of revolutionary–retaliatory violence. Some murders of prison employees since 1970 can be attributed to this source of violence.

Violence as a Function of Organized Gangs

While predatory groups tend to disband with the segregation of their leaders, in the late 1960s California prison gangs began to take on characteristics that would persist for years under a variety of leaders. A quasi-military organizational structure provided continuity to the gang and allowed assumption of power by second-level leaders if the top leadership was segregated. Although membership involves probably no more than 2 percent of the total male felon population, the tight organization and discipline of these groups enable them to dominate much larger numbers of unorganized inmates. Inmates have been the primary targets of the gangs, whose activities are the largest single source of assaults and deaths in California institutions. Gangs are organized around racial-ethnic lines with the Mexican-American groups having the largest membership.

A Closer Look at the California Gangs

Four inmate groups in California prisons have more influence on the tranquility of the system than do the wardens. Biggest and most deadly in terms of numbers of assaults and deaths are the two Mexican-American groups: The Mexican Mafia and Nuestra Familia. Most ideological of the groups, the Black Guerrilla Family, seems more involved in rhetoric than action although the revolutionary ethic they follow is probably responsible for most of the employee murders of the past few years. The Aryan Brothers is a small group of aggressive white inmates whose ideology is theoretically National Socialist, but in practice is no more than a simple antiblack position.

In the manner of conglomerate corporations, these four groups have either assimilated or overshadowed the many smaller regional, neighborhood, or predatory gangs that have always existed in California institutions. The Mexican Mafia incorporates the most aggressive Chicano inmates from the many neighborhood gangs that operate in the East Los Angeles area. Nuestra Familia draws its membership from the smaller, agricultural towns of California's Central Valley, replacing former distinctions between Chicanos from these towns. Some groups such as Maravilla, Inland Empire, and the El Pasos continue to have an identity, but adopt a defensive stance rather than initiating violence. Similarly, the Aryan Brothers attract the most violently inclined members of the motorcycle gangs or the "okies," which result in these groups having a less aggressive role. The number of basic organizations reduces even further through tenuous and temporary alliances, such as Mexican Mafia-Aryan Brothers and Nuestra Familia-Black Guerrilla Family.

Curiously, the existence of these well-organized, highly disciplined groups probably have reduced the chances that large scale intergroup conflict will occur. The dangers in such outbreaks are so threatening that the occasional assaults between individual gang members are often resolved by negotiation. One result has been that most of the serious violence occurs within the groups. The majority of assaults and fatalities involving inmates have been the result of the rivalry between the Mexican Mafia and the Nuestra Familia, with the victims being almost all Mexican-American.

Gang Links to the Outside Community

Some members of the Mexican Mafia and the Aryan Brotherhood have attempted to maintain gang identity on parole, and some criminal activities, particularly narcotics trafficking, have been carried out under the names of these groups. This carrying of gang activities from the prison to the community is a reversal of the more typical process whereby community gangs maintain their identity after imprisonment.

The ideologically oriented Black Guerrilla Family may have links with the Black Liberation Army although it appears unlikely that very many Black Guerrilla Family members continue an interest in revolutionary activities upon release. Both groups express interest in the assassination people, which makes them of great concern to police and prison employees. This concern undoubtedly leads to overestimation of the size and importance of these groups either in or out of prison.

Parenthetically, it should be noted that the Nation of Islam in California prisons has steered a neutral role in gang conflicts, becoming violent only in response to the rare attacks on one of their members, and remaining uninvolved in attempts by other groups to strike out against the prison administration. The Black Muslims relate closely to their outside organization and to the power struggles within that sect. Recruiting measures sometimes become overzealous. In recent months, some members of the Nation of Islam have shown interest in Maoist doctrines so that their roles may change.

Diligent efforts have been made to politicize the gangs by members of revolutionary cadres outside and by some politically sophisticated inmates. The Chicano groups have been particular targets for politicization because of their formidable nature and the great disruptive influence they could have if turned against the administration. However, these efforts have been unsuccessful, partially because the antagonisms run so deep between the Chicano factions and there are so many old scores to settle.

Periodically, there have been attempts to form a popular-front group made up of politically oriented inmates from all groups. The objective of these efforts is to divert the considerable energies inmates expend in assaulting each other for ethnic and interethnic reasons into class conflict between inmates and the prison administration. The reasons for the consistent failure of such attempts are unclear although they undoubtedly involve both some concern about staff reaction and the unstable nature of these interethnic alliances.

1976

The Fantasy World of the Chicano Gangs

The reader of the literature and tables of organization produced by the Mexican Mafia and Nuestra Familia (and the Black Guerrilla Family) will feel immersed in a fantasy world that is composed of excerpts from the Infantry Manual and Alice in Wonderland. This feeling of unreality is heightened by reading the official accounts of these groups written by staff investigators who spend an inordinate amount of time trying to ascertain what rank particular inmates hold in the organization.

Briefly, the Nuestra Familia in all institutions is led by a Nuestra Generale housed at one institution who manages to have his orders transmitted by an elaborate messenger system. Ten captains back up the generale. Lieutenants are next in order, having earned that rank by performing three kills or similar meritorious service. Membership is granted only after serious evaluation of the candidate, who upon acceptance into the group can never resign without fear of being executed.

The suspicion arises that inmates and employees are each feeding the others fantasy lives in an effort to erase the essential bleakness of life generally and prison life particularly. There is no doubt that conspiracies, election of leaders, execution of defectors, and laying of battle plans are far more emotionally involving for inmates than washing dishes or attending school, nor is there any doubt that chasing Nuestra Generales is more stimulating than manning a guard post.

This does not mean that these organizations are not real and deadly. The body count attests to that. However, it may be hypothesized that these gangs are created to meet deep-set needs of inmates and that their perpetuation meets staff needs in fundamental ways. What may be a very loose-knit organization with limited membership can be fantasized as much larger, more deadly, and more purposeful than it really is with the result that the inmate organization becomes exactly what the staff fears it was in the beginning.

Touching Briefly on Solutions

A discussion of solutions to the problem of prison violence can be little more than an overview because the long list of the experts' favorite theories are not matched by a list of satisfactory results. There are many measures that probably reduce violence somewhat, but nothing seems to come close to eliminating assaultive incidents.

Sound, Humane Prison Management

There can be no quarrel with measures that alleviate inmate frustrations as a means of improving the quality of institutional life. However, since the frustration of prison life is not the only source of violence, institutional remedies are incomplete. Additionally, prisoners are subject to the effects of rising expectations so that improvements lead to the hope for more improvement, and the relative frustration level remains about the same. Finally, there is no way to releave the greatest frustration of all, which is the loss of liberty.

Security and Control Measures

California has had nearly two years experience with the application of various restrictive controls including the almost complete shutdown of four major institutions for a period of several months. These controls resulted in the use of more makeshift weapons and a shift of violence from the general population to the security units.

Serious violence was largely restricted to two institutions instead of disrupting all ten male felon prisons. Complete control can be achieved only by reducing activities to nearly zero, a condition that is inherently unstable and ultimately brings about generalized outbreaks of violence.

Segregating and controlling leaders of the Chicano gangs did help to reduce gang-related violence somewhat and to restrict such action to the units in which these leaders were segregated. With the leadership off the yard, some gang members were able to defect although many of these defectors are now in protective custody status.

Efforts are now underway to structure a whole unit in which there would be a maximum of normal programs, but the clientele would be entirely violent inmates, although not those who have been top leaders or the most dedicated followers of gang leaders. Some success has been achieved, in part due to the participation of inmates in solving management problems.

Elimination of the Indeterminate Sentence

The indeterminate sentence has been a major point of contention in California. There is no doubt that the indeterminate sentence as administered has been highly frustrating to nearly all inmates. However, it is highly speculative to say that removing uncertainties about length of prison term will have much influence on levels of violence. The present aim of the California Adult Authority is to grant fixed parole dates for some 80 percent of the inmates. If this is carried out, there will be an opportunity to assess the effects of this new policy.

Providing an Alternative to Gang Membership

Although an alternative is desirable, nothing yet has been found to match the adventure of gang activities or to satisfy the machismo needs of the inmate gang members.

Some efforts to establish Chicano and black cultural enterprises failed because leadership of these constructive groups became pawns in the power struggles of the violent groups. Staff fears of the rhetoric of these groups also contributed to their failure to fill an emotional role for the inmates. A suggestion that inmates be trained in the theory and practice of social change, including the methods of revolutionary change, also proved too threatening to the administration.

Basic Changes in the Prison Cultures of Both Staff and Inmates

Some critics of the system feel that staff machismo needs, loyalties, and a perception of inmates as both inferior and dangerous, all of which creates a vast gulf between staff and inmates, support and encourage violence by inmates. While there is some truth in this position, changes are most difficult to make within the limitations of the institutions. Both staff and inmates have deep-rooted attitudes that are most resistant to change, particularly for violent inmates and for those who must manage violent inmates.

Note that there is almost no problem of violence with milder prisoners housed in institutions of lesser custody. The task here is not to create a therapeutic community type of climate with minimum-custody inmates but to do so in maximum custody units with inmates of demonstrated violent behavior, and with the traditions of particular ethnic groups.

In conclusion, California will apply a variety of part solutions to the problem of violence with the result that the levels of violence will change.

However, no one will know exactly what caused the levels to change. Prison administrators and others will probably believe the change was due to factors that were in fact irrelevant.

It will remain fairly clear that if the only way intense individuals are allowed to define themselves is through violence, then violence will occur. However, it will continue to be uncertain as to which means of personal definition an inmate will adopt given a wide spectrum of choices, a spectrum that in no event can be as wide as the society from which the prisoner came and which, in the majority of instances, was not sufficient to deflect the offender's violent impulse.

Discussion

Park: The role of the Chicano gangs has always been the enhancement of manhood in a prison situation that does take away your manhood, particularly in the Chicano ethic. It becomes very important to define yourself as a man. Once they have this kind of organization going, the staff then comes in and reinforces it by taking it so seriously. We have investigators who do nothing but investigate all of these gang relationships — who the general is, who his couriers are, and who his lieutenants are — because it meets staff needs. Prisons are such terribly dull places when there is no disruption. You see, over and over again, how very mild inmates will tell their visitors what a terrible place this is and describe the war that's going on in great detail. The officers, the guards — they do the same thing. They go to the neighborhood bar where, instead of being a humble, underpaid civil servant, they tell the whole bar about the same terrible war.

Not that the war isn't real. We've got to keep emphasizing that. But the Chicanos didn't envision all of this elaborate structure until staff started asking, "Hey, do you have a plan to cover this contingency?" "Oh yeah, yeah we have a sublieutenant to do that." Violence has this instrumental rewarding function in a very general sense.

Someone mentioned the deterioration in staff's self-confidence. This is very true. Staffs have been confused, particularly under the impact of court decisions, civil rights, and affirmative action. They haven't known what they're supposed to be—counselors, disciplinarians, or what have you. One of the phenomena in most prisons is that, when there's been a violent outbreak and you've shut down the prison and the staff are really in control, their morale goes up tremendously. Even after the worst incident in San Quentin, the George Jackson incident, in which six people died (three inmates and three officers), the staff were not demoralized by the fact that three of their people had been murdered, but were bursting with enthusiasm for this total lockdown at the institution. It is a danger that you have to watch for as prison administrators. For everyone, including the administrator, the disturbance or the incident has this reward of being exciting. It helps you to be someone more important than you really are, and administrators have to make a major effort to control this in themselves and to help their staff work through this kind of reaction.

The problem of the Chicano gangs in California is unique; it could not be related to Puerto Rican gangs in the Eastern prisons. It's a totally different sort of cultural thing. Our Muslims have not been involved in disturbances in California to any great extent. They have very carefully walked around the strikes in 1968. They avoided entanglement, and walked to work. No one dared stop them because they were reputed to have such a tight-knit organization. Apparently this is not true in other prisons.

97

We were concerned about inmate violence but not terribly concerned as long as inmates were getting killed. It was not until staff began to be killed that we really got uptight about violence and started talking about shutting down total prisons, something that we had avoided in the past. This is human nature.

Related to this is the fact that the Chicano war resulted in by far the most casualties. Yet, if you polled line staff, they would be much more afraid of the Black Guerrilla family or other black militant groups who are probably very small in number, who are given to a good deal of rhetoric about killing employees, but very little action. While I would attribute the murder of our 11 employees mostly to this kind of revolutionary ethic that you kill members of the power structure and so forth, in fact, the people that did the killing were probably not connected with Black Guerrilla family or other militant organizations. They simply followed that ethic.

Finally, we've had at least one officer murdered due to the activities of people associated with venceremos. We think that some of these murders were encouraged, either directly or indirectly, by revolutionary cadres. This is a very small group but disproportionately threatening to staff because they seem well organized and sinister, which is probably not true. The factors that cause the Chicanos to kill each other in wholesale quantities are much more worthy of our concern.

As violence increased in the prisons, it was likewise increasing in the community and we are probably dealing with some common causes over which we don't have much control. You can have a prison full of weapons and they are not going to use them unless the climate and the preconditions are right. Staff is rarely assaulted in California prisons and was rarely murdered prior to 1970. You set up a set of conditions and ideologies, ways of thinking, points of view that cause the bricks or the metal to become weapons, and go into action.

Wilsnack: We often make the assumption that violence is socially destabilizing. That doesn't necessarily have to be the case. You can have a stable regime or informal order built on a system of terror. The descriptions given here of what is going on in California resemble accounts of how a very stable social order can be maintained by perceptions of terror and random violence carried out by particular ruling clique. One reason that you may not have collective outbursts of the traditional riot type is that, in fact, by occasional incidents of violence and fear of interpersonal violence within the prison community, you can actually have a very stable, tightly disciplined social order.

Cole: Yesterday's revolt is being interpreted as today's revolution, and yesterday's rioter is being called today's revolutionary. In what sense are these people revolutionaries? Is there a link between groups inside prison with groups outside the prison and for what purpose? What is the goal? Perhaps we label it revolutionary because it is a term that has been used freely by the general public.

Park: We tend to use the term revolutionary too widely. I am reserving it strictly for those people who follow a Maoist or Marxist or some kind of structured ideology about social change through violence. Most of the murders of our 11 officers were the result of a revolutionary ethic to strike out against the masters who are keeping you oppressed. The victims were generally picked at random. They were just ordinary, run-of-the-mill people who happened to be at the wrong place at the wrong time. That is why I say revolutionary–retalitory because they are a little bit different. Maybe they shouldn't be too closely associated. The retalitory ethic has certainly became stronger as California prisons have had an increase in the number of blacks who demonstrate a strong impulse to retaliate against injury to any member of their group.

Cole: It sounds like the FBI cracking down on the Communist party, in the 1950s, or the FBI going after organized crime.

Park: This is the danger, and one source of the problem.

Jacobs: We have to be cautious not to attribute to these prisoners organization abilities and structures beyond what is indicated by the evidence. It is a very open question as to exactly how organized these groups are. What is their capacity for collective action? Could they really co-ordinate and execute a complex plan to "hit" someone? In Illinois prisons the gangs often have great difficulty even making a decision. The situation in California should be critically examined to insure ourselves that much of this is not a phenomenon of attribution by guards, administrators, and scholars, as has apparently been the case in many studies of street gangs. What men believe to be real then becomes real in its consequences. When we treat these prisoners as belonging to highly structured, formal organizations we may be contributing to their formation. Furthermore, a belief in omnipotent organizations may be functional for prison administrators for whom it serves as a cop out. Time and again they say, "How can we possibly do anything? The gang has taken over the Illinois prisons; they have carved up the place; we can't possibly even begin to put in a program when these gangs are tearing each other apart."

Bennett: This is a trap that California fell into while we were ill-prepared to deal with what actually occurred. We were aware of this latent concept, overreaction, the fantasy of staff about the elaborateness of the gang organizations. When we got the prison violence, we looked at our own mistakes from dealing with Black Muslims, where we overreacted. So we were backing off. We actually had a departmental edict that said we will not use the term Mexican Mafia. We were trying to condition staff to avoid this problem of looking at the gangs and creating it via the self-fulfilling prophecy of their own belief system. The end result was that we got caught markedly off base because these people *are* organized. They are much more rigidly organized than we would have ever have conceived from looking at the Los Angeles gangs in the fifties.

Irwin: The big mistake you made in that period was that you didn't see the only thing that could withstand the influence of the gangs would be the various types of organizations you labeled "political." These included any group not employing the most conservative definition of the prisoners' position and problems, and not seeking solutions that were totally accepting of the status quo. This included groups such as EMPLEO (Chicago) and SATE (Black) in San Quentin and other California prisons, which were pursuing "self-help" directions, examining the history of racial prejudice, and occasionally seeking redress for actions they perceived as discriminatory. After the "unity" demonstrations in San Quentin (which were one or a few days, nonrule-breaking strikes), the homicides surrounding the Soledad Brothers case, and then Attica, you lumped all persons involved in general prison or societal reform into the classification of "political" and all forms of planned protest into the classification of "riot." You attempted to suppress both. What this accomplished was to place in segregation most of the persons who could have prevented the emergence and dominance of the gang activity. It also made it so dangerous in terms of length of sentence for other types of leaders whom you defined as "politicals" that they just wouldn't get involved. Now the only process that will establish a new overriding informal system in prison in the face of the heterogeniety and conflict that exists will be some type of political organization formed by a coalition of the different groups.

Ohlin: The notion is that if some other kinds of grievance machinery or contacts had been permitted with the outside you might have been able to control this violence better by building a counterforce against it. It seems to me to be suggested not only by the survey data we gathered, but also by the case studies of 14–16 riots that occurred now and in the fifties.

In regard to what John Irwin is saying about the various types of conflict that occur: inmate–inmate, inmate–staff, the strikes, and "peaceful demonstrations," at no point did he talk about a large-scale, total prison riot occurring in this period. We are dealing really with only two subtypes of collective violence. There are a lot more and you have to look at that very carefully and try to sort out the preconditions of each and identify them as they are emerging in the prisons.

Cohen: The discussion has proceeded almost entirely in terms of what you might call overt or expressed violence, that is, people actually getting hurt or killed.

The question is raised as to whether prisons are really all that violent when we compare statistics on homicide rates within prisons to homicide rates in a comparable population. You could do the same with not just homicide but aggravated assault and mayhem of various kinds, like knifings. It may well be that, amongst prisons, there is a great range of variation in this respect, and that some of them may be relatively safe places in comparison to, say, military units or things of that kind.

But there is another aspect to the question of violence, and that is the extent to which the threat of violence undergirds social organization and helps to account for what happens in a particular social system. You can go from there to all kinds of speculations. For example, it may be that in prisons where there is, in a certain sense, no great problem of violence (there is very little homicide and so on) it nonetheless may be that, in comparison with some other social universe, the threat of violence plays an overwhelmingly important role in determining the shape of things in general. That is, almost all the decisions that people make have to take into account, to some degree, the probability that violence will be exercised, whereas, in other settings, with higher rates of overt violence, this may not be true. For example, it could conceivably be that in prison you have a relatively small number of people, a clique, who are able to impose a highly credible threat of violence, and that these individuals can in a sense terrorize everyone. This is partly in consequence of the fact that in prisons, if you are doing business with someone who is trying to dominate you or exploit you, there may be no way of getting away from him except getting yourself put in isolation. You have your choice of standing your ground, striking back, retaliating – or yielding. In the former case, there might be no visible violence, because the threat is sufficient, whereas in the world outside, there may be many more options available to people: they can remove themselves to scenes, games, social networks, where neither the substance nor the threat of violence plays much of a role. I am not suggesting that, in prisons generally, violence or the threat of violence is the only or even the most important basis for stability and order. For example, in the traditional kind of prison, it may be that the exchange system – the traffic in commodities, and the various other services that people exchange – plays a much more important part generally than the threat of violence in maintaining order. Still, there is a whole range of possibilities here that we have barely touched relating to the part that the threat of violence plays in the organization of the prison and its relationship to overt violence.

Bennett: If someone gets killed once in a while, the threat of violence takes on a new meaning. Also, to go back to an earlier concept about having a new revolutionary ethic, without that in the background, we would not have had staff executions. To call it revolutionary in a sense of being part of an organized system to bring about the deaths may be overstating it considerably. But we have to think of the social–psychological force of approving violence as a method for working toward a solution. The concept of the approval of violent behavior by significant others is extremely important in understanding how quickly a person can loosen up and carry out these very violent acts. The revolutionary ethic must be dealt with, particularly when you look at the historical situation when in earlier times an inmate simply did not consider this as a solution

Megargee: One question hasn't been addressed at all: Why do we have prisons in the first place? Because they're there? Given that they're there, what can we do? How can we devise rehabilitative programs with simply maintaining a base level of security and safety? It's hard to think about any kind of programming, any kind of education, any kind of treatment goals to prepare for life *outside,* when a constant struggle to stay alive *inside* takes precedence over everything else.

Sometimes we talk about prisons as warehouses. The first function of a warehouse is to keep the goods in reasonable condition. If our prisons are not even achieving that, it is pretty depressing. The goals of staff selection and staff training, in this kind of context, makes for a serious problem. If you are an officer in an institution where violence is a way of life, how can you relate to a person in terms of how you can help him when your first concern is, "Am I going to survive this encounter." This whole realm of problems is antithetical to those of us who are trying to think in terms of programming, or using the system in some kind of socially constructive way.

Part III

Ecology of Violence

8

Prison Architecture and Prison Violence
William G. Nagel

I spent a good portion of my life working in a prison, worrying about such everyday concerns as sawed bars, escapes, fights, and other aspects of human misbehavior common to the unnatural setting of the American correctional institution. During those years, I accepted the design of our physical plant as an unhappy given. It was not until John Conrad (then working for LEAA) asked me to make a nationwide study of the state of the art of prison architecture that I gave more than passing thought to the fact that prison design contributed to prison problems, including violence. Since then, in the company of an architect and a psychologist, I crisscrossed this nation looking at its newer prisons—over a hundred of them. In the process, I became somewhat sensitized to the effect of the physical environment upon the individual.

But prisons are full of people who were violent long before they got to prison. Many of them are products of violent homes, with more than a few the reported victims of child abuse. Moreover, many of these prisoners are victims of violent neighborhoods. Not long ago, I visited an architectural nightmare in Chicago called "Cabrini Green." It is a public project. The police station in its midst has solid steel plates over the windows because the neighborhood is so violent. In Philadelphia, gang violence terrorizes the inhabitants of North Philadelphia. In fact, the young in North Philadelphia are safer in our mega-prison at Graterford than they are on the streets of their own neighborhoods. Violent prisoners are also the product of an economic system that is violent and of a nation that has made violence a national ethic. We have been at war for 25 years. That has to have some effect on a generation of Americans. When our government orders a 15,000 ton bomb dropped on primitive Cambodia in order to prove our collective masculinity, the message gets across to young people all over this country. Although most prisoners were violent long before incarceration, architects can make prisons less violent places.

Until five years ago in Philadelphia, prisoners were transported from the police station to the jails, to the court houses, to the prisons, etc., in sheriff's vans. These vans were similar to delivery trucks in that they were without windows. As many as 40 human beings, like so many hind-quarters of beef, would be pushed into these vans. They were infernos in the summer, deep freezes in the winter, smelly all the time, and totally without possibility for supervision. Violence and threats of violence at a bestial level were common place. I read very briefly from the testimony of a 17-year-old youth who, incidentally, had been charged with nothing more serious than being a runaway:

All of a sudden, a coat was thrown over my face and when I tried to pull it off, I was punched viciously in the face for about ten minutes. I fell to the floor and they kicked me all over my body, including my head and my privates. They ripped off my pants from me while five or six of them held me down they took turns fucking me. My insides feel sore, my body hurts, my head hurts, and I feel sick in the stomach. Each time they stopped, I tried to call for help, but they put their hands over my mouth so I couldn't make a sound. They held me and burned my leg with a cigarette. When the van stopped at the prison, they wiped the blood from me with my shirt, threatened my life and said they would get me inside if I said anything and if they couldn't get me inside they would get me the next time I was in the van. When the door opened, they pushed me to the back so they could get out first. I told the guard I tripped and fell."

The design of the van did not cause the violence that this incident represents. The design did enable that violence to happen. Since then, the vans in Philadelphia have been replaced with school busses, which are designed for people, not cattle. In them supervision is ever present. Violence, such as I have just described, is no longer reported. The two lessons from that incident are these: (a) make the environment for people and not for animals, and (b) make the environment one in which supervision is omnipresent.

A second example: On July 4, 1970, we had a very violent disturbance at our prison in Philadelphia. It was a senseless riot. There were no demands. Just plain sadistic behavior. In a period of just over three hours, 29 guards and 43 inmates were beaten, stabbed, and mutilated. A number of inmates were so seriously wounded they were left for dead by the rioters. Attempts were made to dismember one inmate with a meat cleaver, to hang another, and one was disemboweled with repeated knife blows. Butchery became an organized act. Cries of "give me more, give me more," could be heard repeatedly as the rioters collected victims for knifing and beatings. The final index of the violence of that day can be found in the fact that the aggressors were charged with 41 counts of assault with intent to kill, 12 counts of aggravated assault and battery, additional counts of threat to kill, mayhem, and assaults with intent to maim. I was on the commission that was convened to investigate that riot. We concluded that there was no planned purpose other than the venting of violence. It was surely a reflection of a racial despair with the aggressors black and the victims all white (except guards who were cut up regardless of their color). There was incontrovertible evidence that the predators in this riot were men of long-standing violence. Of the predators, 39 had records that included murder; 30 were under indictment for robbery; 2 for rape; 9 for assault with intent to kill. The victims of their assaults were mostly nonviolent people whose offenses included burglary (28), larceny (36), and fraud and forgery (11).

It should be obvious that the prison did not cause the violent character of these men. The prison's design did help the violence to occur. This prison, for example, was built at a time when air conditioning was considered a luxury. Independence Day in 1970 was the hottest in decades. The aggravations caused by that heat were manifold. Moreover, the prison was designed in such a way that prisoners marched to the dining room past the kitchen. The riot occurred in the dining room. In the kitchen there were not sufficient safeguards to control the circulation of meat cleavers, butcher knives, and a myriad of other weapons. This was common knowledge to the prison population. As if the heat and the lack of weapon control were not enough, the prison itself is such a monstrosity that a three-man court later found it to be in violation of the Federal Constitution, the State Constitution, and of 156 provisions of the Pennsylvania statutes. These violations, essentially environmental in nature, helped raise the anger level of violent men.

Ugly, inhuman structures such as Holmesburg provoke violence not only from the kept but from the keepers. Listen to the following testimony from *Bryant* vs. *Hendrick:*

After a time the guards returned, and a series of beatings ensued. Selected prisoners were ordered out of the cells, were compelled to strip, and were beaten by guards. The guards used clubs in the form of nightsticks, table legs, and metal top wringers. Prisoners were beaten to the floor, all over their bodies - heads, legs, backs, groins - until they bled. They were then returned to their cells, only to be ordered out again and beaten again by as many as 25 to 30 guards who lined up on either side of a cell block and beat them with clubs as they ran, or, beaten down, crawled, through the gauntlet. It happened that one such beating was observed by the prison chaplains, including the Methodist chaplain, Reverend David Myers, who testified to this Court.

July 5, 1970. I was at 507 cell and they brought a guy that was on the block back and somebody said that he was a spokesman for the disturbance, and they beat him in front of my cell and he had his pants on and he had his shoes in his hand and they started beating him. He dropped his shoes and his pants had fell down to his ankles and they were still beating him. And they had him by both his arms and his legs stretched up in the air beating him, and he did a number on himself in front of my cell.

Judge Spaeth: He did a what?
Judge Nix: Had a bowel movement, is that what you are saying?
The Witness: Yes, in front of my cell.

Holmesburg, to be sure, is old. Many of the prisons in operation today are old. During the past year, my work with The American Foundation has taken me to many other old prisons including Rahway and Trenton in New Jersey; Huntingdon, Pittsburgh, Graterford, and Bellefonte in Pennsylvania; Canon City in Colorado; Stillwater and St. Cloud in Minnesota; Walla Walla and Monroe in Washington; Statesville, Menard, and Pontiac in Illinois; Carson City in Nevada, and others. Most, in the immediate past, have experienced acts of individual and group violence serious enough to be reported in the national media.

All of these prisons were designed for a different era and for a penology no longer acceptable. Cell blocks house up to a thousand men in mini-cages stacked three, four, and five tiers high. They were created during a period when imprisonment meant two things—solitary confinement and hard labor. Men spent 12 hours per night and all day Sunday in their tiny cells. At a fixed time each morning, they marched in lock step past posts of guards, armed with billy clubs and guns, to their places of congregate employment. At night, in similar fashion, they returned to their cages.

Penology is no longer just solitary confinement and hard labor. It is work, school, therapy, recreation, congregate eating, interviews, vocational training, visits, and a host of other activities necessitating constant movement. The designs of America's mega-prisons provide perimeter security, protecting, for a fleeting time, the general public from the predator. Their designs do not provide the internal security to protect the guard from the prisoners, the prisoners from the guard, or the prisoner from the prisoner. In such prisons, violence is the way of life.

Violence in architecture is not limited to the old, but is a part of much that is new. For example, in a brand new prison in Alabama we saw a deisign that I consider to be more violent than anything that the violent men who were there could possibly have done. The prison was built with one thing in mind—to save money. The biggest item of expense in prison management is manpower, and, therefore, this prison was built to minimize the use of manpower. In each housing unit, one guard sat in a bulletproof capsule where he was charged with monitoring a series of TV consoles. Idleness was structured into the place. Behavior, in that awful prison, was controlled in one of three ways. Compliant behavior was rewarded by assignments to tiny two-man cells. Imagine, if you will, the following conditions representing a reward (I quote from my book, *The New Red Barn* (New York: Walker & Co., 1973):

One prison was built for 500 of the most intractable prisoners of a certain state. Because it has no gymnasium, no classrooms, miserably small dayrooms, and practically no industry, each man spends most of his prison life in a 5½ x 8 foot cell with another prisoner. Each man has less living space than that provided by the surface of a typical bedroom door. There, because of the lack of program and recreational activity, the prisoners vegetate. Privacy does not exist. The cell toilet, for example, is pushed tight against the bottom bunk. As there is only one chair in the cell, the toilet stool serves as a second chair. It was the warden's observation that even a man and his wife require moments of privacy from each other. Here, he said sadly, privacy and human dignity are relentlessly sacrificed. We can think of few more gross forms of humiliation.

Unacceptable behavior was penalized by literally throwing the noncomplying into jungles of dormitories. Men with whom we talked were terrified at the idea of being put in there. Again I quote from *The New Red Barn:*

Tiny and crowded as the cells are, they are infinitely preferred by the prisoners to the congested dormitories where single beds have been replaced with double-decker bunks, where noise and night lights impede sleep, where privacy is non-existent, where one can never be alone, and where television, beds, recreation, toilets, and showers are all crowded into the limited space. These crowded wards are, according to staff and prisoners, frightening jungles where predators assault their fellow prisoners for their possessions or their bodies.

Among the reasons why the dormitories are such dangerous jungles is that officers are not physically present in them. At the end of each series of dormitories or cellblocks, there is a bulletproof cage where a guard sits, able to observe but not to control the living units.

If neither of these two options produced compliant behavior, there were the "dog houses." In these cages, as many as six to eight naked men were confined. The cells were devoid of light, furniture, even blankets. Once more, I quote from my book:

In one institution at the time of our survey, nearly 18% of the inmate population was in some kind of segregation—19 in isolation, 65 in segregation, and an additional 35 in a disciplinary quarantine, flatteringly called the "halfway house." The isolation was especially brutal. As many as eight people have been locked into one of the tiny, dark, airless, and bedless isolation cells for up to 21 days. During our visit these gloomy, bare dungeons contained two, three, and four men sitting naked on the floors. Only the 5-inch holes in the floors, used as toilets, served any human purpose.

The 19 men in the isolation cells were being punished for such diverse offenses as fighting, possessing homemade knives, drinking "julep," and refusing to be transferred from a cell to a dormitory. One man had broken up his cell furniture. His succinct explanation as shown on the disciplinary report was, "I'm tired of this fucking place." Autistic, hallucinating, and psychotic behavior, as well as other serious forms of pathology, are not uncommon.

Fortunately, the Federal Courts have listened to days of testimony about Alabama's prisons from many persons, including myself. In an historic decision in *James* vs. *Wallace* (13 January 1976), Judge Frank M. Johnson, Jr. describes the conditions in Alabama's prisons as representing cruel and unusual punishment. His far-ranging opinion describes the violent conditions that he found. Following are some extracts from that opinion:

Violent inmates are not isolated from those who are young, passive, or weak. Consequently, the latter inmates are repeatedly victimized by those who are stronger and more aggressive. Testimony shows that robbery, rape, extortion, theft and assault are everyday occurrences among the general inmate population. Rather than face this constant danger, some inmates voluntarily subject themselves to the inhuman conditions of prison isolation cells.

In view of the foregoing, the rampant violence and jungle atmosphere existing throughout Alabama's penal institutions are no surprise. The evidence reflects that most prisoners carry some form of homemade or contraband weapon, which they consider to be necessary for self-protection. Shakedowns to remove weapons are neither sufficiently thorough nor frequent enough to significantly

significantly reduce the number of weapons. There are too few guards to prevent outbreaks of violence, or even to stop those which occur.

One 20-year-old inmate, after relating that he has been told by medical experts that he has the mind of a five year old, testified that he was raped by a group of inmates on the first night he spent in an Alabama prison. On the second night he was almost strangled by two other inmates who decided instead that they could use him to make a profit, selling his body to other inmates.

The conditions in which Alabama prisoners must live, as established by the evidence in these cases, bear no reasonable relationship to legitimate institutional goals. As a whole, they create an atmosphere in which inmates are compelled to live in constant fear of violence, in imminent danger to their physical well-being, and without opportunity to seek a more promising future.

The living conditions in Alabama prisons constitute cruel and unusual punishment.

Some new prisons have been designed so as to minimize the environment's contribution to violence while providing both internal and external security. Leesburg in New Jersey is an excellent example. Leesburg is a secure new prison designed to hold approximately 500 adult male felons. All living units are built around open courts, the four sides of which contain outside rooms built in two tiers. These rooms are self-contained and have secure, solid, prison-type doors, which, like the rooms themselves, are painted in various hues. The inside wall of the housing square is glass from ceiling to floor almost giving the impression of no wall at all. The enclosed court is landscaped. One man, recently transferred from the ancient prison in Trenton, said that this was the first time in several years that he had had the opportunity to observe the sky and trees.

Although most prisons we visited were drab and grim and gave us the feeling that all of man's sensory needs had to be sacrificed to security and control in the prison setting, we found Leesburg architecturally different. So did the inmates and guards with whom we chatted. Only time will tell whether all the glass, colorful rooms, and landscaped gardens will survive the rigors or convict occupation. This much we know: In its first three years, violence at Leesburg has stayed at a surprisingly low level.

Two new women's prisons—in Oregon and Washington— demonstrate the contrasting philosophy that architects bring to the design of correctional institutions.

In Oregon we visited a new prison for women. The basic belief behind its design is that women prisoners have to be watched every moment, that they should not be trusted. This prison was surrounded by barbed wire. The housing units were built in the form of a cross so that all corridors could be constantly overseen from one central control room. There were no dayrooms as such, but tables placed around the control room and under the eye of the matron served that function. There the women could play checkers or cards under constant supervision. Although the bedrooms were reasonably large and well glazed, there were no pictures on the walls, no curtains, and no colorful bedspreads. Everything looked very sanitary, dull, and unfeminine. The vista from the rooms included gun towers and concertinas of barbed wire. This plant and its operation reflected a point of view.

In Washington the new Purdy Treatment Center for Women serves an identical purpose and a nearly identical population, but it was conceived and built and is operated according to a completely different point of view. This difference is especially apparent in the living quarters.

Individual rooms are decorated to the tastes of the occupants. Colorful bedspreads and draperies personalize their quarters, which are comfortably furnished. Each grouping of 16 rooms has a carpeted parlor complete with comfortable living room furniture, television, and a handsome fireplace. Adjoining the dayroom is a dinette for snacks, furnished with stove, refrigerator, and coffee percolator. The women hold keys to their rooms. The entire environment spoke the words *trust, individuality,* and *beauty,* and the view from the rooms echoed them.

The great contrast in the morale of those confined in these two institutions was very apparent. Each was designed to handle the entire female penal population of its respective state. A worthy research project might be a comparative study of violence over the next decade in these two new and neighboring women's prisons.

Another interesting comparative study of violence might be conducted in the three adjacent southern states—Georgia, Florida, and Alabama—where three new prisons serving identical function, reception and classification, have been built in the last decade. Two, opened in 1969 and 1970 respectively, were tightly built in the telephone-pole design. These were geared to the fullest possible supervision, control, and surveillance of the inmates. Design and program choices optimized security. Buildings and policies restricted the inmate's movement and minimized his control over his environment. Other considerations, such as individual or social needs of the inmate, were responded to only as they conformed to security requirements. Trustworthiness on the part of the inmate was not anticipated; the opposite was assumed. His compliance was not sought; it was not even necessary.

The third, opened in 1967, is of campus style with several widely separated buildings occupying 52 acres, which are enclosed with a double cyclone fence with towers. Movement is continuous as inmates circulate between the classification building, gymnasium, dining room, clinic, canteen, craft shops, handsome outdoor visiting area, and dormitories.

Men who are not specifically occupied by the demands of the classification process are encouraged to involve themselves in a variety of recreational and self-betterment activities conducted all over the 52-acre campus. An open air visiting patio with picnic tables and milticolored umbrellas supplements the indoor visiting facility, which is used ordinarily only in inclement weather. The relationship between staff and inmates appears casual. Movement is not regimented. Morale appears high and escapes are rare.

We were in general favorably impressed with campus-type facilities. They are much more attractive; they are not congested; and they cause inmates and staff to move in and out continuously, thus providing sensory stimulation so often missing in closed facilities. Moreover, they allow or require inmates to make choices, thus reducing the overdetermination that is characteristic of prisons. At the same time, if designed properly, they provide the security required by properly assigned populations. Most important, one does not become hypnotized by the effects of the endless corridors, the clanging locks.

By the middle of the nineteenth century all the idealism and hope that went into the invention of the penitentiary was replaced by a pragmatism that held that confinement was a valid end in itself. Prisons could not correct or reform, but they could separate the offender from the rest of mankind. No one in this audience will be surprised to hear that this idea preceded James Q. Wilson by a century. A kind of warehousing developed. Economy of operations became the essential element of prison management. The bigger the prison, the more economical the operation. Prisons grew. Penitentiaries to house between 2,000 and 5,000 men were built.

The inevitable consequence was the development of operational monstrosities. It is impossible to remove large numbers of men from the free world, isolate them together in the unnaturalness of huge prisons, and not have management problems of staggering dimensions. The tensions and frustrations inherent in prisons of any size are magnified by the herding together of large numbers of troubled people. The result is the evolution of a prison goal that, when stripped of all the correctional rhetoric, is simply, "Keep the lid on." Dehumanization and violence are major results.

The population of the prison of the future will be no improvement over that which we must deal with today. Quite likely it will be more difficult, more violent, as alternate programs strip away the property offender who today provides a leavening influence. The prison of today will not serve tomorrow's prisoner.

Tomorrow's prison will have to be located in or near the population centers. The reasons are many, but fundamental is the need to attract and hold competent and racially balanced staff. A significant amount of prison violence is a by-product of the racial disbalance between the kept and the keeper. It is reflected in many ways, but one was made vivid to me last week when I visited a large, rural prison in the midwest staffed almost exclusively by white personnel.

In punitive segregation, on the day of my visit, there were 19 blacks and 2 whites. On that same day, administrative segregation had a count of 92 of whom 74 were black.

The facility of tomorrow will have to be small with living units of from 10 to 15. This will enhance security while minimizing the opportunity for and causes of much prison violence.

The perimeter will be secure, but internally there will be freedom made possible by smallness of numbers. Security, then, will be static on the outside, dynamic on the inside.

Each man will have his own room void of the grilles that have rendered the prison of the past so cage-like. It will, however, be sturdy and secure. Dining will be in the living module in small and pleasant dining rooms.

Work shops will be small, and sometimes attached to the living units. Work will be meaningful and pay competitive. Recreational space will be ample and diverse, providing for both "quiet" and "physical" activities. Visiting facilities will be open, attractive, and conjugal.

Such a prison may not reform, but it will do less harm. It will meet the twin needs of punishment and quarantine demanded by today's criminologist, legislators, and judges. At the same time, it will provide the constitutional safeguards against constant threat of violence enumerated in *Woodhous* vs. *Commonwealth of Virginia* and other court cases.

While occasional, isolated attacks by one prisoner on another may not constitute cruel and unusual punishment, Penn v. Oliver, 351 F. Supp. 1292 (E.D. Va. 1972), confinement in a prison where violence and terror reign is actionable. A prisoner has a right, secured by the eighth and fourteenth amendments, to be reasonably protected from constant threat of violence and sexual assault by his fellow inmates, and he need not wait until he is actually assaulted to obtain relief.

Such a prison will be costly, but *Holt* vs. *Sarver* has established beyond doubt that inadequate funding is no answer to the existence of unconstitutional conditions in state prisons.

Let there be no mistake in the matter; the obligation of the Respondents to eliminate existing unconstitutionalities does not depend upon what the Legislature may do, or upon what the Governor may do, or, indeed, upon what Respondents may actually be able to accomplish. If Arkansas is going to operate a Penitentiary System, it is going to have to be a system that is countenanced by the Constitution of the United States.

The Ecology of
Prison Violence
Edith Elisabeth Flynn

To the builders of this nitemare
though you may never get to read these
words. I pity you; for the cruelty of
your minds have designed this hell; if
men's buildings are a reflection of what
they are, this one portrays the ugliness
of all humanity. If only you had some
compassion.

Anonymous (Graffito found in a prison cell)

The specter of violence and the full-scale, bloody riots in prisons of the United States have resulted in intensified efforts to identify some of the causes or correlates of prison violence. It is a sad commentary on our social priorities that every conceivable statistic concerning sports is collected and made available to all who are interested, but there is almost no empirically verified knowledge on the probable causes of prison riots. Nonetheless, a growing body of knowledge in the behavioral sciences and the experience of correctional administrators and on-site observations at institutions experiencing riots permit at least a tentative identification of some of the underlying conditions of prison riots, and an approximation of some of the causal relationships in the patterns of institutional disorders. There are, for example, single case studies,[1] some perceptive qualitative generalizations,[2] data on individual characteristics of rioters,[3] and a quantitative analysis of preconditions for major prison riots,[4] all of which, collectively, provide at least base-line information for systematic analysis.

Upon dissecting the concept of prison violence, one finds at least three analytically distinguishable phenomena: (1) collective violence, (2) violence and counterviolence by agents of social control within correctional institutions, and (3) individualistic violence.

To distinguish between collective violence and other forms of collective resistance, such as work or hunger strikes, collective violence is defined here as an event in which all of the following criteria are present: (1) seizure by inmates through force or violence of some institutional territory where inmates have free access but the staff does not; (2) willful destruction of public property; and (3) pursuit of collective demands by inmates to correctional authorities for the purpose of negotiating some change.

Correctional history in the United States is replete with accounts of institutional riots and collective disturbances that reveal not only a cyclical pattern of periodic flare-ups every decade or so, but also a steady increase in occurrences of disruptive behavior and a change in the seriousness of riots in terms of more severe personal injuries and loss of life.[5] The bloody prison uprising at Attica, during which 43 persons died in September 1971, epitomizes prison violence as no other riot has done previous to that disaster.

The second type of prison violence is initiated or provoked by agents of social control. Counterviolence on the part of staff may occur either in retaliation for previous riotous behavior by inmates, or to suppress an altercation or riot in progress. Knowledge as to the prevalance of this type of violence is scant in comparison with instances of prisoner-initiated collective violence, but there is sufficient evidence to indicate that it is a serious problem in corrections and that violence of retaliation and suppression often surpasses the violence it seeks to suppress.[6]

Individualistic violence, the third type of prison violence, is readily distinguished from the previous two types of violence, since it occurs on a person-to-person basis: among inmates and among inmates and staff. Individualistic violence, which has long been recognized as intrinsic to prison organization, is a daily occurrence in most prisons and reformatories. It occurs because of an almost infinite variety of reasons; it frequently results in severe physical incapacitation or loss of life among inmates, as well as among staff. Prisons are skewed and unnatural microcosms in which inmates are forced to adjust to a highly artificial existence characterized by batch living, movement in blocks, unceasing surveillance, lack of privacy, monotony, enforced idleness, coercion, regimentation, and imposed activities. On a more subtle level, inmates are exposed to abasement, degradations, humiliations, and processes leading to the "mortification of self."[7] Cumulatively, these influences lead to an environment filled with anxiety, tension, hate, and a continuous potential for conflict. The result is an incessant breaking out of violent incidents and crises, which interrupts the deadly prison routine with predictable periodicity.

Toward A Classification of Individualistic Prison Violence

An examination of official reports and past research on the subject of individualistic violence in prisons reveals a relatively common mixture of reasons for its occurrence. In terms of underlying motives, the patterns of violence have been historically categorized to fit one or more of three recurrent themes: (1) homosexuality, (2) racism and political tensions, and (3) hustling.

Homosexual activity has been consistently linked to assaultive behavior in prison research.[8] Recent investigations into the subject substantiate the fact that typical conventional conceptions held by administrators concerning homosexual advances and assaults in prisons are not exaggerated. Typically, a young inmate is approached by an older man who offers food, advice, or protection. The inmate who accepts these offers may find to his surprise that he is expected to reciprocate with sexual favors. The options are limited to fighting or submitting. Thus, by a process of intimidation—usually verbal but occasionally violent—such relationships begin. There is also evidence that "resolutions" of homosexual "triangles" frequently involve assaults.[9]

Racism and political tensions have increasingly been identified in the literature as the cause of much collective and individualistic prison violence.[10] The prevalence of racism in American society is intensified in correctional institutions. This is true not because staff may be more racist than the population at large, but because inmates cannot escape from it. There is no way to avoid confrontations and unpleasant experiences when interaction is always present and quarters are so close. Increasingly, sophisticated and politically minded minority members, whose hopes have been dashed in their fight for civil rights, represent perilous elements in an already volatile prison atmosphere. Long-harbored racial animosities become increasingly linked to outbursts of interracial collective and personal violence, and there appears little hope for abatement.

"Hustling" or "making out," the third common theme that underlies prison violence, has its counterpart in the larger economic system. Since prisons provide only the most basic necessities of life—food, clothing, tiolet articles, and some tobacco—a supplementary inmate system of production and exchange develops in prisons, as a direct response to the officially imposed deprivation of goods and services. The informal production is limited only by the imagination of the entrepreneur and the demands of the clients. Such an economic exchange system requires substantial organization and skill, since contacts must be maintined and a means of transportation and delivery assured at both ends of the supply line. Activities usually include hustling of homosexuals, gambling, information exchange, and a variety of contraband: drugs, alcohol, pornography, as well as protection services. The type of hustling most frequently associated with personal violence involves appreciable investments of money (Currency or more frequently, the currency of the prison realm: cigarettes) and the defense of personal reputations.[11] Finally, since both alcohol and drugs are integral parts of the prison setting, and since both have been consistently related to personal violence,[12] their consumption undoubtedly contributes significantly to assaultive behavior in correctional institutions.

The identification and elaboration of the three patterns of individualistic violence in prisons discussed above, that is, homosexuality, racism and political tensions, and hustling, have helped to further our understanding of this type of violence. The same knowledge offers at least the potential for controlling such violence. But there is substantial evidence that this taxonomy is incomplete and it is therefore suggested that the listing be expanded by two additional categories: situational grievances and ecological factors. It is our purpose here to focus on these two issues.

Situational Grievances

Recently generated research results[13] indicate that unresolved inmate grievances, imagined or real, are related to incidents of individual violence. The term "situational grievance" is proposed to reflect the relative combination of circumstances at certain moments of institutional life, which lead to grievances of the "day-to-day irritant" kind. Prison life is full of problems and frustrations. In addition to general dissatisfaction with food, housing, and lack of programs, institutional life means idleness, festering racism, degradation, and humiliation. There is a lack of many of the necessities of life, an absence of choice, physical and mental harassment, threats to personal safety, a myriad of rules governing every aspect of behavior from dawn to dusk, perpetually changing regulations and procedures, all of which lead to uncertainty, misunderstanding, and mounting anxieties. The lack of prompt and fair resolution of such grievances and disputes tends periodically to lead to the use of more disruptive methods on the part of dissatisfied and frustrated inmates, to make their distress and suffering known.

A closely related issue is the absence of due process in many prison disciplinary procedures. The equitable administration of correctional institutions requires, at the minimum, clearly stated rules and regulations, which should be published, periodically updated, and made known to inmates. The application of rules should be equitable. Restrictions on an inmate's behavior should be limited only to what is absolutely necessary to maintain institutional order and safety. Certainly, they should not be based on administrative convenience. Few institutions meet these basic requirements.[14]

A survey of disciplinary procedures applied within American correctional institutions shows a mixed set of circumstances.[15] Arbitrary authority continues to be exercised in many institutions. Some improvement has occurred in view of judicial interventions,[16] and through voluntary adoption of more equitable procedures by correctional administrators. Yet, few institutions meet the basic requirements of due process: (1) written notification of the charges, (2) impartial hearing, (3) right to representation at the hearing, (4) opportunity to present and cross-examine witnesses, (5) right to rebut the evidence, (6) impartial adjudication, (7) written findings, and (8) substantiated conclusions. Worse, there are still a number of administrators who maintain that all civil rights, including guarantees of "due process," are lost when an inmate enters the correctional system.[17]

The accumulation of unresolved greivances—especially in the absence of an effective communication system—has been consistently linked to collective violence. Also, the format in which grievances are presented appears to be related to the form that prison resistance will take.[18] For example, riots are more often preceded by escapes and an absence of grievances related to inmate groups, whereas prison unrest, other than rioting, occurs when such unrest is preceded by peaceful presentation of grievances. Finally, the excessive use of administrative and punitive segregation facilities as an outcome of disciplinary procedures has been empirically linked to prison violence.[19]

The implications of these findings are clear. Unresolved situational grievances are major factors underlying individualistic prison violence, and they must be considered in any administrative or legislative attempts to deal with the problem of violence in correctional institutions. It would be prudent for administrators to concern themselves with the development of grievance procedures and the institutionalization of due process in matters of discipline.

Ecological Factors

The effects of the physical environment of correctional institutions on inmate behavior has rarely been investigated.[20] This is all the more surprising when we consider the archaic, dilapidated, and frequently inhuman physical structures in which most of this country's jail and prison inmates are housed. Such basic issues as crowding, privacy, and sensory deprivation urgently await experimental investigation. If the work of biologists in their studies of animal populations has any applicability to the prison setting, we may find that crowding is related to acts of violence, sexual perversions (including homosexuality), decreases in the life span of individuals, and to the general breakdown of customary social order.[21] There is also an impressive amount of research to show the negative effects of deprivation. These include an inability to concentrate and think clearly, boredom, high degrees of restlessness, exaggerated emotional reactions, cognitive inefficiencies, speech impairments, temporal disorientation, anxiety, hunger, and sometimes loss of contact with reality.[22] Finally, the lack of privacy in correctional institutions increases the vulnerability of inmates to fall prey to unprovoked assaults and homosexual attacks.

Research has lagged, but there has been unprecedented activism on the part of the courts affecting administrative practices and conditions of incarceration. The traditional "hands-off" doctrine, practiced by the American judicial system, has been replaced by the recognition that inmates, as individuals, continue to possess many basic constitutional rights, regardless of their legal status in the criminal justice system. An impressive body of case law is now on hand, relating time and again certain attributes of the physical environment to frustration, violence, and ultimately to cruel and unusual punishment, constituting thereby clear violations of the Eighth Amendment. Gross overcrowding, lack of sanitation, and punitive isolation have been consistently declared unconstitutional by the courts. For example, *Jones* v. *Wittenberg*[23] found incarceration in a county jail to be cruel and unusual. The jail was an overcrowded nineteenth-century structure featuring toilets with leaking soil and waste; inmates who, because of overcrowding, had to sleep on the floors on which the waste leaked; solitary confinement cells with no drains or sanitary facilities of any kind; a kitchen, into which sewage leaked, and which had no equipment to sanitize the dishes; a complete lack of ventilation and illumination; and no privacy. In *Hamilton* v. *Love*[24] the court declared incarceration unconstitutional in a jail that was overcrowded, had inadequate toilet and sanitary facilities, insecure cells with no protection against inmate assaults and homosexual attacks, no classification and rational separation of inmates, and was overrun by rats, roaches, and poisonous insects. In *Holt* v. *Sarver*[25] the rampant incidents of homosexual rape in barracks, which staff could not or would not control, were singled out in the finding that being incarcerated in the Arkansas prison system constituted cruel and unusual punishment.

Neither the accelerating involvement of the judicial system nor the urgent need for factual information seems to have stimulated research efforts specifically designed to relate the phenomenon of prison violence to variables of the manmade physical environment. At best, studies investigating prison violence mention the dilapidated physical conditions of prisons and jails, which form the backdrop for the periodically spawned turmoil that such settings engender. At worst, the studies ignore the impact of the physical environment completely, Interestingly, a degree of environmental awareness in sociological analysis can be traced to such early social theorists as Max Weber and Georg Simmel.[26] Subsequently, concern with environmental issues receded and remained dormant until the 1960s. For example, Parsons' action frame of reference is defined as "the orientation of one or more actors to a situation."[27] It is to be noted that Parsons deliberately chose the term "situation" to "environment," to avoid confusing that term with the biological meaning of environment.[28] Yet, it is increasingly difficult for a number of behavioral scientists to ignore the fact that behavior always occurs within the limits of specific physical surroundings and is to a certain degree affected by it. Recent recognition of the importance of this self-evident fact has led to studies specifically designed to relate various aspects of behavior to the physical spaces in which they are observed.[29] All of these studies use an appropriately expanded frame of reference containing at least three elements: (1) the actor, (2) the behavior, and (3) the physical setting in which the behavior takes place.

The remainder of this chapter discusses one such study, which sought to identify environmental determinants of inmate behavior in correctional institutions. The intent is to bring to bear the special power of sociological and ecological thought on the identification of environmental determinants of person-to-person violence and on how such determinants may provoke, invite, or facilitate violence.

With violence-promoting factors in the institutional environment tentatively identified, we seek to establish those environmental determinants that could conceivably contain, control, and reduce person-to-person violence in correctional institutions. For this purpose we draw upon a rich body of data assembled during a nationwide controlled study of American prisons and jails. The study sought to isolate specific effects of surveillance techniques within correctional institutions.[30] Of particular use for the purpose at hand was the study's effort to investigate environmental variables that would either increase or decrease the personal safety of inmates and staff.

The study design employed a variety of methodological approaches and test instruments consistent with the need for multiple operationalism, whenever theoretically interrelated components are studied.[31] It included behavioral mapping, interviews, and attitude and perceptual surveys. Instrumentation consisted of semantic differentials, alienation, and institutional impact scales as well as extensive demographic data. Statistical techniques included factor analysis and analysis of variance. In all, 98 of 120 major state-operated correctional institutions (identified by the 1972 *Directory of Correctional Institutions and Agencies*, American Correctional Association) responded to a standardized survey questionnaire that listed a variety of demographic data: institutional function, prisoner-to-staff ratios, levels of security; as well as information on programs, circulation and residential space; and inmate and staff characteristics. Twenty institutions were subsequently selected for more detailed study. These represented generally the range of institutions, identified in the earlier survey, in terms of such variables as population size, institutional function; maximum, medium, or minimum security; background of inmates; staff characteristics; and geographic location. Direct observation, personal interviews, and questionnaires were used at each of the 20 facilities, in an effort to study the critical variables in considerable detail. Most importantly, observations were made of behaviors; and some of the methods and techniques first advanced by ecological psychology were applied.

The ecological perspective, which focuses on the interrelationship of organisms and their environments, was first brought into focus in the late nineteenth century by biologists who emphasized the interdependence of plants and animals occupying the same habitat.[32] Park[33] and the Chicago School of Sociology subsequently expanded ecological theory in an attempt to develop a comprehensive model of human ecology, defined as "the study of the form and development of the human community".[34] Barker's[35] research in ecological psychology has particular application here since it represents an extension of ecological principles from the macro (or community) level of analysis to the consideration of microsocial phenomena. Barker's concept of "behavior setting," defined as an environmental–behavioral unit, and characterized by cyclical patterns of activity that occur within specific time inervals and spatial boundaries, facilitates the analysis of human behavior in specific environments, including correctional institutions. Barker's research also focuses on differences in overt behavior rather than on continued reliance on the analysis of perceptual or cognitive differences. Using this particular approach, 40 behavioral maps based on 40 physical settings were generated in the process of studying the 20 institutions.

Findings and Discussion

The debate as to the purpose of corrections (incapacitation, punishment, rehabilitation, or reintegration) still rages unabated, but there is agreement among scholars and administrators on one point. Corrections, especially correctional institutions, should provide a safe environment for staff and inmates alike. The "goods" should not be damaged any further by the process than they are already. Yet, we know that institutions fail dismally in this most basic and universally accepted responsibility. Individual and collective violence, disturbances, and injuries are common occurrences in institutions and bear witness to the fact that staff and inmates cannot be adequately protected from physical harm.

An analysis of the safety and security concepts that are applied in most correctional institutions reveals that for decades the issue of security has remained almost exclusively in the hands of custodial staff. Consulting services perpetuate this custom, since they rely chiefly on such persons as hardware specialists who represent steel companies or similar manufacturers, retired administrators in the consulting business, or custodial experts from other facilities.

Conceptually, two types of security are discernible in institutions: perimeter security and internal security. Perimeter security refers to the outer limits of an institution. Unauthorized persons are kept out and inmates are kept in. Thick walls, chain link fences, barbed wire, guard towers, and attack dogs epitomize perimeter security measures. Recent improvements in military hardware have produced their own kind of fallout for corrections by adding underground movement sensing devices, radar and movement sensors on fences, and closed circuit television to the arsenal of perimeter security.

Internal security refers to the inside area of an institution and the staff's ability to control the behavior of inmates. The physical safety of staff and inmates, the prevention of violence and riots, the protection of staff and inmates from one another, and the peaceful settlement of conflict are included in this concept. Even a precursory examintion reveals that correctional institutions have consistently overemphasized perimeter security and neglected issues of internal security ot the latter's detriment. Worse, the physical layout in most institutions actually impedes internal security. For the past 150 years, economic considerations have determined the manner in which correctional institutions have been constructed. A maximum number of inmates should be controlled by a minimum number of staff at minimum cost to the public. Such misplaced economy has proved disastrous for corrections. The problem is compounded by yet another fundamental error that may be the basis for the problems of inadequate security and safety in American correctional institutions: perimeter security concepts have been consistently applied internally. This has led to the overuse of security hardware such as maximum security cell construction, reinforced concrete walls, catwalks, closed circuit television, sally ports, security vestibules, and similar devices to control and isolate inmates. Preoccupation with security and overindulgence in hardware have failed to achieve cost effectiveness. Maximum security construction costs are three to four times the cost of more normative correctional institutions. The classic, multitier cellblock is a perfect example of ineffective security design: long rows of cells, stacked six or eight high, to insure surveillance of as many as 600 inmates by one correctional officer. Such a design insures safety and security for only as long as there is one inmate per cell and as long as inmates remain confined in their cells day in and day out. This is one reason why correctional administrators tend to resort to "lockup" measures (i.e., keeping inmates in their cells continuously, sometimes for many months) whenever violence and disturbances reach such endemic proportions that they can no longer maintain order in their institutions in any other way. However, normal operations require that inmates leave their cells for work, program activities, sustenance, recreation, etc. The architecture of today's prison and jail, which has remained essentially unchanged for 200 years, is simply not capable of supporting such "normal" activities. Nor are the descendants of the Pennsylvania and the Auburn systems particularly designed to facilitate effective staff intervention, whenever the life and safety of inmates or fellow staff are endangered. The time-honored and deliberate separation of staff from inmates has brought on many problems. Violence and destructive behavior occurring in dormitories, bullpens, or at the far end of long corridors can be observed but not stopped by staff, without unduly endangering the observing officer. By the time assistance is summoned, it is frequently too late to prevent injuries or save lives. The lack of visibility and the long distances involved often make it impossible to identify those responsible for assaults or other deviant behavior. As a result, subsequent disciplinary proceedings become exercises in futility. Correctional architecture and environments in this sense become the breeding grounds for violent, anti-social, and criminal behavior—the cultural medium in which the deviant, informal prison subculture flourishes.

Proceeding now from macroscopic considerations of the effect of the physical environment of correctional institutions on inmates, the study seeks to define more closely the actual determinants of security as they apply to all security contexts. Eight determinants of security were identified; these are presented in hypothesized form. It should be noted that the concepts are partially validated by the findings, but they remain to be fully tested in subsequent, more elaborate research. Ideally, the testing should be under experimental conditions.

Security-inducing and Violence-reducing Determinants

In general, physical environments, including correctional facilities, promote safety when they suggest an atmosphere of "normalcy." The typical correctional facility conveys an institutional look. Long colorless corridors, noisy, gray dayrooms; cagelike cells; and impersonal administrative spaces—all these create an environment that destroys hope and initiative. Such environments do not foster the normal behavior deemed necessary for the successful reintegration of offenders into society as law-abiding citizens. The determinants now to be discussed should help to create correctional environments that have a normal appearance both inside and out. To achieve this normalcy, populations would have to remain small, because large-scale institutions, excessive numbers of inmates, and regimented day-to-day routines dehumaize individuals and foster abuse. "Normalcy" means abstention from traditional security concepts such as unceasing surveillance, erection of physical barriers, deterrence by intimidation, and "target hardening."

Normative Stimuli

Psychology, in its development of conditioning and learning theory, has established that the relationship between the physical and social environment and behavior is a function of perceived stimuli and responses. Whereas specific responses to stimuli will be affected by such intervening variables as differential learning experiences, diversity of cultural background, and differing personal experiences, it stands to reason that if corrections wishes to foster normal social behavior of inmates, it must provide normative stimuli in the correctional environment. The implications of this hypothesis are clear. The old concrete and steel bastilles must give way to facilities and housing that resemble normal, group-living arrangements in society. The indestructibility of the steel bunk bolted to the wall, and the prison-type toilet that requires straddling to gain access to a miniature steel washbowl must be replaced with normal furniture. Depersonalized prison garb should be outmoded in favor of everyday clothing. Rigid, quasi-militaristic interactions between staff and residents should be substituted by normal demeanor and verbal communication that reflect the fact that offenders—even though they have broken the law—are still human beings. Room decorations should be permitted, and the individualizing of living spaces by means of partitions or furniture should be facilitated. Dining areas, critical space in terms of resident satisfaction (or violence), should be normalized through subdivisions, partitions, booths, and tables and chairs in group arrangements. Bathrooms and toilets, also one of the most dehumanizing areas in prisons and jails today, should be converted to facilitate safety and privacy commensurate with requirements of human decency.

Personal and Group Investment

Experiences with public housing and student dormitories indicate that when groups or individuals have built or worked to improve their living quarters, they tend to protect those segments. Group members will exert pressure on nonconforming individuals to abstain from destruction or vandalism of the common property. There is evidence to support the fact that these experiences are equally applicable to the correctional environment. The study observations were closely tied to the concept of "territoriality," which is only one behavioral aspect of the spatial environment that has been amply defined and experimented with in psychology and anthropology. The definition of that concept indicates that as a result of a combination of biological and cultural forces, various species (including the human species) display a need to identify and defend certain areas that have meaning for the individual or the group.[36] In juvenile corrections, for example, the concept of territoriality becomes most striking in the manner in which youths will hang up posters and strew clothing on furniture in attempts to maintain their "turf." In dormitories, prevailing rules for the use of territory suggest that the definition and defense of one's turf becomes crucial, particularly since there is little opportunity to gain privacy or a sense of self-identity. Corrections has characteristically given negative connotations to the concept of territoriality, but there are indications that when certain spaces, particularly in the living and socializing areas, are identified with small groups possessing positive orientations, the concept of territoriality is consistent with safety and the reduction of violent or destructive behavior. A reduction of "incidents"—assaults and inmate altercations—has been noted in institutions where inmate privacy and some demarcation of personal areas were allowed.

It should be noted that most facilities do not lend themselves readily to permitting residents to build or modify their own environments. Painting one's cell and posting pinup pictures are simply cosmetic attempts to humanize correctional facilities. Such approaches have not shown any observable degree of success and may serve to delude staff into thinking that staff has humanized the institution. Probably only extensive renovation or new facilities will permit a design that is flexible enough to allow individuals to build and modify their environments to the degree that such environments are able to reflect the many life-styles prevalent in our society. Suffice it to say here that an individual's attempt to change his or her environment contributes to a sense of well-being, permits investment of time, effort, and resources; lowers initial construction costs; and, most importantly, reduces violence by enhancing security.

Positive Reinforcement of Acceptable Behavior

Positive reinforcement (along with the amount of reinforcement) has long been recognized in psychology as a means to increase desirable behavior. Yet, prison systems operate essentially on a basis of negative reward systems. For example, good time allowances and parole eligibility are granted automatically but are quickly lost by bad conduct. An inmate who does not "cause any waves," will go unnoticed, but inmates who "act out" will get considerable attention. Attention is a powerful reinforcer.

In addition to practicing negative reinforcement, correctional institutions are also severely restricted in their environment. Most institutions provide general population housing and an area for disciplinary segregation, isolation, or "adjustment." Certainly, there are no opportunities for residents to progress to new, more normal, and better environments. If such options were available, positive behavior could be reinforced to improve living arrangements. The obverse would be feasible for destructive behavior. In this manner, the correctional environment would take on a normal aspect and be a constructive tool in the motivation for self-improvement of inmates.

The time interval between stimulus and response is another major issue. Since the writings of Beccaria,[37] the swiftness of punishment for crimes has been deemed a crucial factor in reducing recidivism. Yet, neither society nor correctional administrators have heeded that recommendation. Infractions of rules, such as assaults, are conventionally handled by locking individuals into isolation cells pending disciplinary procedure. After a period of waiting, the individual is punished by being sent back to isolation for several more days, weeks, or months. It stands to reason that swiftness of action may be more important than severity of punishment, and that if such behavior could be negatively sanctioned immediately after its occurrence, it might reduce the incidence of bad behavior. It is not our purpose to outline a course of action that would conflict with the requirements of due process discussed earlier. The kind of negative sanctions envisioned are limited to a removal of the individual from the general population for but a fraction of one day to isolation rooms within the general housing area. This would facilitate easy access, supervision, and quick return of the individual to the general population. Performance contracting could determine, in advance, negative as well as positive sanctions and would have a priori agreement by all participating parties. This, in turn, would facilitate the application of sanctions when needed and obviate lengthy hearings.

Another observation is pertinent. The indestructibility of the average prison environment effectively removes any feedback for negative, destructive, and violent behavior. Vandalizing, scratching, and kicking of steel bars or concerete walls have few visible consequences for the inmate—or the wall. In contrast, a resident who has destroyed his easy chair or reading table suffers the deprivation of functional and comforting objects and thus experiences a tangible inconvenience, if not a loss. It is interesting to speculate that the very indestructibility of the correctional environment may be an important element in inmate violence, since fellow human beings are the only targets left in such environments against whom frustration and despair can be vented. When viewed from this perspective, the provisions of an environment that is more vulnerable to the venting of hostility could conceivably help to reduce the amount of violence that occurs in institutions.

Environmental Consistency

The protection of individuals from assaults and violence demands that environments and social interactions between staff and inmates, and among inmates be consistent to the degree of predictability. There are few physical differences in correctional institutions between general population housing areas and isolation cellblocks. Both areas are bleak and sparsely furnished. Inmates are subject to assaults almost everywhere, and residents commonly request segregation or lockup for reasons of personal safety. If normal and peaceful behavior is to be promoted, a safe, secure, and reasonably pleasant environment must become an obtainable goal for residents, one that, when removed, produces immediate and significant consequences for them. Activity spaces should communicate clearly through architectural means (such as types of building material, interior decoration, color schemes, acoustic treatment, partitions) programmatic differences; and access thresholds and doors should convey to residents the type of social area he or she has entered. At a minimum, three programmatic areas should be differentiated in these terms: (1) individual or single rooms; (2) dining, recreational, and social activity space; and (3) program and work space.

Additionally, well-defined and clear guidelines for staff activity and intervention should accompany the establishment of normative environments and "safe zones." The guidelines should be made known to residents to insure predictability of staff reactions to previously described and defined behavior and situations.

Supportive Spatial Arrangements

To enhance the safety and well-being of residents as well as staff, spaces should be provided in which they feel safe and comfortable. With such provisions, individuals can control and sometimes "own" a certain territory. Some progressive correctional institutions are facilitating this kind of development by providing residents with keys to their cells or rooms (with staff having overriding master keys). In this way, a threatened inmate can always retreat to that one space for protection. Similarly, staff should be provided with lounging or rest areas in which they can feel secure. In addition, familiarity and predictability of the whole correctional environment would increase the general sense of security in the institution and help to identify those areas that represent danger. Movement and circulation patterns should be functional so that residents need not go through potentially dangerous areas. Three major techniques have been identified by which areas can be demarcated and made known as safe and secure: (1) physical control through enclosure, either through physical barriers or behaviorally, through movement; (2) the creation of visible access points, whereby residents can see potentially dangerous areas or sense the presence of dangerous individuals; and (3) the creation of an architectural advantage, such as one-way visibility or spatial differences. Elevated or sunken spaces would permit inmates and staff to anticipate or identify potentially dangerous situations.

Scale

The concept of scale refers to the proportion between two sets of dimensions. Applied to the correctional environment, scale should reproduce the quality and look of the normal environment outside the institution. The issue of scale relates to all areas of a correctional facility. In general, correctional facilities are characterized by abnormally large scales: buildings of towering proportions, serving huge populations, and overwhelming and dehumanizing the individuals they contain. The National Advisory Commission on Criminal Justice Standards and Goals recommends that no correctional facility be designed for more than 300 persons. By that definition, most correctional institutions are outdated. Yet, it stands to reason that a facility of 300 inmates may still be too large to permit normalcy and to guarantee safety. Physical scale relates not only to facility size but to room dimensions, functions, furniture, circulation space, and to the quality of social and personal relationships within an environment. Since there is a strong relationship between scale and dimensions of institutions, and between reduced resident security and violence, facilities should be subdivided into the smallest possible components (or modules) that replicate more closely ordinary residential scales. Self-sufficient programmatic entities serving groups of residents of no more than 16 to 20 should provide the safety and security so badly needed.

Increased Choice for Inmates

Most correctional facilities are characterized by an almost total lack of choice for inmates as far as programs and activities are concerned. Certainly, correctional institutions do not foster the development of responsibility and initiative that are essential for personal development and individual safety. Traditional approaches to security require that staff intervene in dangerous situations. Inmates are pawns and have no options. However, there are some indications that provision for a range of choices for responding to desirable as well as to undesirable situations fosters individual and group safety. Giving residents a choice in programs, in kinds of work, and in types of residential quarters fosters commitment to meaningful activities. A number of architectural options helps to facilitate decision making by reproducing within the facility environmental cues found in society. A range of physical environments can be made available, and an inmate's choice would reflect his ability to negotiate increasingly complex options.

Experience with handling such options should assist the individual in a gradual return to free society.

Purposive Activity

Idleness, passivity, and lack of purpose characterize the correctional institution. These, in turn, are related to tensions, frustration, disturbances and violence in facilities. Purposive activity has a number of advantages: (1) it develops a positive self-concept; (2) it fosters normative environmental stimuli conducive to positive social interaction; and (3) it creates a high level of visibility, which, in turn, acts to reduce potentially dangerous behavior. Again, a number of environmental design techniques are available that serve to promote personal safety and security. Changes in scale, visibility, judicious location of intersection and circulation patterns, changes in texture, and truncation of spaces all help to promote purposeful activity in previously unused areas that may have been marked by endemic violence. For example, placing a well-lighted television area at the far end of a dormitory, where much physical abuse has occurred, could appreciably reduce the opportunity for such behavior. A mixture of stationary activities with routes for staff would promote security. A combination of activity and programmed space could create natural supervision for areas that would otherwise be dangerous for those who venture into them.

Purposive activity, the final violence-reducing determinant in this discussion, has special potential for increasing safety in correctional institutions. Although the physical environment is characteristically difficult to change, the implementation of activities and programs can do much to reduce violence and destructive behavior of inmates. It should be noted, however, that such programmatic changes would still be futile if they are not totally accepted by the correctional staff. Among the techniques that can be used to reduce violence are the placing of popular activities beyond a problem zone, thereby increasing intrinsic surveillence through added movement; and by converting problem areas into spaces used for high frequency popular activities.

Conclusions

In addition to broadening the existing taxonomy of individualistic violence in correctional institutions by adding the categories of situational grievances and ecological factors, we have sought to identify environmental determinants of violent inmate behavior. Eight such determinants were pinpointed: normative stimuli, personal and group investment, positive reinforcement of acceptable behavior, environmental consistency, supportive spatial arrangements, scale, increased choice for inmates, and purposive activity.

The discussion offers many suggestions for the containment, control, and reduction of person-to-person violence in correctional institutions. It also gives preliminary findings in the form of hypotheses to facilitate testing and experimentation. The principal motive of this chapter is to reduce violence and physical harm to staff and inmates alike, mainly because violence is intrinsically harmful and inflicts devastation on the minds and bodies of those who come in contact with the corrections system, be they keepers or the kept. By no means are the suggestions to be viewed as providing answers, the implementation of which would justify the perpetuation of the megaprison. The congregate prison is clearly out of touch with the reality of our times, and no correctional strategy should be developed to provide for its continuation as a correctional solution.

Corrections today is a house divided. There are those who call for the abolition of prisons. Others call for the incarceration of only the hard-core, reticent, violent offender, and the placement of the remaining population into community-based correctional programs. But rarely are criteria offered on the basis of which such a division might be accomplished. Finally, there are those who call for an increased use of incarceration and for even more punishment and tougher measures in dealing with offenders. While a minority of jurisdictions have succeeded in reducing the number of their correctional institutions, the majority of states are experiencing spiraling incarceration rates and bulging prison populations. It becomes increasingly clear that the implementation of correctional reform is a slow and painful process. Changes in corrections and in the criminal justice system must be accompanied by changes in the social perception of the causes of crime, as well as by changes in the method in which the public wants the system to deal with offenders. Such changes characteristically come slow. It is hoped that the implementation of the procedural and environmental changes proposed in this chapter will make the process of change less painful and less costly for all of us.

Notes

1. Gresham M. Sykes, *Society of Captives* (Princeton: Princeton University Press, 1958); Richard H. McCleery, "The Governmental Process and Informal Social Control," Donald R. Cressey, ed., *The Prison: Studies in Institutional Organization and Change* (New York: Holt, Rinehart, and Winston, 1961), 149–88; New York State Special Commission on Attica, *Attica: The Official Report of the New York State Special Commission on Attica* (New York: Bantam Books, Inc., 1972); John F. Spiegel, "The Dynamics of Violent Confrontation," Paper presented at Meeting of the Society of Medical Psychoanalysis, New York, New York, 1971.

2. Frank E. Hartung and Maurice Floch, "A Social-Psychological Analysis of Prison Riots," *Journal of Criminal Law, Criminology, and Police Science*

(May-June 1956), 51-57; Clarence Schrag, "The Sociology of Prison Riots," *Proceedings of the American Correctional Association,* 19th Annual Congress, 1960, 136-47; Vernon Fox, "Why Prisoners Riot," *Federal Probation,* 35 (March 1971), 9-14; Hans W. Mattick, "The Prosaic Sources of Prison Violence," Occasional Papers, Chicago: The Law School, The University of Chicago, 1972; G. David Garson, "The Disruption of Prison Administration: An Investigation of Alternative Theories of the Relationship Among Administrators, Reformers, and Involuntary Social Service Clients," *Law and Society Review,* 6 (May 1972), 531-61.

    3. W. Douglas Skelton, "Prison Riot: Assaulters verses Defenders," Archives of General Psychiatry, 21 (September 1969), 359-62; Herbert E. Thomas, "Regressive Behavior in Maximum Security Prisons," Paper prepared for the American Association for the Advancement of Science (January 1973) (unpublished).

    4. Richard W. Wilsnack and Lloyd E. Ohlin, "Preconditions for Major Prison Disturbances," Paper presented at the Meeting of the American Sociological Association, New York, 1973; Richard W. Wilsnack, "Explaining Collective Violence in Prisons: Problems and Possibilities," Paper presented at the Conference of Violence in Prisons, Durham, New Hampshire, 1975.

    5. Garson, "The Disruption of Prison Administration"; William D. Leeke, "Prevention and Deterrence of Violence in Correctional Institutions—Research Efforts to Date," *Prevention of Violence in Correctional Institutions* (Washington, D.C.: National Institute of Law Enforcement and Criminal Justice, Law Enforcement Assistance Administration, 1973).

    6. James D. Crawford, "The Report of the July 4, 1970 Riot at Holmesburg Prison," Philadelphia, 1970 (unpublished report); Mattick, "The Prosaic Sources of Prison Violence"; New York State Special Commission on Attica, *Attica.*

    7. Erving Goffman, *Asylums* (Garden City: Doubleday and Co., Inc., 1961).

    8. Donald Clemmer, *The Prison Community* (New York: Rinehart, 1958); Sykes, *Society of Captives*; Arthur V. Huffman, "Sex Deviation in a Prison Community," *The Journal of Society Therapy,* 6 (1970), 170-81; Rose Giallombardo, *Society of Women: A Study of a Women's Prison* (New York: John Wiley, 1966); Esther Heffernan, *Making It In Prison* (New York: John Wiley and Sons, 1972); New York State Special Commission on Attica, *Attica*; Peter C. Buffum, *Homosexuality in Prisons* (Washington, D.C.: National Institute of Law Enforcement and Criminal Justice, Law Enforcement Assistance Administration, 1972); Anthony L. Guenther, "Violence in Correctional Institutions: A Study of Assaults," Paper presented at the Meeting of the American Society of Criminology, 1974.

    9. Guenther, "Violence in Correctional Institutions."

    10. Edward Bunker, "War Behind Walls," Harper's Magazine, 244 (February 1972), 39-47; Edith Elisabeth Flynn, "Sources of Collective Violence in

Correctional Institutions," *Prevention of Violence in Correctional Institutions* (Washington, D.C.: National Institute of Law Enforcement and Criminal Justice, Law Enforcement Assistance Administration, 1973).

11. Guenther, "Violence in Correctional Institutions."

12. Manfred S. Guttmacher, *The Mind of the Murderer* (New York: Farrar, Strauss and Cudahy, 1960); John Lanzkron, "Murder and Insanity: A Survey," American Journal of Psychiatry, 119 (1963), 754-58; Everett H. Ellinwood, "Assault and Homicide Associated with Amphetamine Abuse," *American Journal of Psychiatry,* 127 (1971), 1170-75.

13. South Carolina Department of Corrections, *Collective Violence in Correctional Institutions: A Search for Causes* (Columbia, South Carolina: South Carolina Department of Corrections, 1973).

14. U.S. National Advisory Commission on Criminal Justice Standards and Goals, *Corrections* (Washington, D.C.: U.S. Government Printing Office, 1973).

15. South Carolina Department of Corrections, *Collective Violence.*

16. M.A. Millemann, "Prisoner Disciplinary Hearings and Procedural Due Process—The Requirements of a Full Admininistrative Hearing," *Maryland Law Review,* 39 (1971), 41.

17. South Carolina Department of Corrections, *Collective Violence.*

18. Wilsnack and Ohlin, "Preconditions for Major Prison Disturbances."

19. South Carolina Department of Corrections, *Collective Violence.*

20. Robert Sommer, "The Social Psychology of the Cell Environment, *The Prison Journal,* 51 (Spring-Summer 1971), 15-21.

21. J.B. Calhoun, "Population Density and Social Pathology," *Scientific American,* 206 (1962), 139-48; J.J. Christian, V. Flyger, and D.E. Davis, "Factors in Mass Morality of a Herd of Sika Deer," *Chesapeake Science,* 1 (1960), 79-95.

22. M. Zuckerman, "Perceptual Isolation as a Stress Situation: A Review," Archives of General Psychiatry, 11 (1964), 225-76; W.H. Bexton, W. Heron and T.H. Scott, "Effects of Decreased Variation in the Sensory Environment," *Canadian Journal of Psychology,* 8 (1954), 70-76; J.P. Zubeck and M. MacNeill, "Perceptual Deprivation Phenomena: Role of the Recumbent Position," *Journal of Abnormal Psychology,* 72 (1967), 147-50; John Rasmussen, *Man in Isolation and Confinement* (Chicago: Aldine Publishing Co., 1973).

23. Jones v. Wittenberg 323 F. Supp. 93 (N.D. Ohio, 1971).

24. Hamilton v. Love, 328 F. Supp. 1182 (E.D. Ark., 1970).

25. Holt v. Sarver, 309 F. Supp. 363 (E.D. Ark., 1970), aff'd, 442 F. 2n 304 (8th Cir. 1971).

26. Max Weber, *The City,* D. Martindale and G. Neuwirth, eds. (New York: The Free Press, (1958); Georg Simmel, "The Metropolis and Mental Life," *The Sociology of Georg Simmel* (New York: The Free Press, 1950), 409-24.

27. Talcott Parsons, *The Social System* (New York: The Free Press, 1951), 4.

28. Talcott Parsons, "The Social System: A General Theory of Action," Roy R. Grinker, Sr., ed., *Toward a Unified Theory of Behavior* (New York: Basic Books, 1956), 55–56.

29. Oscar Newman, *Defensible Space* (New York: The Macmillan Company, 1972); C. Ray Jeffery, *Crime Prevention Through Environmental Design* (Beverley Hills, California: Sage Publications, 1971).

30. F.W. Benton et. al., *Prison and Jail Security* (Urbana, Illinois: National Clearinghouse for Criminal Justice Planning and Architecture, The University of Illinois, 1973).

31. E.J. Webb, D.T. Campbell, R.D. Schwartz, and Lee Sechrest, *Unobtrusive Measures: Nonreactive Research in the Social Sciences,* (Chicago: Rand McNally and Co., 1966).

32. F. Clements, *Research Methods in Ecology* (Lincoln, Nebraska: The University of Nebraska Press, 1905).

33. Robert Park, "Human Communities: The City and Human Ecology," Robert Park, ed., *Human Ecology* (Glencoe, Illinois: The Free Press, 1936).

34. A. Hawley, *Human Ecology: A Theory of Community Structure* (New York: Ronald Press, 1950), 68.

35. Robert Barker, *Concepts and Methods for Studying the Environment of Human Behavior* (Stanford: Stanford University Press, 1968).

36. Robert Sommer, *Personal Space: The Behavioral Basis of Design* (Englewood Cliffs, N.J.: Prentice Hall, Inc., 1969).

37. Cesare Bonesana Beccaria, *An Essay on Crime and Punishment* (Philadelphia: P.H. Nicklin (1819).

10

Population Density and Disruptive Behavior in a Prison Setting

Edwin I. Megargee

As the world's population has soared with no concomitant increase in its land mass, social scientists and laymen alike have become increasingly concerned with the problem of overpopulation. In a recent review of the literature, Zlutnick and Altman[1] reported that crowding had been blamed for a plethora or social problems including crime, physical and mental illness, drug and alcohol addiction, family disorganization, and acts of aggression ranging from homicide and riots to war.

However, Schaar[2] recently maintained,

Despite popular opinion and professional conjecture, the body of research evidence relating to the actual effects of crowding fails to indicate such negative outcomes. Instead, studies show that humans appear to be relatively unharmed by populous conditions. The apparent inconsistency can probably be attributed to the paucity of relevant human crowding research, to an unfounded, ominous and premature prognosis of over-crowding's effects, and to a too-common trend of paralleling the results of animal crowding studies with humans.

As Schaar pointed out, the findings on the relation between population density and human behavior are indeed more ambiguous than the results of animal research. Different investigators studying the incidence of social pathology in areas differing in density have reported positive, zero order, and negative correlations.[3]

Similarly observational studies of hospital patients and of children in groups varying in size have reported inconsistent results.[4] Individuals consistently interacted less in larger groups, but the findings with regard to aggression differed, with Loo reporting less aggression in the denser situation and Hutt and Vaizey more.

Experimental investigators have placed different sized groups into rooms varying in size and observed the effects on such variables as subjective feelings of anxiety and the attitudes and behavior of group members toward one another.

This research was supported in part by USPHS grant MH 18468 (NIMH: Center for Studies of Crime and Delinquency) and in part by the Federal Bureau of Prisons. All statements and opinions expressed are those of the investigator and should not be construed as representing official policies, opinions, or attitudes of the Public Health Service Bureau of Prisons.

The investigator is grateful for Marilyn Sempert Saur's help in reviewing the literature and her critical reading of an earlier draft of this manuscript, and for Karen Moorhead's assistance in obtaining temperature data. A revised and condensed report of this study is to be published in the *American Journal of Community Psychology*.

The results of these studies have differed as a function of the sex of the subjects, the tediousness of the task on which they worked and external conditions such as noise level and room temperature.[5] Integration of the findings of these studies is difficult, not only because a variety of designs were employed, but also because the measures of such dependent variables as aggression and anxiety differed from study to study.

In the course of this research, it has become clear that several conceptual distinctions must be made. Stokols[6] pointed out that one must distinguish *density,* a physical condition, from *crowding,* a subjective feeling. Spectators densely packed into bleachers at a sporting event may not experience crowding, whereas people in a bus may feel quite crowded even though they have more space. Unfortunately these two terms are used interchangeably in much of the literature including the recent article by Schaar.[7]

Linder[8] also pointed out that *density,* the number of people in a given space, should be differentiated from *numerosity,* the sheer number of people with whom one might interact.

Loo proposed a distinction between *spatial* and *social* density. "Spatial density research compares the behavior of groups of the same number in spaces of differing sizes while social density research compares the behavior of groups of differing numbers in the same sized space."[9] He also inquired, "Does increasing the density by *reducing* available space have the same effect as *increasing* the numbers of individuals in the same given space?"

A final conceptual issue is whether the density is perceived as *temporary* or *chronic.* Whereas most of the concern about overpopulation is with regard to the long-term effects of chronic high density, most of the human research has investigated the temporary high-density conditions that can be produced in a laboratory. This temporal difference could account for some of the differences between the results of human and animal research.

The present study was designed to investigate the relation of population size and population density on the incidence of disruptive behavior over a three-year period in a prison for male youthful offenders. As Paulus, McCain, and Cox recently pointed out, prisons afford a unique opportunity for population research.[10] Unlike laboratory subjects, prison residents are coping with long-term, chronic conditions rather than a temporary situation that will end within an hour or so. Moreover, since the behavior of the residents is routinely observed and recorded, unobstrusive study of naturally occurring behavior patterns is possible.

In the institution in question, notable variations in population size took place over the three years; moreover, renovation of the living quarters during the second and third years caused significant variations in the amount of personal space available for the inmates.

Method

Since 1970 I have maintained a laboratory and have conducted an extensive program of research at the Federal Correctional Institution (FCI) at Tallahassee, Florida, a medium-security institution for male offenders aged 18 to 25. From the data accumulated as part of this ongoing program, which has been described in detail elsewhere,[11] the following variables were extracted for study in the present investigation:

Population

The number of inmates in residence every day is routinely recorded by the FCI staff. In the present study the mean monthly count for the 36 months from November 1971 through October 1974 was used.

Space

Overall, the FCI encompasses some 21 acres, including recreational fields, an educational industrial complex, utility and administrative buildings, and a central lawn bordered by four living units. For the present study, the amount of actual living space was the critical variable since the overall area of the institution did not vary.

FCI inmates are housed in four buildings, each of which contains two dormitories. Study of the blueprints showed that at the outset of this period each of these eight dormitories had 5,080 square feet of space available for the inmates, 3,744 square feet in the sleeping area, 450 square feet in the bathroom area, 437 square feet in the TV room, 288 square feet in the game room, and 161 square feet in the vestibule, for a total of 40,640 square feet of inmate living space in the eight dorms.

In January 1973 one dormitory was closed for renovations and the inmates were relocated in the remaining seven, thus reducing the available space by 5,080 square feet to 35,560. During the renovations, the barracks-like atmosphere was reduced by installing privacy screens around each man's bed and nightstand; the ceilings were lowered and better lighting was provided. However, the amount of living space was reduced from 5,080 square feet to 4,695 square feet since the game room and part of the TV room were converted into offices so that treatment personnel could be more accessible to the residents. When the first dormitory was completed and the work begun on the second, 4,695 square feet of space were restored but another 5,080 removed, leaving a total of 35,175 square feet. By studying the progress of the renovation program, the number of square feet of living space available to the inmate population was thus determined for each month.

Density

Density was calculated by dividing the number of square feet by the monthly population to determine the number of square feet of living space available per man per month.

Incident Reports ("Shots")

When an FCI staff member observes an inmate engaging in disruptive behavior, he may write an incident report charging the inmate with a disciplinary violation. This report is filed with the lieutenant of the watch, who investigates the alleged misconduct and records his evaluation. Later a formal hearing is held during which the inmate is allowed to offer his version of the events. A finding of "innocent" or "guilty" is made and, in the event of a guilty verdict, an appropriate penalty is assessed.

These incident reports (called "shots" by the staff and inmates), range from fairly minor infractions such as refusing to report for work or insolence to an officer to quite serious offenses such as assault with a deadly weapon or attempted escape. As part of the ongoing research project, copies of all the shots written at the FCI were collected. The total number of shots per month served as the measure of disruptive behavior.

It was hypothesized that there would be (a) a significant positive correlation between the mean population and the number of shots and the rate of shots per 100 inmates, (b) a significant negative correlation between the total number of square feet of living space and the number and rate of shots, (c) a significant negative correlation between the density index (number of square feet per resident) and the number and rate of shots.

Results

The basic data are summarized in table 10-1. It can be seen that there were noteworthy variations in all three of the major independent variables. The mean population waxed and waned through the three-year period, ranging from 523.6 to 589.0 in the first 12 months, from 543.6 to 627.9 in the second year, and from 530.3 to 571.4 in the third. Thus, population changes were not confounded with time and any effects of population size are independent of changes

Table 10-1
Summary of Basic Data

	Mean	S.D.	Range
Population	557.86	25.22	523.6 – 627.9
Total living space (square feet)	38,443.06	2,322.68	34,405 – 40,640
Space per resident (square feet)	69.10	5.77	55.41 – 77.62
Total number of disciplinary reports	73.94	19.42	45 – 128
Number of disciplinary reports per 100 residents	13.23	3.29	3.29 – 20.40

in administrative policy or the type of inmate admitted over the three-year period.

As luck would have it, the population tended to be highest during the renovation periods when inmate living space was reduced. In fact there was a significant negative correlation ($r = -0.33$) between the mean population and the total number of square feet available in the institution over the 36-month period. This was reflected in the density index computed by dividing the available space by the number of residents. The data show that this index varied from a high of 77.62 to a low of 55.41 square feet of space per inmate. This means that throughout the study we were dealing with crowded living conditions, especially when one considers that the space available included communal areas such as the bathrooms and showers. The amount of personal space each man could regard as his own territory was considerably less than this average figure and at times of peak density extensive double bunking was required. To place this in context, the National Advisory Commission on Criminal Justice Standards and Goals recently recommended that in constructing correctional facilities, "The design of the institution should provide for privacy and personal space by the use of single rooms with a floor area of at least 80 square feet per man. . . ."[12] At the same time it should be pointed out that most of the daylight hours were spent off the dormitories in shops, classrooms and recreational areas. However, the educational, vocational and recreational resources were not adequate to handle the periods of peak population and at these times an excessive amount of idleness could be observed throughout the institution. It is a correctional maxim that idleness breeds discontent and disruptive behavior.[13]

Each of the three independent variables—population, total space, and space per resident—was correlated with the total number of disciplinary violations and the rate of violation per 100 residents. Because population and space were significantly correlated, we also computed the partial correlations of population with the number of shots and shot rate holding space constant, as well as the partial correlations of space with the two dependent variables with population held constant.

These results are presented in table 10-2. It can be seen that there was a significant correlation between the mean monthly population and the number of shots ($r = 0.39$; $p = 0.01$); the significant partial correlation ($r = 0.28$; $p = 0.05$) indicated that this association was not an artifact of the correlation between population and space. However, it is trivial to demonstrate that disciplinary violations increase when there are more men in an institution. It is more important to determine whether the *rate* of violations increases with the population. This did not prove to be the case; the correlation between population and shot *rate* was not significant ($r = 0.08$; $p = 0.33$) when the covariation with space was partialled out.[a]

The amount of living space available for the residents was significantly associated with both the number ($r = -0.46$; $p = 0.002$) and the rate ($r = -0.42$; $p = 0.005$) of disciplinary violations. The partial correlation coefficients ($r = -0.38$; $p = 0.013$) showed that the significance of this relationship was not attributable to the covariation between space and population.

It had been anticipated that population density, the average number of square feet of living space available per resident, would bear the closest relation to disciplinary violations. This proved to be the case. The density index correlated

Table 10-2
Correlations and Partial Correlations of Population
Space and Density to Disciplinary Violations

Independent Variables		Dependent Variables	
Primary Variable	Covariate	Total Number of Violations	Rate of Violations per 100 Residents
Mean population	None	0.39[a]	0.21
Mean population	Total space	0.28[b]	0.08
Total space	None	-0.46[a]	-0.42[a]
Total space	Mean population	-0.38[a]	-0.38[a]
Population density	None	-0.52[c]	-0.40[a]

[a] $p < 0.05$

[b] $p < 0.01$

[c] $p < 0.001$

[a] All p values are two-tailed.

significantly with both the number ($r = -0.52$; $p = 0.001$) and the rate ($r = -0.40$; $p = 0.008$) of disciplinary violations.

A scattergram of the relation between density and disciplinary showed a curvilinear pattern resembling the "twisted pear" distribution first described by Fisher.[14] During months when the density was relatively low, there might or might not be a high rate of disciplinary violations. Months with high density, however, typically had high rates of misconduct. In short, high density appeared to be a sufficient but not a necessary condition for high rates of disruptive behavior.

Overall inspection of the data showed that high rates of disciplinary violations were most frequent in the summer months. Griffith and Veitch[15] had reported that uncomfortably hot temperatures exacerbated the adverse effects of crowding so a post hoc analysis of the relationship between heat and disciplinary violations was undertaken. Data from studies by Gadge, Stolwijk, and Nishi[16] and by Rohles[17] indicated that at the humidity levels customarily found in Tallahassee a dry bulb temperature of 85 degrees or higher would be regarded as uncomforable by most individuals in the unair-conditioned FCI domitories, a figure that corresponds fairly closely with subjective experience.

Data provided by the U. S. Weather Bureau at Tallahassee indicated that the number of days per month when the temperature equaled or exceeded 85 degrees ranged from 0 to 31 with a mean of 13.17 and a SD of 12.86. The number of hot days did not correlate significantly with either the number of shots ($r = 0.21$; $p = 0.11$) or the rate of shots ($r = 0.10$; $p = 0.28$), nor was there a significant partial correlation of the number of hot days with the rate of violations when the density index was held constant ($r = -0.08$; $p = 0.32$). In short, heat did not contribute to the association between density and disciplinary violations in this institution.

Discussion

The results of this study are in sharp contrast to the results of laboratory research indicating no adverse effects associated with crowded conditions among humans. In a prison setting, where crowded conditions are chronic rather than temporary and where people prone to antisocial behavior are gathered together, there is a clear association between restrictions on personal space and the occurrence of disruptive and aggressive behavior.

Since this study used representational design in a field setting, it was not possible to manipulate spatial and social density independently. However, it was clear that the changes in available space correlated more strongly with disruptive behavior than did changes in the number of residents. It would appear at first glance that, in answer to Loo's[18] query, there are different effects associated with reducing available space and increasing the number of individuals in a given space. However, it should be pointed out that in this particular instance the effect of the space reduction was to move individuals from a dorm undergoing renovation to other areas within the institution. This involved territorial intrusions and disruptions of friendship ties as well as mere reduction in personal space.

The present study suggests a number of avenues for further research that should help clarify that influence of the various independent variables studied. Behavioral scientists in prison settings could attempt to replicate some of the laboratory studies on crowding that have been performed using college students to determine whether temporary crowding has the same effects on incarcerated individuals. If so, the present results may be attributable more to the chronicity of the conditions than the personality patterns of the participants. If not, then it may be that personality patterns are more important. The importance of the personality dimension could also be clarified by field studies involving relocations and changes in density among noncriminals in military barracks or summer camp settings.

Territoriality and friendship ties also deserve further study in the crowding literature. When a group has been together long enough to establish a dominance hierarchy and claims to certain areas, the addition of new residents is probably resented more than when the same number of strangers are brought together in the same sized space for the first time.

Concepts such as "territoriality" and "dominance hierarchies" are more closely associated with animal than human research, and have received little if any attention in the crowding studies performed with humans in laboratory settings. In a short-lived group brought together solely for the artificial task of participating in an experiment, such constructs are relatively unimportant. But when people are crowded together in an ongoing living situation, the issues of who gets the lower bunk or the spot nearest the window or furthest from the loud snorer become very important. Such books as *Andersonville,* the *House of the Dead,* or the *Gulag Archipelago* may not be replete with tables or statistical tests, but they nonetheless should be considered by social scientists making generalizations on the benign influences of high-density conditions.

Notes

1. S. Zlutnick and I. Altman, "Crowding and Human Behavior," *Environment and the Social Sciences: Perspectives and Applications,* J. Wohlwill and D. Carson, eds. (Washington, D. C.: American Psychological Association, 1972), 44-60.

2. K. Schaar, "What's Bad for Rats May Be OK for Humans," *APA Monitor,* 6 (1975), 7.

3. O. Galle, R. Grove, and M. McPherson, "Population Density and Pathology: What Are the Relations for Man?" *Science,* 176 (1972), 23-30; R. Schmitt, "Density, Health, and Social Disorganization," *Journal of the American Institute of Planners,* 32 (1966), 38-40; P. Spector, "Population Density and Unemployment: The Effects on the Incidence of Violent Crime in the American City," *Criminology,* 12 (1975), 399-401; H. Winsborough, "The Social Consequences of High Population Density," *Law and Contemporary Problems,* 30 (1965), 87-115.

4. C. Hutt and M. Vaizey, "Differential Effects of Group Density on Social Behavior," *Nature,* 209 (1966), 1, 371-1,372; W. Ittleson, H. Proshansky, and L. Rivlin, "Bedroom Size and Social Interaction of the Psychiatric Ward," *Environment and the Social Sciences: Perspectives and Applications,* J. Wohlwill and D. Carson, eds. (Washington, D. C.: American Psychological Association, 1972), 95-104; C. Loo, "Effects of Spatial Density on Social Behavior of Children," *Journal of Applied Social Psychology,* 2 (1972), 372-81; P. McGrew, "Social and Spatial Density Effects on Spacing Behavior in Preschool Children," *Journal of Child Psychology and Psychiatry,* 11 (1970), 197-204.

5. J. Baxter and B. Deanovich, "Anxiety Arousing Effects of Inappropriate Crowding," *Journal of Consulting and Clinical Psychology,* 35 (1970), 174-78; J. Desor, "Toward a Psychological Theory of Crowding," *Journal of Personality and Social Psychiatry,* 21 (1972), 79-83; J. Freedman, S. Klevansky, and P. Ehrlich, "Effect of Crowding on Human Task Performance," *Journal of Applied Social Psychology,* 1 (1971), 7-25; J. Freedman, A. Levy, R. Buchanan, and J. Price, "Crowding and Human Aggressiveness," *Journal of Experimental and Social Psychology,* 8 (1972), 528-48; W. Griffith and R. Veitch, "Hot and Crowded: The Influence of Population Density and Temperature on Interpersonal Affective Behavior," *Journal of Personality and Social Psychology,* 17 (1971), 92-98; R. G. Heimberg, "Social and Spatial Density Effects on Anxiety, Interpersonal Attraction and Perceptions of Crowding," Master's thesis, Florida State University, 1974; J. Ross, B. Layton, D. Erickson, and J. Schopler, "Affect, Facial Regards, and Reactions to Crowding," *Journal of Personality and Social Psychology,* 28 (1973), 69-76; M. S. Saur, "The Effects of Noise and Density of Subjective Feelings of Crowding, State Anxiety, and Interpersonal Judgment in Female Subjects," Master's thesis, Florida State University, 1974; S. Smith and W. Haythorn, "The Effects of Compatibility, Crowding, Group Size and Leadership Seniority on Stress, Anxiety, Hostility, Annoyances in Isolated Groups," *Journal of Personality and Social Psychology,* 22 (1972), 67-79; D. Stokols, M. Rall, B. Pinner, and J. Schopler, "Physical, Social and Personal Determinants of the Perception of Crowding," *Environment and Behavior,* 5 (1973), 87-115.

6. D. Stokols, "On the Distinction Between Density and Crowding: Some Implications for Future Research," *Psychological Review,* 79 (1972), 275-77.

7. Schaar, "What's Bad for Rats."

8. D. Linder, *Personal Space* (Morristown, N. J.: General Learning Press, 1974).

9. C. Loo, "Effects of Spatial Density on Social Behavior of Children," *Journal of Applied Social Psychology* 2 (1974), 372-81.

10. P. Paulus, G. McCain, and Z. Cox, "A Note on the Use of Prisons as Environments for Investigation of Crowding," *Bulletin of the Psychonomic Society,* 1 (1973), 427-28.

11. E. I. Megargee, "Applied Psychological Research in a Correctional Setting," *Criminal Justice and Behavior,* 1 (1974), 43-50; E. I. Megargee, J. E. Hokanson, and C. C. Spielberger, "The Behavior Research Program at the Federal Correctional Institution, Tallahassee, I. Goals and Initial Data Collection Procedures," *FCI Research Reports,* 3 (1971), 1-48; E. I. Megargee, et al. "The Behavior Research Program at the Federal Correctional Institution, Tallahassee, II: Later Data Collection Procedures," *FCI Research Reports,* 4 (1972), 1-34.

12. National Advisory Commission on Criminal Justice Standards and Goals, *A Strategy to Reduce Crime* (Washington, D. C.: Government Printing Office, 1973), 358.

13. M. A. deFord, *Stone Walls* (New York: Chilton Publishing Company, 1962).

14. J. Fisher, "The 'Twisted Pear' and the Prediction of Behavior," *Journal of Consulting Psychology,* 23 (1959), 400-405.

15. Griffith and Veitch, "Hot and Crowded."

16. A. T. Gadge, J. A. A. Stolwijk, and Y. Nishi, "An Effective Temperature Scale Based on a Simple Model of Human Physiological, Regulatory Response," *ASHRAE Transactions,* 77 (1971), 247-62.

17. F. H. Rohles, Jr., "The Model Comfort Envelope and Its Use in Current Standards," *Human Factors,* 16 (1974), 324-32.

18. C. Loo, "Effects of Spatial Density."

Discussion

Sumner: In California we have a problem in that San Quentin is antiquated and really shouldn't exist. The other prisons are now overcrowded. What are the alternatives?

Flynn: I would be less opposed to prison construction if it were paired with the absolute destruction of the existing facilities. What usually happens is that additional buildings are built and the old ones exist, and when you have an overflow, the net result is the incarceration of more people. If you destruct at the same time as you construct I have no objection.

Toch: There is one additional item in this relationship between people and environments. All these things—crowding, privacy, sense of ownership over space, and so on—are fairly reliable dimensions. When it comes to inmate concerns, say, for physical safety, there is tremendous consistency in that type of concern. But when you look over populations, you discover that inmates vary substantially in their environmental requirements.

Their dominant concerns, for instance, the need for activity, for stimulation, are not the same as the concern for the feeling of discomfort when a person feels crowded, or where there is a lot of noise. Some inmates have tremendously intense concerns with overstimulation. As a matter of fact, it is very extreme when you are dealing with people who are very tense, and sort of schizoid: that they can experience a very acute discomfort because of noise level and the number of people. It is just a terrible source of pain to them. But they are willing to exist in that cell. On the other hand, some people become panic-stricken when they have nothing or little to do.

It turns out that you really have to think of environmental concerns as a classification problem. When one works within a range of available options, one of the things that one ought to be paying attention to in classification is the kind of things that inmates seem to be able to tolerate, or seem especially to need by way of environmental dimensions. There are some strong differences here—in terms of the extremes (like male vs. female) or when you look at people who have certain types of background characteristics, etc.

Flynn: Another example would be that the amount of space you need depends on your level of aggression. There was a very interesting study that showed aggressive people have to have more space.

Toch: We have an institution that has done something quite revolutionary, one of those things where the staff became very much involved—the guards and the inmates together built the dormitory so that each inmate now, instead of being out there in the bed, has a sort of cubby-hole construction around him. It became a community project for the inmates and the guards. There was tremendous esprit de corps, the morale was high and inmates found that type of dormitory extremely comfortable. There was very high praise for that sort of living arrangement compared to what they experienced prior to this.

145

Nagel: I can't help but think of the unrelatedness between research and reality. It's a shame. Some while ago, for example, a study was made of space requirements for aggressive people. They learned that the aggressive people required more space rather than less, that when a person comes within X number of feet of them their whole nervous system begins to get excited. But the reality of imprisoning aggressive people is that they are put in maximum-security prisons, which are more expensive to build than medium- and minimum-security institutions, and therefore space is condensed for cost factors. You end up with all the most aggressive people in facilities that provoke their aggression.

Part IV

Policy Implications

11

The Study of Violence in California Prisons: A Review with Policy Implications

Lawrence A. Bennett

The problem of violence in prison has long been a concern to prison administrators but it has been only fairly recently that the cold searching light of research has focused on the issues. Two factors appear to play a part in this situation: First, the repressive controls available to those managing prisons were reasonably effective in insuring a relatively calm climate amongst the compliant inmates of the day. Second, it is only in the immediate past that scientific methods have been used to gain understanding of correctional problems in general, let alone the very difficult dilemmas presented by prison violence.

Some Differing Emphases

Three distinct approaches can be identified when an attempt is made to describe the causal basis for prison assaults. First, the motivation for violence may be postulated to be within the individual. This may take one or more of the following forms: The individual may be viewed as highly explosive—"a bomb waiting for a place to go off." He is explosive because "he has low frustration tolerance"—he is psychologically maladjusted. The foregoing approach may be pushed even further to suggest that hostile and aggressive inmates are seriously disturbed emotionally. Along with this view would be the possibility that the inmate who lacks frustration tolerance may have some organic brain pathology or glandular dysfunction that interferes with normal controls. Similarly, the psychological, individualistic approach encompasses a wide variety of social background factors—broken homes, early delinquent associates, overly severe discipline—which are often seen as related to a predisposition toward violence.

Second, a more sociological view can be considered. This approach would emphasize the socioeconomic background of the individuals participating in violence within the institution, the organization of the social structure of the prison, and the activity of the individuals in quasi-political–revolutionary groups that are sometimes ethnically oriented.

The third aspect available for exploration places the emphasis on the structural, physical, and psychological environment of the institutional setting—such things as architecture, space, color (or lack of), obstructions, and regimented patterns of traffic flow.

The study of any given area usually involves some aspects of other approaches and, as will be seen later, it seems likely that attempts to understand prison violence will require complex multivariant analyses, involving the simultaneous consideration of all three approaches.

The 1960 Study of Violence

While prison violence has become more severe in recent years and thus of more immediate concern to prison administrators, there has been a long-standing interest in studying the nature and causes of violence, and methods of control of this type of behavior. Illustrative of the concern is the fact that shortly after the establishment of a formal, recognized research unit in the California Department of Corrections, one of the first projects to be undertaken was a study of violence.

San Quentin Prison was selected as the site for the study involving a detailed look at violent behavior.[1] This insitution, one of the largest in the system and housing a population heavily laced with problem inmates, provided ample material for statistical study. The study defined violent acts as any physical act of harm to another, such as stabbing, choking or beating—with or without a weapon—plus threats and intent to harm. Individuals exhibiting such behavior during 1960 were compared with inmates whose records were discipline free (see Table 11-1). Twelve variables were able to differentiate between the two groups

Table 11-1
Variables Significantly Different Between
Violent and Nonviolent Prisoners:
San Quentin, 1960

1. Younger in age
2. Ethnic background: nonwhite
3. Home broken before age 16 by divorce or desertion (63%)[a]
4. Principal father figure: none, many, alcoholic, criminal, or abusive (60%)
5. Measured grade level 6.5 or lower (55%)
6. Prior institutional violence (63%)
7. Four or more institutional disciplinary infractions (63%)
8. Prior institution history of one prison commitment, two jail or juvenile commitments (58%)
9. Age 12 or under at first arrest (65%)
10. First arrest for robbery or burglary (55%)
11. History of epilepsy (100%)[b]
12. Some suicide attempts or self-mutilation (75%)[b]

[a]Number in parenthesis represents the percentage of all those in the sample with this attribute who exhibited violent behavior.

[b]Frequency of occurrence so small as to make variable of little practical value.

at a level with a low probability of being chance occurrences. The characteristics suggest a combination of negative social background items plus indicators of a heavy involvement in criminal and disruptive behavior. Two of the 12 characteristics are present in so few cases that practical utility is lost.

Equal concern must be directed toward those characteristics examined that *did not* discriminate between the two groups. As shown in table 11-2, neither the most serious commitment offense nor prior violent behavior outside seems to be related to violent and aggressive behavior within the institutional setting. It should also be noted that individual psychological characteristics, as measured by the Minnesota Multiphasic Personality Inventory (MMPI), for example, failed to discriminate between the two groups. Also, hostile attitudes, family criminal record, hostility toward parents, or psychopathic traits were of little value in differentiation. In general, one could say that in terms of the findings of this study, individual personality characteristics do not represent the major or unique source of violent behavior. At the same time, disciplinary difficulties and prior

Table 11-2
Variables Not Significantly Different
Between Violent and Nonviolent Prisoners:
San Quentin, 1960

1. Family criminal record
2. Hostility toward parents
3. Opiate use
4. Employment instability
5. Alcohol use
6. Hostile attitude
7. History of mental hospitalization
8. Psychopathic traits
9. High Pd Scale score on MMPI
10. High Ma Scale score on MMPI
11. High Pa Scale score on MMPI
12. Escape record
13. Prior cultural violence
14. Age at latest imprisonment
15. Commitment status
16. Prior criminal violence
17. Prior pathological violence
18. Prior situational violence
19. Prior accidental violence
20. Most serious commitment offense

institutional violence *are* related. Findings of this type, while providing some credence to the notion that the potential for violence resides within the individual also raises doubts by the observation of seemingly separate bases for violent behavior in the community and in the prison. While providing no direct evidence, the possibility is presented that some portion of causality is related to some aspect of institutionalization—whether social-psychological or physical remains to be determined.

The 1965 Task Force to Study Violence

The next effort was a major one. The 1965 Task Force to Study Violence was carried out by the Research Division under the direction of top-level departmental administrative staff. The effort was augmented by such knowledgeable individuals as Hans Toch and James Park. Methodology for this particular study involved the examination of data concerning violent incidents occurring in six major institutions with analyses directed toward shifts in patterns between 1963 and 1964, and a comparison of the characteristics of both the aggressors and victims with their respective residential populations. For the purpose of the study, a violent act was defined as "Assault by inmates using either fists or any weapon which resulted in injury to himself or others and which was deemed serious enough by the institution to report it in an 'Incident Report'." Incidents against staff and among inmates were treated separately as were the California Department of Corrections inmate group and the Youth Authority wards housed in adult correctional institutions.

A large number of findings resulted. In summary, the amount of violence was on the increase in medium-custody institutions. From 1963 to 1964 minor injuries to staff from blows and major injuries to inmates from weapon assaults more that doubled. The characteristics of violent inmates show some parallels with the earlier study but also some decided shifts. (See table 11-3.) While a history of prior institutional violence still showed the strongest relationship to present assaultive behavior and nonwhite ethnic background (in this case Mexican ethnic origin) maintained a strong relationship, we now see family criminal record and high MMPI Paranoia Scale scores positively related whereas previously these items were nondifferentiating.

An attempt was made to unravel the motivational aspects of the incidents. Labeled "Causal Factors," the findings showed that 35 percent of the inmate-to-inmate assaults seemed to stem from accidental, real, or imagined insult combined with hypersensitivity. Twenty-five percent were associated with homosexual activities while 15 percent seemed to be related to so-called "pressuring" activities—the use of force or threat of force to persuade weaker inmates to part with their possessions. Racial conflicts accounted for 12 percent of the incidents with the remainder (16 percent) being divided between informant activities (9

Table 11-3
Characteristics of Violent Inmates:
Folsom, CMF, San Quentin, CTF, DVI, and CMC-East
1963-64

1. Prior institutional violence
2. Born in California
3. Mexican ethnic origin
4. Family criminal record
5. Juvenile escapes
6. Never married
7. High MMPI Paranoia Scale score
8. Last imprisonment under age 25
9. Maximum or close custody

percent) and retaliation for past assaults (7 percent). Despite the fact that three of the institutions under study—California Medical Facility, California Mens Colony, and San Quentin—house large numbers of emotionally disturbed inmates, the emotional condition of the individual was apparently not seen as a significant causal factor in the reported assaultive behavior.

Another factor to be considered when reviewing this study must be the relative contribution of a few inmates to the problem of violence. In the detailed examination of kinds of incidents and differing motivations, the fact can be easily overlooked that the incidents under study were perpetrated by only 2 percent of the inmate population. The foregoing is not to minimize the seriousness of the problem but rather to note the serious statistical constraints encountered when one is faced with predicting the rare event.

In terms of time and place, it would appear that violent incients are more likely to occur in the spring and, during the period of this study, were more likely to occur in the living and recreational areas. Work and dining areas only accounted for about 15 percent of the violent incidents.

Attacks on staff occurred most often at California Medical Facility—our mental hospital for the Department of Corrections—again raising the question of the possible relationship between emotional disturbance and assaultive behavior. A second finding was that Youth Authority wards participated five times as often as adult inmates in violent assaults on staff. The preceding findings are examined later in conjuction with related data. Attacks on staff, for the most part, occurred during apprehension or processing of an inmate suspected of being involved in some disciplinary infraction.

When aggressors were compared to victims, with both Youth Authority wards and Department of Corrections inmates combined, it was found that more aggressors than victims had the following characteristics:

First arrest under age 25
Inmate described in records as hostile
History of prior institutional violence
Gang leader at time of incident

When adult offenders only were used in the comparison, more aggressors had the following characteristics than did victims:

Born in California
Mexican ethnic origin
Family criminal record
Juvenile escapes only
Never married
High MMPI Paranoia Scale score (60+)
Last imprisoned under age 25
Incident while individual under age 25
Maximum or close custody status

Aggressors among Youth Authority wards differed from the Youth Authority victims on a number of characteristics but these are not explored inasmuch as the emphasis here is upon an understanding of adult prison inmates.

As noted earlier, a past history of violence, especially institutional violence, seems fairly strongly related to the aggressive behavior noted during the period studied. The foregoing becomes more apparent when identified aggressors are compared with the prison residents (see table 11-4).

As can be seen, both the largest actual difference and the largest relative difference between the groups was on the variable of past institutional violence (the incidence of a history of prior institutional violence is roughly four times as great among assaultive inmates as among the populations from which they come).

The report continues,

Among other indications of the psychologically distinctive nature of institutionally assaultive inmates is their repeated tendency to become involved in any kind of institutional rule violations. Similarly, the prior escape rate for the adult correctional inmate aggressors is striking if one recalls that most of this group have only jail or juvenile commitments previous to this commitment.[2]

At all institutions, regardless of the average age of the resident inmates, the younger the offender, the greater his participation as aggressor in violent incidents. At the institution housing a large number of Youth Authority wards, Deuel Vocational Institution, the Youth Authority wards participated more than four times as often as adult inmates in violent inmate to inmate incidents; five times as often in violent incidents against staff.

Table 11-4
Identified Aggressors Compared with Prison Residents

	Identified Aggressors	Resident Population
Any prior violence	87.6%	71.9%
Prior criminal violence	60.9	47.0
Prior institutional violence	48.9	12.9
Prior cultural violence	44.9	18.7

The report appropriately focuses on the critical issue of the apparent relationship between youthfulness and assaultive behavior with the following analysis,

The comparatively serious violence record of Youth Authority aggressors raises the question of whether this relative viciousness is a function of age, or whether Youth Authority wards in adult correctional institutions are a unique problem group. To help answer this question, Youth Authority wards in California Training Facility (Soledad), Deuel Vocational Institution (Tracy), and California Medical Facility (Vacaville) were compared with the adult felon inmates at these three institutions who fell into a roughly comparable age bracket of 20 to 24. The major finding in these comparisons is that the two groups are very much alike. The only statistically significant exceptions to this rule are: (1) proportionately more Youth Authority wards have backgrounds with personal opiate use and family criminality; (2) comparatively more Youth Authority wards have prior institutional violence recorded; while (3) fewer of the Youth Authority wards show prior criminal violence. These differences, however, may be produced by discrepancies in case history records.[3]

Out of such consistent findings one must conclude that youthfulness has a positive relationship to violent aggressive behavior. Speculation offers two explanatory possibilities: The first might be the heightened vigor of the young offender who is at the prime of his physical and sexual potential that demands some sort of active interaction with the environment. Despite the extensive opportunity for physical release through exercise and sports activities, apparently the psychological as well as the physical restrictiveness of the prison leads to aggressive outbursts. The alternate concept would suggest that younger inmates must struggle to make their mark, to "earn their spurs" in an all male environment where older inmates maintain their status on the basis of a past reputation for toughness. As is often the case in the human situation, it may well be that both concepts contain a part of the truth.

Aggressive History Profile

Such terms as "cultural violence" are drawn from an instrument developed by Conrad.[4] Designated the "Aggressive History Profile," the attempt was to summarize quickly the history of violent, aggressive behavior of each individual through a system of categorization of kinds of acts committed by an individual plus provide some index as to degree of involvement. The categories are cultural, criminal, accidental, situational, pathological, and institutional. Thus, an individual whose history revealed only a single instance of a threat to do violence associated with some sort of subcultural conflict would be rated lower than an individual who has been involved in several overt acts of aggression. No single numerical index can be offered, however, for there is no known way in which to determine the relative weights of cultural vs. criminal violence. At any rate, with this scale a general profile of an individual's history of aggressive behavior could be easily depicted. It was designed to be used in attempting to predict postinstitutional violence. The application of this measurement to institutional violence represents more of an attempt to take advantage of all readily available information rather than to develop it out of any theoretical system that suggests that past violence of any kind is a great predictor of subsequent violence in an institutional setting.

Three Reports on Behavioral Observations

Rather than being the usual approach of the ex post facto retrospective study, three reports were the outgrowth of an attempt to gather comprehensive information as it occurred about a large number of adult male inmates, starting from their entry into the system.

The first report provided a detailed description of who people were in terms of background characteristics and what they did during their first year in prison.[5] Along with the large percentage who became involved in vocational training, institutional work assignments, and academic training, a small number became involved in violent incidents. The definition of violence used in this study included threats of violence as well as the inflicting of injury. It was found that about 7 percent of new admissions and 4 percent of readmissions (those returned from the community as parole violators, either as a result of a new felony commitment or because of a violation of conditions of parole) were involved in violent acts as defined. The percentages found are considerably higher than the 2 percent of the resident population previously noted. One could argue that differing time periods are under consideration. However, such a view cannot be supported, for the 1965 Task Force study dealt with 1963 and 1964 incidents while the study under discussion made use of 1964 admissions—the resulting incidents would be occurring during 1964 and 1965. Thus, the conclusion must be considered that those inmates newly entered into the system contribute disproportionately more to the disruptive behavior of the institution than do those who have been in residence for some longer period.

One of the recommendations growing out of the 1965 report was that a "violence participation proneness scale" be developed. The statistical problems inherent in predicting the rare event have already been mentioned. Rather than attempting the nearly impossible task of predicting violent behavior, two subsequent reports dealing with approaches to predicting institutional disciplinary difficulties were undertaken. First, MMPI test scores were used.[6] No scale scores were sufficiently precise to be of value. Using item analysis, a three-item scale was derived from the MMPI that was significantly related (r_b=0.53) to two or more disciplinaries (40 percent of this sample; 19 percent had four or more disciplinary reports within the first year). However, the scale failed to be useful for predictive purposes in that, when applied to a validation sample, the relationship between the scale and disciplinaries was nonsignificant.

A second effort, using background characteristics, fared somewhat better. A six-item scale resulted in statistically significant relationships for both the consturction and validation sample (r_b=0.68; r_b=0.42) with the shrinkage in correlation coefficient being expected (see figure 11-1). The two items carrying the greatest weights were a history of juvenile commitments and age 29 or younger at time of admission. The scale was able to predict group percentages in that the percentage of those who incurred two or more disciplinaries within the first year did increase as scores increased.

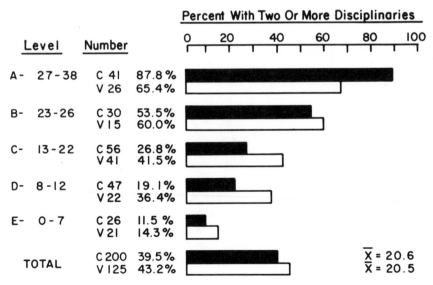

Figure 11-1. Disciplinary Prediction Scale I for New Admissions by Construction and Validation Samples.

It would appear that of those scoring above 23 on the scale (the 35 percent or so of the most disruptive), some 65 percent are likely to become involved in two or more disciplinary difficulties.

For readmission inmates, no predictors of significant stability could be found, either in terms of MMPI scores or in terms of background characteristics.

Institution Violence and Parole Outcome

While the focus of this review is upon the causes of violence in the institution, it seems acceptable to touch briefly upon how such behavior relates to subsequent adjustment on parole. Two efforts have addressed this issue, among others. Continuing the analysis of the behavior during the first year of incarceration, it was found from a study of 325 new admissions that *neither the number* of disciplinary actions *nor any violence* displayed during that first year *has any bearing on parole outcome.*[7] A second study involved some of the same subjects but examined their entire institutional adjustment, relating this adjustment to length of incarceration and to subsequent parole outcome. The presence or absence of disciplinary actions was found, not too surprisingly, to be related to time served in the institution for a sample of inmates convicted for First Degree Robbery and for Second Degree Burglary. However, this variable was related to parole outcome only in the case of the armed robbery group. A similar pattern was found for a *history* of institution violence; such a history was related to parole outcome for armed robbers; not related to parole outcome for the burglars.[8]

A review of Parole Work Unit Reports (a California parole program designed to assess the effectiveness of assignment of parolees to caseloads related to the amount of supervision effort required) for those released to parole 1968 through the first half of 1972 revealed very little difference between those with a history of aggressive behavior and those with lesser patterns in terms of subsequent aggression on parole—defined as murder, manslaughter, assault, rape, and kidnapping. Differences were statistically significant at the two-year parole outcome level however, with the more aggressive parolees revealing roughly twice the potential for subsequent involvement. The consequence of the finding loses impact when closer examination reveals that less than 2 percent of those with a history of major aggressive acts become reinvolved in violence—the overall average for the total release cohort seldom exceeds 1 percent. Since the historical accumulation takes into account any and all aggressive acts, it can be seen that institution violence can account for only a small portion of those characterized as having an aggressive history. Thus, by indirection, it seems fairly safe to conclude that institution violence is not strongly related to subsequent aggressive offenses during the parole period.

The Department of Finance Study

In an attempt to move from strict financial analyses toward a more programmatic review, a team from the California Department of Finance volunteered to undertake studies considered by the Department of Corrections as being of crucial significance. The two areas addressed were classification and violence. The classification study, needed to develop uniform definitions to allow for budgetary descriptions of the total population, soon was abandoned as the fascination of prison violence gripped the investigators. Initial efforts grew out of a statistical model of social motivation, which soon became ensnarled in the tangled realities of information limitations and operational constraints.[9] However, out of this effort emerged an interactional model that may well serve to move research toward improved understanding of the problem.[10]

First, characteristics of institutions were considered as well as the kinds of individuals involved in disruptive behavior. Using such indexes as might be revealed by the study of the characteristics of those involved in prison violence, institutions were measured as to their potential for explosiveness. Such items as the percentage of individuals under age 25, the percentage of inmates of Mexican ethnic background, the percentage of inmates whose most serious commitment offense was of an aggressive nature, all combined to provide a measure that could be related to periods marked by a high level of turbulent behavior. Preliminary assessment suggested a positive potential.

A secondary set of findings grew out of an attempt to assess the extent to which an individual inmate's expectations for self-development were fulfilled or thwarted by the programs offered or by the classification process. Again, *time constraints and informational limitations* caused a shift in emphasis with the result that a quasi-predictor of aggressive potential was postulated. The resulting set of characteristics was viewed as being valuable to the counseling staff in indicating which inmates might require special attention. It was postulated, and some support for this view was provided, that the extent that positive and negative "strokes" were applied would play a central role in whether the potential for obstreperous action would gain behavioral expression. The number of disciplinary reports would, of course, fall into the negative category. Laudatory chronological entries in the case history would be on the positive side as would high grades in a school or training program or the earning of a certificate. Transfers from tight custody institutions to more minimum settings would be a plus while a transfer, other than for administrative reasons, toward a more controlled setting would be a negative stroke. The implications of these preliminary findings are discussed in terms of further research to be undertaken as well as potential applications in the operational area.

Recent Ongoing Efforts

While not designated as a formal research project, the problem of violence engages one in a constant examination of possible clues.[11] The accumulation of data and speculation as to acceptable explanatory principles are seen as laying the groundwork for future research activities of a more comprehensive, directed nature. It is in this vein that the characteristics of identified aggressors have been studied over the period of 1960 to the present. (See table 11-5.)

Some stabilized patterns emerge. The Mexican–American Chicano group has rather consistently been overrepresented among the aggressors as contrasted to the total population from which they are drawn. Violent behavior seems to be related to youthfulness. In more recent years, aggressive attacks have been carried out by individuals who in many instances have entered the system with

Table 11-5
Characteristics of Male Felon Aggressors
in Stabbing Incidents, 1960-74

	1960 (N = 27)	1965 (N = 44)	1970 (N = 73)	1972 (N = 117)	1973 (N = 203)	1974 (N = 197)
Offense						
Assault:						
Designated aggressors	7.4	9.0	20.5	15.4	15.3	13.4
Institution population[a]	3.7	5.0	7.3	7.3	7.3	7.5
Homicide:						
Designated aggressors	11.1	11.4	19.2	21.4	22.8	18.4
Institution population	7.0	8.6	11.9	14.7	14.5	14.8
Ethnic Background						
White:						
Designated aggressors	51.9	40.9	34.3	35.9	35.6	36.3
Institution population	57.5	55.0	52.6	49.8	48.5	47.2
Mexican (Chicano):						
Designated aggressors	22.2	29.5	30.1	48.7	32.6	37.4
Institution population	17.1	16.4	16.6	16.7	17.6	18.1
Black:						
Designated aggressors	25.9	27.3	32.9	13.7	31.1	24.0
Institution population	23.1	26.9	29.8	32.0	32.3	33.0
Percentage Under Age of 25						
Designated aggressors	24.0	45.5	56.2	45.3	46.5	52.5
Institution population	18.5	19.2	20.6	21.9	20.2	20.5
Prior Jail or Juvenile Commitments Only—No Prior Prison						
Designated aggressors	51.9	61.4	72.7	73.5	71.8	73.7
Institution population	40.7	43.7	44.0	48.2	49.1	49.8

[a]Population characteristics are measured as of December 31 of the year under study.

a commitment offense that could be characterized as violent. An example of this phenomenon is the shifting pattern of homicide offenders. In the early 1960s, this group was minimally represented in those identified as attackers; in 1973 they were overrepresented among the violent aggressors. Inasmuch as the characteristics of all the various offense groups are changing over time, it seems probable that those entering the system convicted of the offense of homicide also have changed in terms of extent of involvement in criminality and past assaultive behavior.[12] Further, exploration of this possibility is currently being conducted.[13]

Another aspect being reviewed is the relationship between violent, disruptive behavior, and whether the individual has an established release date. Time constraints prohibit any extended discussion of the value and meaning of the indeterminate sentence. Suffice it to say that one aspect propounded by some is that the requirement to demonstrate readiness for release raises the level of anxiety in a group of people believed to be sociopathically oriented and thus anxiety free. Such anxiety arousal is believed necessary for positive changes to occur. In our most recent exploratory venture, the hypothesis was that not only is anxiety aroused that could be used for self-improvement but also it leads to frustration. When high levels of frustration occur in individuals who have high levels of aggressive potential, the crowded situation of most institutions creates an environment where minor encounters, which ordinarily might be brushed aside, get escalated into major confrontations. In figure 11-2, the pattern of incident reports and parole board denials tends to parallel each other for quite a period.[14] As this period was the first examined, hopes ran high that a major causative factor had been uncovered. However, the clarity dissipated when a longer period was considered. Such a finding does not mean necessarily that the relationship observed earlier was spurious; rather, it must be accepted that the relationship, if it exists, did not hold up over time.

A constant monitoring is maintained of the kinds of incidents occurring, their location, and an attempt is made to categorize the basis for assaults. As might be expected from earlier presentations, a high percentage during any period of review—month, quarter, or year—is related to gang or clique affiliations. The separation of activities attributable to allegiance to an organization and those related to strife between ethnic groups is often difficult inasmuch as some organizations are related, in part, to ethnic background. Kinds of weapons are also classified with the continued hope that they will become less and less lethal and move toward the more ineffective, makeshift type.

In December 1973 extreme operational controls were ordered in the major medium custody institutions of the California Department of Corrections. The clampdown was a reaction to a continued increase in inmate-inmate assault and attacks on staff. The latter occurrence was beginning to increase the level of apprehension on the part of staff. Administrators became concerned that such fears would lead to a total breakdown of communication between staff and

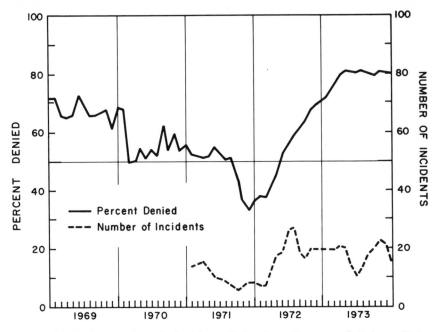

Figure 11-2. Inmate Assault Incidents Related to Percent of Release Dates Denied by Adult Authority.

inmates, further disrupting the smooth management of the institutions. A detailed statistical study of the first 11 months of the lockdown, based upon the routine data collected, revealed that no overall statistically significant reduction in violent incidents was in evidence.[15] Most of the assaults became confined to two of the institutions and tended to occur more often in lockup units than in general population situations. The interpretation of this latter finding is not at all clear. Some would contend that the assaults in the lockup units confirms that proper classification has been achieved, that the right (most assaultive) inmates were being separated from the rest of the inmate population. Those more inclined toward environmental explanations of behavior could just as easily explain the observed phenomenon on the basis that the obstreperous behavior occurred because the inmates were in lockup, increasing tensions and frustrations.

Additional Efforts at Control and Management

Two special efforts are worthy of mention. The first is a plan developed at Soledad. By the use of selected inmate leaders, communication links are established between, among, and within the various factions, gangs, and organizations within the Management Control Unit at California Training Facility-North. No formal research has been attempted to unravel the effective mechanisms involved; the routine counts reveal that the number of incidents is far below that expected considering the youthful, volatile, and aggressive inmates housed in the unit.

The second effort occurred earlier this year, at Deuel Vocational Institution, second only to San Quentin in terms of contribution to the growing number of assaults. The leaders felt something must be done. Conflict Resolution Training has been provided for a limited number of staff by the U. S. Department of Justice under a special LEAA grant. The application of the learned skills had been attempted by small teams relating to staff morale problems. It was decided to test the mettle of the approach by applying the techniques to the problem of intergroup conflicts. Initial success was pronounced with rival gangs participating in mutual problem-solving sessions. During this brief blissful period, assaults dropped off markedly. Subsequently one of the groups has broken off all negotiations and refused to participate. Violence seems, however, to be increasing, but slowly. It is still early to tell if significant effects have been achieved.

Policy Implications

If one looks at this collection of research findings, there is little that suggests direct official action that will suddenly reduce violence. When one reads between the lines of the research findings, it soon becomes clear that the nature of assaultive behavior in California prisons has shifted from behavior arising out of individual-to-individual conflict toward a significant portion of the violence being related to quasi-political organizations that have many of the characteristics of the underworld gang. Thus, the individual motivational factors must still be taken into consideration but no one must jump to the conclusion that corrective measures developed to deal with such problems will significantly affect the kinds of behavior dictated by gang membership. Near kamikaze attacks have been encountered with little or no effort made to avoid detection. No remorse or contrition is expressed, with the view that behavior in the name of the cause is legitimate and retaliatory, or restrictive measures are simple attempts at political repression.

Despite the many limitations of available research findings, there are some actions that can be contemplated. Some of these have already been initiated, others are in the planning stage, while others may be proved inapplicable when subjected to the test of feasibility.

First, it would appear that sufficient knowledge is available to attempt to control the mix of people with certain kinds of characteristics that reside in a given institution. The accumulation of too many youthful offenders with a history of violent behavior and assaultive offenses is likely to result in a high potential for explosive behavior. The application of this technique, however, is fraught with danger and must be attempted with caution, for to change the composition of one population will modify the mix of characteristics at other prisons; often institutions that have been operating trouble-free because of the kinds of inmates housed there. The indices, previously mentioned, could be refined to provide an early alert system that might head off potential problems.

Inmate involvement in the development of rules and procedures may provide a mechanism for at least ameliorating some of the strong hostility generated by tight custodial controls. The work at CTF-North must be seen as pioneering; whether it is something that can be applied in other settings remains to be seen. However, from a variety of other research, the variable of *involvement* seems to underlie positive shifts of attitude.[16] Further, research on the Watts riot suggests that a feeling of powerlessness is related to a willingness to loosen social controls.[17]

In terms of individual characteristics and subsequent adjustment, care must be taken not to rush into a predictive device, for on the one hand such procedures assume immutability of the personality and adjustment, and on the other hand lead to preventative action likely to be inappropriately applied because of the large number of false positives inevitable when one attempts to predict the rare event.[18] However, it now seems possible to develop a device that reflects a changing potential as conditions shift or as frustrations accumulate. Such an instrument should provide a barometer that can signal the need for special counseling that might be of value in averting the anticipated disruption. Currently in the planning stage, a control group approach is being contemplated to insure that the procedure actually results in fewer disciplinary reports and violent incidents.

Enhancing the opportunities for each inmate to express his individuality is seen as a worthwhile attempt to reduce discontent. The Committee to Implement Recommendations of the Task Force of Violence has made a number of valuable suggestions along this line. Supplying paint of different colors and allowing inmates to paint their own cells in a color of their own choosing might well make life more meaningful for some inmates. It should be noted that there is no naive assumption that such a measure will induce a disruptive inmate to become a model prisoner but such efforts might reduce the number of essentially conforming inmates who inadvertently find their way into difficulties through frustration, discontent, and a sense of hopelessness.

Offering a life-style as challenging as inmate organizational activity represents a real stumbling block to administration. The opportunity to attend school or learn a trade pales considerably when compared to the prestige of being a captain of enforcers in a well-organized group.

Future Research Needs and Plans

As can be seen, it has been only recently that there has been a shift away from the emphasis upon the individual as the source of motivation for violence toward looking at aspects of the social, psychological, and physical environment that impinges upon that individual.

An examination of the effectiveness of a changing status indicator has been mentioned. While the assumption is that the potential for violence rests with the individual, there is a recognition that the inmate is involved in an interaction system; that what happens to him affects how he views himself and how he reacts to the world around himself. It seems likely that further experience with such an instrument will lead to additional refinements, markedly enhancing its usefulness.

Among identified aggressors, the Chicano group has been overrepresented as compared to the general departmental population in each study examined from 1960 to the present. While clinical observers would insist that the nature of their involvement has changed over the extended span of time, the fact of their overinvolvement cannot be avoided. Considerable efforts have been expended to ameliorate the situation but have proved to be ineffective thus far. Correctional programs of the past have reflected the prevailing cultural standard that anyone whose native tongue is different from English should immediately give up their natural mode of communication and "speak American" and adopt the folkways of the Anglo group. More recently, attempts have been made to understand the macho and machismo needs of the Mexican male. Special cultural self-study groups have been formed and more recognition has been given to the cultural heritage of the Chicano. Menu preparation has taken into account the taste preferences of different cultural groups. However, our knowledge is far from complete in this area. Thus, one likely area of future research might be a cultural-anthropological study of the Chicano in prison with the aim of improved understanding and the development of accommodation maneuvers to minimize the need for members of this group to express their frustrations through violent behavior.

The longer range research efforts must be directed toward the development of a complex interactive model. Involved in such a model would be a combination of individual predispositions and institutional stresses, cross-laced with situational intrusions. The research model for an approach of this nature has been developed by Ellis, Grasnick, and Gilman.[19] By a series of correlational coefficients arranged in a directional fashion, some sense of causality can be deduced. The results of such efforts might well increase understanding of violent behavior in the correctional institution and might even lead to practical guides for action. For example, a configural analysis might result that would provide a rough probability guide to decision makers that would include the kinds of variables mentioned. A Chicano, under age 25, might have a 7 percent probability of being involved in assaultive behavior, no matter into what institution he is placed. However, if placed in California Training Facility at Soledad or in Deuel Vocational Institution at Tracy, the probability of involvement might rise to 10 or 12 percent; if, on the other hand, he is placed in a forestry camp or in California Institution for Men at Chino, the likelihood of his becoming involved in disruptive behavior might drop down to around 2 percent. Placement in the trade training of his choice might also reduce his aggressivity quotient by say another 2 percent. The probabilities are fictional but there appears to be a sufficient accumulation of findings and an adequate availability of data to make the development of such a system within the realm of possibility.

A natural experiment is already under way. Earlier the notion was explored that not knowing the date of release to parole might be viewed as frustrating by a prisoner. Recent changes in procedures by the Adult Authority, the parole board in California, have resulted in a high percentage of release dates set at each hearing. By February of next year, between 80 and 90 percent of all inmates in the various institutions will know the expected date of their release whether in the near or distant future (as contrasted to the 12 to 15 percent during late 1974 and early 1975). If earlier speculation has any relationship to reality, there should be a steady reduction of assaultive behavior over the next few months with a most peaceful climate in existence by March or April of 1976. The plan is to eventually determine the length of institutional stay very early in the inmate's career, perhaps at the end of reception-center processing.

While these future research plans look somwhat sketchy, especially considering the gravity of the problem being confronted, the major effort, the second one mentioned above, should provide major findings of significance to the field. The project as outlined will require extensive expenditure of manpower, a comprehensive planning program and considerable mathematical, statistical analytic power to bring it to completion. The third element, we believe, has been identified. The first two then become a matter of time and muscle to move forward. The culmination of such a project should lead to valuable insights and pave the way for further progress toward viable solutions.

Notes

1. Dorothy R. Jaman, Patricia Coburn, Jackie Goddard, and Paul F. C. Mueller, *Characteristics of Violent Prisoners (San Quentin, 1960),* Research Report No. 22, Research Division, California Department of Corrections, Sacramento, 1966.

2. State of California, Department of Corrections, *Report of the Task Force to Study Violence in Prison,* 1965, p. 6.

3. Ibid.

4. John P. Conrad, "The Nature and Treatment of the Violent Offender: A Typology of Violence," *A Typology of Violent Offenders,* Carol Spencer, ed., Research Report No. 23, Research Division, California Department of Corrections, Sacramento, 1966.

5. Dorothy R. Jaman, *Behavior During the First Year in Prison, Report I–Description,* Research Report, No. 32, Research Division, California Department of Corrections, Sacramento, 1968.

6. Dorothy R. Jaman, *Behavior During the First Year in Prison, Report II–MMPI Scales and Behavior,* Research Report No. 34, Research Division, California Department of Corrections, Sacramento, 1969.

7. Dorothy R. Jaman, *Behavior During the First Year in Prison, Report III–Background Characteristics,* Research Report, No. 43, Research Division, California Department of Corrections, Sacramento, 1972.

8. Dorothy B. Jaman, Robert M. Dickover, and Lawrence A. Bennett, "Parole Outcome as a Function of Time Served," British Journal of Criminology, 12 (January 1972), 5–34.

9. Otis D. Duncan, Archibald O. Haller, and Alejandro Portes, "Peer Influences on Aspirations: A Reinterpretation," *Causal Models in the Social Sciences,* H. M. Blalock, Jr., ed., (Chicago: Aldine, 1971), 219–44.

10. Burt Cohen, Rich Gould, Sandra Felderstein, Leroy Bell, John Broussard, and Curtin Rogers, "A Study of Violence," California Department of Finance, Sacramento, 1975.

11. Lawrence A. Bennett, "A Brief Analysis of Characteristics of Male Felon Inmates Designated as Aggressors in Stabbing Incidents," Research Division, California Department of Corrections, Sacramento, 1974 (mimeo).

12. Robert M. Dickover, "A Study of Trends Among Newly Admitted Male Felons, 1960-1973," Research Division, California Department of Corrections, Sacramento, 1974, (mimeo).

13. Victor Bluestein, "Homicide Offenders and Stabbing Incidents," Study Proposal Submitted to Departmental Research Advisory Council, Research Division, California Department of Corrections, Sacramento, 1975.

14. Bennett, "Characteristics of Male Felon Inmates."

15. Howard Bidna, "Effects of Increased Security on Prison Violence," Research Division, California Department of Corrections, Sacramento, 1974, (mimeo).

16. J. Douglas Grant and Joan Grant, "Contagion as a Principle in Behavior Change," *Unique Programs in Behavior Readjustment* (Elmsford, N. Y.: Pergamon, 1970); Stuart Adams, *The San Quentin Prison College Project: Final Report,* School of Criminology, University of California, Berkeley, 1968.

17. H. Edward Ransford, "Isolation, Powerlessness, and Violence: A Study of Attitudes and Participation in the Watts Riot," *The Dynamics of Aggression,* Edwin I. Megargee and Jack E. Hokanson, eds. (New York: Harper and Row, 1970), 145–59.

18. Ernst A. Wenk, James O. Robinson, and Gerald W. Smith, "Can Violence Be Predicted?" *Crime and Delinquency,* 18 (October 1972), 393-402.

19. Desmond Ellis, Harold G. Grasnick, and Bernard Gilman, "Violence in Prisons: A Sociological Anslysis," *American Journal of Sociology,* 80 (1974), 16-43.

12

Dealing With Prison Violence
George W. Sumner

Much of the progress that has been made to reduce violence at Soledad during the past 18 months is in jeopardy at the time of this writing. Approximately 25 Mexican-American inmates in one of the sections have attacked and stabbed 7 whites. One man is dead, and 2 are near death. This is a serious setback for the program and policies that we have been pursuing. Before this happened, we had had only about 5 stabbings in 18 months. Now we have 7 in 1 day with the possibility of retaliation by the whites looming. But even with this setback, we have made progress at Soledad and it will hopefully continue into the future.

During the past two years an attempt has been made to reduce the level of violence by encouraging the development of a cadre of inmate leaders who could be counted on to maintain lines of communication and to work with the staff to stop the stabbings and other forms of violence. This Social Catalyst Program is based on the assumption that peer pressure can be used to reduce violence; but it requires the commitment of all—superintendent, staff, and inmates.

By almost any standard, Soledad is a large, maximum-security facility. It currently holds about 3,300 men divided into three units: north, containing about 1,200; central, with 1,600; and south, with almost 500. Not only is there a racial and ethnic mix, but these inmate groupings have been well organized— Hells Angels, Aryan Brothers, Mexican Mafia, Nuestra Familia, Black Guerrilla Family—they all have members in Soledad. Soledad has had a history of racial violence in recent years; besides the well-publicized murder of George Jackson, there has been a continuous stream of fights and stabbings that have made portions of the institution unsafe.

An Approach to Prison Violence

About two years ago a new superintendent arrived and announced that his number one goal was to stop the violence. This was his direction to staff and to inmate population. He immediately established himself as a man of integrity and credibility who was truly interested in the needs of the inmates. He allowed inmates to wear personal clothing, he relaxed the hair and mustache regulations, he permitted radios and TVs in the cells, and he brought a number of trailers onto the grounds for family visits. These actions helped to reduce many of the minor, tension-causing irritants of inmate life and to demonstrate that this superintendent was a man interested in positive change. However, his most important strategy was to develop a policy of encouraging rapport between the staff and a selected group of inmate leaders—indiviuduals who had the respect of the others and who were tired of the warring and stabbings, persons who could act as social catalysts or mediators between inmates or between inmates and staff.

In the North Unit we began by meeting over a period of time with about 30 of these inmates who had been selected by the staff because: (a) they were the official or unofficial leaders of their racial groups; (b) they had the respect of the hardcore element of their group; (c) they were thought to be men of principle who would live up to their word; and (d) they had a desire to reduce violence. They were not the verbal pseudo-intellectual inmates who usually sit on advisory committees, but we sought the quiet individual who had settled arguments in the past. We found that often the best selectees were men who had been involved in gang violence and were now tired of it—an analogy would be the old gunfighter who wants to hang up his guns.

We met with these inmates for a considerable time and emphasized that we were not interested in placing blame but mainly in preventing violence. We tried to convey the message that we were striving to create a healthy atmosphere. Although maintaining control was necessary, it was recognized that reasonable privileges and a certain amount of freedom was desirable. Inmates were encouraged to make recommendations for change that would improve the situation. In turn, administrators worked through these inmates when changes were contemplated.

Eventually six of these inmates with ties to each of the racial groups were selected to act as communicators and liaison between the administration–custodial personnel and the inmate population. These social catalysts were encouraged to call us any time, day or night, at home or on the job, whenever they heard of inmate problems. First, the problems were relatively minor and concerned visiting, family crises, and work situations—the type of problem that was not being handled by the case worker or by the uniformed staff. The procedure was for the catalyst to bring the problem directly to a key administrator. Staff were instructed to make themselves available and to take action immediately. In time more serious matters were brought to our attention—inmates needing protective custody, those with debts or sexual pressures, those needing a transfer to another unit.

Within a few months, inmates from the general population of the North Unit were bringing their problems to the representatives so that the staff could learn about needs that could not get up through the maze of the bureaucracy. When there were changes in procedures or programs, or new dictates from Sacramento, we would, in turn, inform this inmate group of what we were doing and why. We would give them written statements that they could pass around to other inmates to let the entire population know that was happening. We were thus using them as our communicators. This became more and more refined so that generally the catalysts were able to build a consensus among the general population that violence was going to be avoided.

This formula has been strengthened so that the catalysts are able to play a more basic role in conflict management. If there is a fight, they will physically separate the combatants. They will help parties settle debts. If there are problems between two inmates because of something that happened on the outside—perhaps one has been living with a common-law partner while on the outside—the mediators will come to us to discuss the situation and to decide which one should be moved. If men are transferred into the North Unit who belong to a faction of one of the warring groups, the mediator will probably tell us that man does not belong here and we will transfer him out. He is usually very willing to move. If the problem is interracial the mediators from those groups will get together, then check with members of their own race, and then meet again together to work out a solution. All of this is healthy. It has been accepted by the general body of inmates and has reduced the violence. Where another major California institution had approximately 90 stabbings last year, we had 3.

Some may ask why an inmate would be willing to assume this role of social catalyst. There are probably some who truly believe that they are performing an important function and are willing to do it on that basis. However, it is also important that they get recognition and rewards for putting themselves on the line. We assign them to this job as full-time workers with an office and pay. They receive $32 a month, the highest inmate pay in the institution. When they are paroled we attempt to place them in jobs commensurate with their abilities. I was able to get one appointed as a counselor in the Monterey County Boys Ranch. Another is an employee at the Correctional Training Facility as canteen manager, and a third is now in a civil service position at our Departmental Training Academy in Modesto as an administrative assistant. While at Soledad, these men have a lot of status with both inmates and staff. When they go before the Adult Authority we write recommendations pointing out that they have been a mediator for the period of time, that they have endangered their lives and have had to walk the narrow line between their fellow inmates and staff.

The Role of Staff

The key to this approach is staff acceptance. You have to have a very flexible, loyal, willing staff at all levels or this method will not work. The staff must be trained so that they will have a sense of the importance of the plan, will support it, and will change their behavior accordingly. They must become attuned to human relations and be willing to support the inmate catalysts even if it goes against the grain of traditional norms. The catalysts will often have to go out on a limb for you in their relations with staff and fellow inmates. If they voluntarily bring inmate problems to you for solution, you cannot demand that they inform. You must respect their confidences and conversations with you. If you ask them unreasonable questions or make unreasonable demand such as telling you who stabbed whom, you impugn their integrity and they become ineffective. Their effectiveness or their lives cannot be jeopardized by indiscriminate talk among staff members that will surely get back to the inmate body. In addition, staff must also not get the idea that the inmate facilitators can be coopted into becoming pseudo-officers.

What we had to do was to be very demanding of the top staff to get them to accept the approach and to bring people in at the lieutenant's level who could carry out our goals. We picked officers who had their college degrees and preferred those from minority groups. We encouraged them to be counselors for a year and then transferred them across as lieutenants. As a result, all of our recent appointees have been counselors and have been selected on the basis that they are going to carry out our approach and work with the people. The whole emphasis is on working with inmates.

The idea that you are going to consult inmates is very threatening to some staff. Inflexible lieutenants at the watch commander level are not going to listen or are not going to give up their power to inmates or accept suggestions for change with an open mind. That is why we have the younger, more flexible type of second-line supervisor to implement our procedures. Recruitment, selection, and training of staff are essential to this approach. We recruit staff statewide by going to the colleges and looking for good officer material. We tell them that they can work for effective change within the system by working for the Department of Corrections. We have brought our minority staff members from 6 percent to 27 percent, and this is a steady progression.

The training of both recruits and in-service personnel has to be drastically altered away from the standard routine of firing range, restraint, counts, locking devices, etc., to one where human relations, ethnic culture, techniques of supervision, and the functions of a manager are emphasized. Training must not take a back seat. This means that your instructors have to be committed to their work and the students must recognize that the training they receive will help them in their work. They must be able to see their place in the goal of reducing violence and lessening tension. In addition, the staff must recognize that unprofessional behavior that is demeaning, prejudiced, or overly moralistic will not be tolerated. Inmates must be viewed as fellow human beings and individuals. Whatever actions are taken are directed at the behavior, not the person. Discipline must be firm but fair.

When Violence Occurs

Nothing is more weakening to efforts made to reduce violence than for staff to be unconcerned when it breaks out. You must demonstrate that you sincerely care about lives. If a stabbing or murder of an inmate occurs it must be investigated and handled in exactly the same way as if the victim was a correctional officer or administrator. Immediately seal off the exits, search for weapons, bloody clothing, etc. Interview in private all inmates who had access to the area. Show your concern by asking why it happened and what can be done to prevent it from happening again. Good results will follow if the members of the investigative team have demonstrated that they are persons of integrity and have established relationships with the inmates through their regular work contacts. If they have been abusive, moralistic, or indifferent they will not receive much information. Lock the inmates down who had access to the area and have the inmate catalysts walk the tiers talking to the inmates to get a feel for the situation and ascertain if further violence is likely if they are released prematurely. In other words, when violence occurs you must take it seriously and show that you really care.

Summary

On the basis of our experience, this is a realistic approach to the problem of prison violence. Gang membership has declined and there are some former members who have disassociated themselves from these groups. I have been able to travel to the different institutions throughout the state and pull out over 100 inmates from various adjustment centers, people who could not move freely within the general population, and brought them to our Departmental Management Control Unit at Soledad. The approach that we have developed is an alternative to keeping people locked up 23 hours a day—for their own protection or that of others. Violence has been reduced because the entire inmate body is exerting peer pressure to eliminate armed assaults.

Postscript, December 1975

Two inmates died and several others suffered serious injuries in the attack that occurred as this chapter was being prepared. The attack was by members of the Mexican Mafia on white inmates that resulted from an earlier fist fight between whites and Mexican-Americans. The catalysts had assurances from the inmates that the hard feelings resulting from the fist fight had been resolved. Because the commitments to remain peaceful had been broken there was a great deal of suspicion and animosity between the white and Mexican-American catalysts after the stabbings. This undermined the foundation of our catalyst program, which is based on mutual acceptance and cooperation.

Neither my staff nor I could ascertain if the white catalysts were planning revenge and if the Mexican-American catalysts had been involved in planning the knife attack. Both groups requested polygraph examinations of the other. All of the catalysts were tested and passed in a positive manner. A leader of the Mexican Mafia was given a polygraph examination and failed. We then began to help the catalysts regain each other's trust and to urge them to assist us in our efforts to prevent retaliation by the whites. We were successful and the catalyst program is stronger and more effective than it has ever been. Soledad continues to have a greatly reduced rate of violence and improved racial harmony.

One or two members of the conference voiced their concern that the catalyst system would create more gang members. This has not been the case. Members of the Nuestra Familia in the general population of the Correctional Training Facility severed relationships with the statewide gang because of its insistence on perpetuating stabbings. This was followed by the members of the Black Guerilla Family disassociating themselves from the statewide gang because of stabbing contracts being sent on individuals at North Facility. Recently the leaders of our Muslim religion have declared themselves supportive of our efforts to reduce violence and have offered their assistance. I consider these to be immense steps in reducing the prison gang's effectiveness.

One possible problem with the inmate catalyst program is the undermining and/or diluting of the authority (real or imagined) of line personnel. To negate this problem, the administrator must establish and maintain an aggressive, open method of communicating with line personnel, and between line personnel and the inmate catalysts. If the second-line supervisors (lieutenants) and first-line supervisors (sergeants) believe the administration is bypassing them by conducting business directly with the inmate catalysts, the entire program will be in great jeopardy. When the inmate catalysts are responsive to the needs of the line correctional officer, and line personnel perceive the program as beneficial to their day-to-day operation, the use of inmate catalysts will be successful. A high degree of trust must be developed. An atmosphere must prevail in which neither party (staff or inmate) feels that he or she is being used—taken unfair advantage of.

The Social Catalyst Program is simple in design, but requires total dedication and implementation if any appreciable results are expected. The key is credibility and application. The administration, from the superintendent down, must verbalize and actualize commitment to the program. This has been the key to successfully reducing violence in our specific facility.

We have also indicated the extreme importance of staff selection and the makeup of the men who actually implement the program on a day-to-day basis. As evidenced by the anecdotes and narratives of past successes and failures, the catalyst program is an extremely sensitive and dynamic process by which both staff and inmates benefit. When observing or analyzing the process, the casual observer fails to grasp the intricate balance between success and failure when dealing with highly emotional and volatile inmates. It is difficult to operate successfully a business or system of well-balanced, motivated people. Imagine for one moment attempting to rehabilitate several hundred inmates who have already demonstrated their inability to conform to the rules of society—inmates who have psychological and developmental problems, who have a total disregard for the well-being or the safety of themselves and their fellow beings. To coordinate such a program is a task that cannot be understood unless directly involved in its implementation.

We are not stating that this program will work in other institutions if drawn exactly from our design. The concepts and principles, however, are the basic rudiments of managing violent inmates in a volatile situation. In the final analysis, the rewards and failures cannot be measured to a degree that you can rate as success or nonsuccess. The rewards come from within, and are the result of people dealing with people in a situation that often determines whether a person will live or die.

Discussion

Irwin: I have reservations and fears about the direction of your approach. The period of peace that you have experienced is going to be followed by a period of enhanced violence, which to some extent is going to be of your own making. You've taken the rather ephemeral, informal social structure of these gangs and have crystalized them in an official way which is going to be much more difficult to back off from. You have not paid attention to the many studies of working with the gangs in New York. Over and over again these studies have shown that the more attention you pay to the gang, the more gang-like it becomes. The more they endure, the more they participate in the kinds of behaviors that they were accused of. It is a self-fulfilling prophecy. Moreover, you've ignored, and made it more difficult, almost impossible, for nongang members. One fault is your method of selection. If you are going to create a position of inmate leader, it is as if you went into New York to hold an election for the mayor, went around to the toughest bullies, and said, "O.K. come up with your toughest bullies," and we would have a Mafia mayor.

If we are to seek inmate participation in the decision-making process we have to be committed to constitutional principles. There must be an expression from all sections of the population as to who is to be their leaders. I would insist upon a secret ballot by all of the inmates. This notion that you are going to select someone bothers me. I know how the system works. You may pick an inmate leader, he has the job for six months, and then when he is ready to go out you ask him to recommend some people. He goes around and picks all his friends. You check on them and pick the one you think is most talented. You are probably perceptive in picking who is an inmate leader, but still you have no idea what segment of the population is being totally ignored by this guy. Little cliques of people take over little sections of the prison and they perpetuate themselves, and they make sure that all their friends get the jobs. That is what you are catering to. Moreover, it is inevitable that you are going to have the kind of violence that you are having. You're going to prolong the period of terror that came in with all that gang stuff. I recommend that you ignore those gangs—they are not a basis on which to build a political and social structure—even if it means a period of letting them fight it out for awhile. But any official recognition of the gangs is going to mean that it is going to take that much longer to get out of the mess.

Sumner: We don't recognize the gangs. The selection process was to take the leadership, not of the gangs necessarily, but of the inmates that were there at the time. We picked the 20 or so individuals what we thought were the leaders out of the 600 people there. Reduce that down to 6. Most of the 6 are not members of a gang. We selected 2 from each race.

Conrad: There seems to be a great deal of dependence on the personality and the discretion of the wardens running a program like this. Some wardens could do it, while there are other wardens that couldn't. I wonder how much interest there is among your colleagues, among your wardens.

Sumner: They sent representatives from another institution to look at our program, and I advised them not to do it. I don't think it would work at that institution any way at all, because of the entrenched lieutenants that are there.

Toch: What Soledad is doing is reminiscent of our efforts to reduce violence in the Oakland Police Department. The strategy was almost completely parallel. We took the most violence-prone police officers that we could find and set them to solve the violence problem. They not only instituted a program where there was peer review of incidents but we built a subculture there, which sounds very much like yours. Of our original seven officers, six were promoted to sergeant and one of them, as a matter of principle, didn't want to be a sargeant. They are all now in very substantial positions in the department.

The experience with gangs is the issue of maintaining cohesion or breaking them up, the problem of who gets coopted, which showed up very substantially in the Chicago expeiences, and has to do with the maintaining of the structure but not too much monitoring of the direction. One is dealing here with a matter of the subcultures, and it is a fact that one is stuck with. You didn't segregate these people. The Department of Corrections in California has taken the position of dealing with violence by having wolf versus wolf settings instead of wolf versus sheep settings. There are different strategies when one deals with these two types of settings. But once you have a wolf-wolf setting you are stuck with the composition and informal normative system and everything else that goes with it. At that point one's hope is in reversing the violence in that subculture if one can. Then one has to deal with the pushes and pulls of the larger subculture. Obviously under those circumstances one has to select people of both strength and credibility. The danger is that of creating a kind of subsegment that gets bypassed within the subcultural base, or even worse, creating something that then gets built into the ongoing warfare. That does not necessarily occur if two conditions are met: one, there is a kind of problem-solving emphasis where everyone says, well we've got a violence problem here and these social catalyst people have some kind of formal role but it's all our problem, we are all going to be very aware of this from day to day.

Another thing that one has to pay very close attention to is, how does one protect what is going on from the reward system that is involved? One can do this among other things by a continuing, open communication system, and also by making entirely sure that one is aware of when that subculture forms. There are other things that one can do and we have a whole catalogue of them.

Sumner: I have been around to the various adjustment centers in the state and pulled a great number of inmates out and into this unit that otherwise would be locked up 23 hours a day. Our gang membership is being reduced. What this unit does provide is an alternative to keeping inmates locked up 23 hours a day. It is an attempt by the administration to reduce violence and reduce inmates from being unnecessarily locked up.

Park: There is the general problem of selection of inmates if you are going to have inmate participation in management. So far we have not had a process at work to elect people who are really respected by the inmates. The hoodlums determine what happens on the yard anyway and you need to respond to this. What we really need is more than just Soledad's operation but systematic experimentation of how you do it. But if we let the Prisoner's Union in, we would have the same problem of the inmate politican getting elected and I don't believe he represents the other inmates.

Also, one of the problems—where six inmates can call the deputy superintendent—is that you've got to take account of the correctional officer who is walking his beat, who also needs some access to the power structure.

Wilsnack: What is valid is that there may be something provocative in the very fact that there is growing inmate organization within this section of the prison, such that the young Chicano prisoners coming in engage in violence as a declaration of independence from a structure that is presented to them as, "this is the way things are, take it or leave it." So in a sense, the conditions work against violence that is organized and yet they serve to provoke new inmates to try and engage in unorganized and spontaneous violence as sort of a declaration of independence.

Irwin: I find it peculiar that the California Department of Correction responded so unbelievably and unreasonably to the reliable, responsible organizations such as the prisoner's union. Yet, they have built this system on the gangs.

If you respond to a gang like this you will never get a request for any structural change. All you will get is an argument over who is guilty of the games that are quite common in prison. None of those men ever came up and talked to me about the indeterminate sentences. You took the men who maybe had some potential for developing a broader perspective and made them little big shots. It is the perfect system of cooling out any potential person who may have emerged as a responsible human being. If you take some good men and make them into self-help people they become more serviceable to the system—a very conservative, successful approach. Whenever you have a group of people who lack privileges, and lack power, if you pick out their leader and give them a little job, and let them become part of the system, then you reduce the strength of the potential protest. That is what you've done. You may not have thought of this but the reason that you have been allowed to do this experiment is because it is not threatening to the overall system. If it were found out that you catered to the prison union members in there, and they had a contact outside, I would guarantee you that the message would come from Sacramento: "Stop that nonsense. We don't want any part of that prisoners union." Even though the men would be working with you in an entirely different fashion. There wouldn't be any murders involved. It would be something entirely different. It would be the fact that they are now bringing up issues that are going to require structural changes, and that is intolerable.

Jacobs: In Illinois the Soledad policy was attempted for several years at Pontiac; the results were far from salutary; there was a great deal of violence and fear. A further disturbing possibility is the strengthening of these proto-organizations to the point where they will develop into criminal syndicates that will move into areas of organized crime. We have already begun to see this in Illinois and, in part, it was a consequence of government policy. First, the federal government gave grants to illegitimate structures like the Black P Stone Nation and then they were deferred to by some prison people the way you are describing here, legitimizing their organizations and leadership. The end result may be a serious crime problem on the streets. What responsibility do the prison authorities have to prevent this from happening?

Sumner: On the other hand, the morale of the uniform staff is extremely high. I am not dealing just with the gang members. There are a lot of other people involved that we are working with. But what we have said is that just because a man is a gang member he is not rejected from our program. The fact that he is a gang member is very real and we are listening to him the same as anyone else that has some leadership qualities.

Wheeler: To the extent that energies get concentrated on what is going on inside the institution, and to the extent that the staff is spending its time organizing what is going on inside, it is preventing disruption. But to the extent that one promotes the salience of what goes on inside there will be an absence of promoting the development of the inmate's relationship to the outside world, which is what one ought to be trying to work on while he's in. There is a limit as to what can be done, but by recognizing the legitimacy of inmate groups, of gangs, you build up the reality of those things in their life. In doing that you loose something else. If the same amount of staff energy were going into promoting the relationship of the outside world around the prison to what is going on inside, so that the inmate was more worried about jobs outside, about relatives outside, about everything else outside, the inmate would be better prepared for his return to the community. What you want to do is to make the institution much less rather than much more. The concentration of energy in this particular direction may do exactly the opposite.

Ohlin: It is hard for us to judge to what extent this sort of reeducation and legitimacy of the gangs is going to amount to anything. There is ample evidence that this is not happening. We need better understanding of what the criteria are by which we are going to recognize whether that phenomena is taking place. You have to look at the total system. You are describing a part of a very large system of corrections. The strategy is to segregate the violent offenders but what has this done to the rest of the system? In appraising whether you want to legitimize these gangs you have to take account of all the costs and benefits across the total system, and not by focusing on what is going on in this particular unit.

Author Index

Author Index

About the Editors and Contributors

Robert G. Bailey received the master of public affairs degree in correctional administration from The University of Connecticut. He is currently assistant ombudsman to the Connecticut Correctional System.

Lawrence A. Bennett is chief of research, California Department of Corrections, having served in a variety of positions in the correctional field of that state beginning in 1952. He is the author of articles published in professional journals. Dr. Bennett has been a consultant to a number of organizations, including the National Institute on Law Enforcement and Criminal Justice, the United States Army Retraining Command, the National Council on Crime and Delinquency, and the Institute for the Study of Crime and Delinquency.

Albert K. Cohen is a university professor and a member of the Sociology Department of The University of Connecticut. He is author of *Delinquent Boys: The Culture of the Gang* (1955) and *Deviance and Control* (1966).

George F. Cole is an associate professor of political science and director of the Corrections Program at The University of Connecticut. His published works include *Politics and the Administration of Justice* (1973), *Criminal Justice: Law and Politics* (1972), *Politics and the Administration of Justice* (1973), and *The American System of Criminal Justice* (1976).

John P. Conrad is a senior fellow of the Academy for Contemporary Problems, Columbus, Ohio. His career in correctional occupations began as a California parole officer in 1946. He was chief of research of the United States Bureau of Prisons from 1967 to 1969, and chief of the Center for Crime Prevention and Rehabilitation in the National Institute of Law Enforcement and Criminal Justice from 1969 to 1972. He has taught at the University of California at Davis, the University of Pennsylvania, and Ohio State University.

Edith Elisabeth Flynn is associate professor of criminal justice at Northeastern University. She is co-founder of the National Clearinghouse for Criminal Justice Planning and Architecture and was a member of the Task Force on Corrections, National Advisory Commission on Criminal Justice Standards and Goals. Her extensive research and writing has focused on the collective violence and the influence of environment on criminal justice goals.

James B. Jacobs holds a joint appointment as assistant professor of law and sociology at Cornell University. His interest in prison organization grows out of his doctoral and postdoctoral research at The University of Chicago. Between 1972 and 1975 he conducted several related studies of Stateville Penitentiary, Joliet, Illinois.

Edwin I. Megargee, professor of psychology at Florida State University, is the author of 4 books and has contributed approximately 40 articles to professional journals. A past president of the American Association of Correctional Psychologists and a member of the Board of Directors of the American Correctional Association, he has been a consultant to the Bureau of Prisons since 1967.

Kenneth E. Moyer is professor of psychology at Carnegie-Mellon University. The author of numerous scientific articles and five books, including, The Physiology of Hostility (1971), *You and Your Child—Primer for Parents* (1974), and *The Psychobiology of Aggression* (in press), Dr. Moyer is editor in chief of the international journal *Aggressive Behavior.* He is a fellow of the Division of Psychopharmacology, American Psychological Association, and a fellow of the American Association for the Advancement of Science.

William G. Nagel, author of the widely cited book *The New Red Barn: A Critical Look at the Modern American Prison,* is executive vice-president of The American Foundation, and director of its Institute of Corrections. Mr. Nagel's professional career has been primarily in the field of corrections, having worked for the Pennsylvania Prison Society, the New Jersey Department of Correction, and the National Council on Crime and Delinquency. He served as consultant to the President's Commission on Law Enforcement and the Administration of Justice (1967) and was a member of the National Advisory Commission on Criminal Justice Standards and Goals (1973).

James W.L. Park began his professional career with the California Department of Corrections as a clinical psychologist at the California Institution for Men at Chico. He was chief psychologist for the Department from 1956 to 1962; associate superintendent, Correctional training Facility, Soledad, from 1962 to 1964; associate warden at San Quentin from 1964 to 1973; and is currently chief of research and planning services for the Department of Corrections.

George W. Sumner has had an extensive and varied career with the California Department of Corrections. Since 1972 he has been deputy superintendent of the Correctional Training Facility—North, Soledad, California.

Hans Toch, professor of psychology at the School of Criminal Justice, State University of New York—Albany, is the author or editor of seven books, including *The Social Psychology of Social Movements* (1965). A fellow in the

American Psychological Association, his current research focuses on violence in the criminal justice system.

Richard W. Wilsnack is assistant professor of sociology at Indiana University. He received the Ph.D. from Harvard University. His major research interests are in collective behavior and deviance. He is currently studying the preconditions of prison disturbances, general characteristics of collective behavior episodes, and (with his wife, Sharon, a clinical psychologist) drinking patterns among high school students.

Related Lexington Books

Tabasz, Thomas F., *Towards an Economics of Prisons,* 224 pp., 1975

Berkson, Larry C., *The Concept of Cruel and Unusual Punishment,* 256 pp., 1975

Strickland, Katherine G., *Correctional Institutions for Women in the United States,* forthcoming

Brodsky, Stanley L., *Families and Friends of Men in Prison,* 352 pp., 1975

Chappell, Duncan, and Monahan, John., *Violence and Criminal Justice,* 176 pp., 1975

Curtis, Lynn A, *Violence, Race, and Culture,* 128 pp., 1975

Curtis, Lynn A., *Criminal Violence: National Patterns and Behavior,* 255 pp., 1974

Dodge, Calvert R., *A Nation without Prisons,* 288 pp., 1975

Smith, Joan, and Fried, William, *The Uses of American Prisons: Political Theory and Penal Practice,* 192 pp., 1974

Simon, Rita James, *Women and Crime,* 160 pp., 1975

Carlson, Rick, J., *The Dilemmas of Corrections,* forthcoming